How Businesses
Buy Legal Services

LARRY SMITH

DIRECTOR OF BUSINESS DEVELOPMENT
LEVICK STRATEGIC COMMUNICATIONS, LLC
WASHINGTON, D.C.

Copyright © 2001 NLP IP Company,
ALM Publishing, a division of
American Lawyer Media, Inc.

www.lawcatalog.com

Cover Design: *Michael Ng*

Interior Page Design & Production: *Amparo Graf*

Library of Congress Cataloging-in-Publication Data

Smith, Larry, 1949-
    Inside/outside : how businesses buy legal services / by Larry Smith.
        p. cm.
    Includes bibliographical references.

    ISBN 0-9705970-5-3

    1. Corporate legal departments—United States. 2. Law firms—United States.
        3. Legal services—United States. I. Title.

    KF1425 .S634 2001
    340'.068'8—dc21   2001053567

"A superb exploration of the behind-the-scenes decision-making that goes into buying outside legal services. Larry Smith has a keen sense of the unspoken factors and considerations that affect our thinking. Attorneys in both law firms and corporate law departments will find this book a revelation."

Jeff Kindler, President, Partner
Brands, McDonald's Corporation

"This book should be called 'What inside counsel want.' Smith has gotten past the buzzwords and has drawn an accurate picture of what matters to large consumers of legal services. I wish all our law firms would read it."

John Liftin, Senior Vice President and
General Counsel, Prudential Financial

"A comprehensive analysis of the most important current developments in the delivery of legal services by large law firms, filled with pertinent pro and con arguments as to why and how law firms should consider modifications in their structure. The hours I have spent reading it have been extremely helpful to my understanding of law firm innovations. My strong recommendation: BUY IT AND STUDY IT."

"Smith trains his sights on how clients distinguish one firm from another and zeroes in on the key turning points in the decision-making process. His insights are a gift for every lawyer who wants to know what clients really think of when it comes time to hire a firm."

PREFACE

Some time around the turn of the twentieth century, American law schools expanded their course of study from a two-year to a three-year program; in the late 1960s they changed the name of the degree they awarded from Bachelor of Laws (LL.B) to Juris Doctor (J.D.). But nowhere in this expanded curriculum, or during the twentieth century, did law schools teach much more than a federal approach to the practice of law. As essential as this intellectual ground work may be, it leaves graduating lawyers at an extreme disadvantage, particularly in a competitive, global legal marketplace.

At this writing, there are no requirements for business, sales, market research, advertising, public relations, and marketing strategy classes specifically designed for the lawyer. There are merely discussions of such possible curricula at a very few law schools in the United States and the United Kingdom. And so they go forth, these newly minted attorneys, marching off in record numbers, nearly half of them to larger law firms, expecting to make partner.

Somewhere along the line, whether in a down economy when associates are laid off, or when the partner track is stalled, this next generation of lawyers will start thinking about what too few of their partners know enough about to teach: "How do I develop business? What do buyers of legal services care about? What makes them buy and want to buy from me?"

One of the most interesting dynamics in the marketplace is the difference between how in-house counsel say they buy and how they actually buy. Larry Smith's book points eloquently to the frequent assertions by buyers that they are impervious to most law firm marketing. Often they really are. But other times they're just posturing, and are really very susceptible indeed to the better business development efforts of the more capable law firms. The mystery of marketing is finding what actually works, whether or not the buyers acknowledge that it does.

When marketing is successful, it is invisible. Consider Santa Claus, who shares the red and white colors of Coca Cola, a similarity resulting from a 1922 marketing campaign to fight declining winter soda pop sales. And the diamond engagement ring? A marketing campaign by DeBeers at the beginning of the last century. Mother's Day? Wannamaker's. Rudolph the Red-Nosed Reindeer? Montgomery Ward. The universality of blowing out birthday candles? A Kodak moment.

Marketing can work and work brilliantly, but not because the buyer says it does. It works when it is done properly and becomes woven into the decision-making process of the buyer. One of the most interesting aspects of *Inside/Outside* is that, like *Fantastic Voyage* three decades ago, Smith takes you inside the heads of the buyers. *This* is what they are thinking.

The one area where marketers can feel safe investing their money and time is in any form of marketing that creates value for the buyer. This is where the buyer is willing to more comfortably acknowledge susceptibility to law firm marketing. Marketing that merely trumpets a name is less effective than something that leaves the buyer better off at the end of a day. In this book, buyer after buyer talks about seminars, roundtables, or whatever provides helpful—and free—points of substantive law.

In the 2001 version of the Corporate Legal Times-PriceWaterhouseCoopers annual survey of the purchasing of legal services, general counsel said they want to hear about "what problem is coming next in my industry." In other words, the buyers' message to the sellers is: "We already know you are smart. Please don't tell us where you've gone to school or how well you did. Tell us what we need to worry about next in *our* industry and how we can avoid that problem. That makes you a true partner."

As a marketing media strategist, I was struck by how Mr. Smith contrasts branding as a profession-wide trend to the increasingly frequent "sales training" of lawyers. These are trends you don't normally see contrasted, but, as he points out, they represent the polar opposites of marketing. Branding doesn't necessarily bring value to the client, at least in the form offered by some firms that are now attempting it at the firm-wide level. (At the practice-group level, branding can be an effective, client-friendly tool.) In contrast, sales training, because it allows the seller to crystallize and address the buyer's underlying business problem, results in a sales process that helps the buyer whether or not a sale is finally made. It makes it worth his or her time.

In many ways, this book provides a historical perspective such that the buying/selling dynamics described, and the relationship management described, are of permanent interest. In other words, you won't find any quick fixes or flavors of the month here. For example, as presented by the author, the in-house revolution begun in the 1980s at General Electric is as fresh and interesting today as it was then.

For the same reasons, marketing takes time. When a managing partner says, "For this year, we want to brand the law firm," it's like saying, "Let's overtake Federal Express with our new mail service before the end of the quarter." Non-spontaneous purchasing decisions—and legal services are almost always purchased non-spontaneously—are influenced by many things. Good work and relationships are chief among them, followed by the beliefs and perceptions prevalent in the marketplace. Studies of in-house buying patterns (such as the FGI/Greenfield/Belser studies referenced in this book) continuously show that, for example, what a legal buyer reads helps to influence his or her decision. This begs the question, "Why wouldn't a lawyer want to be featured in the publications that a legal buyer reads?"

To permeate the minds of buyers with a near universal recognition of a lawyer's strong selling position takes time. It means communicating in many different ways—advertising, public relations, public speaking, direct mail, websites, sponsorships, etc.—continuously over long periods of time. The very reactions that Larry Smith traces in this book are a validation of this truth of time. As Coca Cola marketing executive Robert Ball said, as recently as 1974, "If we stopped marketing, you'd forget who we are in ten days."

Inside/Outside provides a range of noteworthy cases. For instance, we learn in these pages how small or mid-sized firms can play the game as effectively as the big boys, by picking their targets and developing honest partnerships with corporate America. And, we also see how a megafirm like Jones, Day, Reavis & Pogue can plan a global strategy on behalf of a full range of clients that works as seamlessly across two oceans as if it were a single office in a single city.

The lessons learned from this book should be integrated with the business development approach *and* the marketing efforts. The lessons that are true for large firms are true for the small ones. If you are going to sell widgets, market them. For every Jones, Day or Howrey Simon Arnold & White that has integrated marketing with its practice management and practice development plans, there's a small firm that can learn and apply the same lessons. No-one who reads this book should ever say, "Sure, but that's Jones, Day," or "But that was a decade ago." Every firm of every size at every point since legal marketing in the United States began to grow into a cottage industry over two decades ago has faced significant challenges. Smith's work tells you how to think like a buyer so you can get closer to success faster and more economically.

Larry Smith doesn't present anything as absolute wisdom. An experienced journalist, he will present the revolutionary convergence model pioneered at DuPont in all its glory. He will respectfully elucidate the best practices that evolve from such buying models. But he will just as respectfully show us how and why both the convergence strategy, and the resultant best practices, failed at a company like Prudential.

Indeed, there is nothing cut and dried in this book, because the inside/outside relationship can never be a cut and dried dynamic. We see in these pages example after example of how management is at least equal parts art and science. The science part is relatively easy. After reading this book, make sure to grab your paint brush.

Richard S. Levick, Esq.

President, Levick Strategic Communications, LLC

September, 2001

CONTENTS

CHAPTER 2

CHAPTER 3

CHAPTER 4

CHAPTER 5

The Extracurricular Equation: How Lawyers Who Solve Non-Legal Problems May Revolutionize the Legal Profession

CHAPTER 6

Law Firm Accountability: A Review of State-of-Art Budgeting and Case Management Oversight

CHAPTER 7

"Convergence": The Decade's Dominant Inside/Outside Event

CHAPTER 8

How GE's In-House Revolution Changed an Inside/Outside Dynamic 213

CHAPTER 9

Beyond Convergence: How Law Department Culture Affects Corporate Legal Purchasing 237

CHAPTER 10

"Next Economy" Legal Buyers: What Fortune 500 High-Tech Corporations Expect from Outside Counsel 285

How Buyers of Legal Services Think Today: Global Response to a Millennial Study

L et's start with some data.[1]

For over fifteen years, FGI, Inc., a market research company in Manassas, Virginia, has been conducting studies of how corporations buy legal services. One of the most recent such studies was presented by FGI, Inc., along with co-sponsor and producer Greenfield/Belser Ltd. of Washington, D.C. at a 2000 meeting in Barcelona of the European chapter of the American Corporate Counsel Association ("ACCA").[2] It is of particular interest that the survey provides material that is clearly of global significance. Most Fortune 500 legal officers do, after all, purchase on a global basis these days. It is also fortuitous that the ACCA meeting provided an opportunity for a number of international buyers to respond directly to the FGI/Greenfield/Belser findings.[3]

The first focus of the survey is how professionals have treated each other regarding the inside/outside relationship in the past—their courtesy, their responsiveness, their flexibility. But the survey looks forward as well toward new forces in the marketplace, often Internet-based, that will have an increasingly decisive impact

---

[1] Data used by permission of FGI, Inc. and Greenfield/Belser Ltd.

[2] FGI, Inc. and Greenfield/Belser Ltd., "How General Counsels Buy and Will Buy Legal Services," American Corporate Counsel Association (ACCA) (European chapter, Barcelona, Nov. 2000).

[3] The survey results may be found in the Appendix to this chapter, *infra*.

on how buyers and sellers find each other, and what happens afterward.

From the buyer's standpoint, the data in the survey can be divided into (1) how as buyers they "find" counsel and (2) how they then "choose" outside counsel. From the seller's standpoint, these steps translate into (1) "marketing," which is how outside counsel are found, and (2) "selling," which is how they get chosen. The "finding" step is what leads to a short list of qualified providers, explains Dr. Mark T. Greene, FGI's Managing Director for Research/Quality Consulting.

Not all buyers are active buyers. The greatest force in the universe is inertia, and the greatest temptation is to do what has always been done. "That is consistent with the way most legal services are given out to law firms," says Greene. "The firms that you have been using are the firms that you will use when the next matter crosses your desk."

To some extent, surveys such as the FGI/Greenfield/Belser— and, for that matter, books like this one—are therefore studies of the exceptions. But they are the exceptions that ultimately change buying habits across the board. When we examine DuPont in Chapter 7, for instance, we'll be looking at an idiosyncratic situation that prompted an off-the-charts response by the in-house client. Yet it was a response that re-created the inside/outside dynamic of the late 1990s. Today, if ninety-seven of 100 in-house lawyers scoff at, say, the online purchasing of legal services, the really significant fact may be that there are three who do *not* scoff.

Some inertia is justified. Corporate counsel often have good reason to prefer the devils they know. They understand the strengths and weaknesses of the law firms they're accustomed to using, and they'll keep them on their short lists because matters for which those firms are suited will likely arise. Some matters, moreover, don't require excellence. Competence is sufficient, and frequently anything more cannot be cost-justified.

Susie Flook, Group Intellectual Property Counsel with The Body Shop International PLC, a UK cosmetics multinational, describes this profession-wide inertia as a kind of managerial efficiency. Relationships, as well as dependable competence, justify this approach. "After searching long and hard for a law firm that can provide the services needed, I do tend to stay with the devil I know because I can get myself to a situation with a law firm where I always have one contact partner that I deal with," she says. "It does not matter if it is litigation, environmental, M&A, or intellectual property."

The contact partner will know The Body Shop's business to a greater extent than anyone at a new law firm that might overall offer greater breadth or depth of legal services. Such knowledge of the client could cover a multitude of non-crucial deficiencies. The contact partner will know the client's key managers, and those relationships further enable the in-house lawyers to confidently let outside counsel manage itself in terms of work assignments, budget, technology, etc.

The devil-you-know strategy should also mean better cost control. In later chapters we'll see how, in the mid-1990s, the revolution at corporations like DuPont put more legal work volume in fewer hands. The client was thereby able to wrest significant concessions on how the work was billed. These companies "converged" the use of outside counsel because they were emerging from a situation where they'd been inefficiently using far too many law firms. Flook is describing a more contained situation wherein the existing law firm (the "devil she knows") is already susceptible to that kind of pressure, because the relationship with The Body Shop is long-standing and important to the firm. Presumably, she's already in a good bargaining position.

For example, Flook "absolutely refuses" to have standard hourly rate agreements. Instead, she sits down with the contact partner and figures out the commercial value of an important matter to The Body Shop. That discussion leads to an appropriate fee agreement. It's a salutary example, especially since The Body Shop isn't just negotiating in this way with hungry young law firms that really need the work. To the contrary: Flook says colleagues have wondered "how the hell I get a [global] law firm like Clifford Chance [to do work] for piffling costs."

The answer, she advises, is to keep fee negotiations pegged to the value equation. If you allow law firms to expend $10 million in billable hours on a case where the exposure is $9 million, they will. However, by establishing the value of the case at the get-go, outside counsel knows the rules of the game at the beginning—and the contact partner can start thinking, at that time, about how the firm must manage its resources for this work. In turn, Flook can take the budget to her own client at The Body Shop, knowing that it's grounded in the kind of value-for-value language that businesspeople understand and approve.

After the concept of simple habit, referrals account for most of the names on corporate short lists, especially when these referrals are from familiar and respected lawyers at other companies. Significantly, such referrals seldom address capabilities, backgrounds, wins versus losses, or even fees. The question most corporate counsel ask their colleagues when they call for a reference can be boiled down to, "Is this person good to work with?"

A critical moment occurs when the in-house buyer doesn't actually know who to call. Suppose there's no law firm on the approved list with expertise in the needed area, or one that has enough geographical breadth to handle the work. For whatever reason, there's also no colleague at another law department who has a quick referral at hand. This is the kind of moment when law firm marketing actually means something. Suddenly, whatever efforts a firm has made to get its name out, or to make that name trigger certain associations among possible purchasers, pay off. This is when a "brand" can pay off. This is when getting quoted in *The Wall Street Journal* pays off. This is when hosting a seminar on construction law or ERISA or hostile takeovers pays off.

In these situations, even a listing in *Martindale-Hubbell* can mean something. A listing will at least get the firm found, even if the road to getting chosen is still a long one. The online searches are also causing considerable interest as of this writing. In some ways, they represent an automated extension of the old *Martindale-Hubbell* searches, insofar as buyers are looking for new and often unfamiliar firms, or firms with which they've never worked before. Buyers can go on the Internet and get the name of a law firm or lawyer to handle a case in some obscure jurisdiction. They can even start vetting the prospect online.

It's hard to find in-house buyers, especially among the older GCs, who will admit to using this automated resource. Their caveat is that the personal dimension, by which they mainly define the inside/outside relationship, is missing. "I'm going to want to know somebody who knows these people," says Flook. "I'm going to want to have that personal reassurance that this guy is okay. 'He did a job for me, and he is okay.' "

Yet online exchanges or sites such as eLawForum and iBidLaw are growing apace. Older GCs cite user numbers that belie the knee-jerk disapprobation so often heard from corporate buyers. Among those numbers, there were industry estimates of $222 million in legal services that would be purchased on the Internet in 2001. Even if that sum was greatly exaggerated, the trend is pretty clear. Part of the growth is based on the fact that, for many corporate buyers, the personal dimension isn't quite so important at the first stage of hiring counsel. The exchanges are mainly important as a way to find counsel. At the same time, although exchanges such as eLawForum provide boilerplate examples to help in-house counsel draft Requests for Proposals ("RFPs"), the "personal" dimension *is* sometimes facilitated as well. That's because referrals are a major item on those boilerplates, so potential buyers can typically go offline and telephone those references as part of the finding process.

Getting chosen is another matter, however. Toward that end, the legal exchanges and other high-tech innovations are just the first step. And when it is time to sell rather than market, the media appearances and substantive public forums don't count for much either. However, brand names may still matter at this point.

A disputant will hire an aggressive litigation firm such as Washington, D.C.'s Williams & Connolly just to scare the bejesus out of the other guy.

Or the sale may be an IBM- or AT&T-type sale, by which we mean a "safety sell." Here, the matter is too large to entrust to a law firm the buyer hasn't heard much about. So the in-house lawyer hires the brand name, the Skadden or Cravath or Kirkland, and, even if the matter goes south, the buyer has still protected himself because the buying decision was judicious and predictable. More often, though, the issues aren't quite so critical, and subjective factors therefore become paramount at the actual selection stage.

Sometimes, the more recondite the matter, the more subjective the sale—since, at that point, the buyers can't necessarily determine which law firm might be a little bit better at handling some obscure transaction. Also, as Greene suggests, personal chemistry may actually be more important in the legal business than in most other businesses (as Flook's comment on the legal exchanges suggests). The buyer, after all, could wind up working alongside the seller at 2:00 a.m. Who wants to be working alongside somebody they don't particularly like at that hour?

This model—of objective finding and subjective choosing—is eminently compatible with the results of the survey research over the last fifteen years, according to Greene. But narrow expertise, the survey finds, does become a more saleable commodity when boutiques sell to in-house specialists. In 1994, "expertise" was identified, along with reputation, as one of the two most important considerations when FGI asked in-house counsel how they shop for financial, property, and other specialty services. In 1996, the survey data suggested that in-house lawyers were more likely to evaluate expertise than were nonlawyer executives. That's hardly surprising, but it does show a somewhat bifurcated picture on the buyers' side. On the one hand, clients need hand-holding, friendship, chemistry, and compatibility. On the other hand, in certain situations, they'll hone in on specific legal skills as the determinative factor.

Fast-growing companies, especially in technology, face a similar conundrum in the current market. The nature of the technology industry demands specialized knowledge by outside counsel, but these buyers aren't usually lawyers. In fact, there often is no in-house counsel capable of assessing the extent to which prospective law firms have that specialized knowledge. At the same time, fledgling companies need *consiglieres*, all-purpose business/legal advisors rather than merely legal practitioners.

According to Greene, in 1999 FGI again found that expertise and personal relationships were the leading interrelated factors driving retention decisions. Yet there seems to be an intrinsic tension between these two factors—the need for a trusted advisor versus the need for something like a necromancer's mystic knowledge—that complicates the buying process on both sides.

The survey data unveiled in November 2000 is helpfully broken down by industry groups, and by size of organizations. Not surprisingly, legal services buyers at biotech and infotech companies emphasized expertise as a buying criterion. At larger companies, there was an assumption that expertise can always be found whenever it might be needed, so that personal chemistry with outside counsel is the real premium.

The 2000 survey queried which specific traditional tactics, referrals, or contact media continue to be effective selling mechanisms. One persistent theme was, "I came to respect somebody that I met while he [or she] was representing the competition." Brochures—those most disdained of marketing aids in the professional services—were still cited, as were directories, including *Martindale-Hubbell.* Significantly, some clients even said they had hired lawyers who had, if not quite cold-called, made the buyer's acquaintance through personal channels other than traditional referrals.

Even the most cursory review of such data suggests that marketing tactics thought to be antiquated, scattershot, or otherwise ineffective may still have some use. For example, future clients (as well as current clients) read articles and direct mail updates on the law. Seminar appearances are similarly effective. Indeed, we will see in future chapters how even the most skeptical in-house attorneys acknowledge that, if there is one way a law firm can get on their corporate radar screens for the first time, it's by hosting or appearing at CLE-type functions. All of which is not to suggest, however, that referrals from trusted sources are in any way less the predominant influence on how corporate buyers pick outside counsel than they were fifteen years ago, when FGI first started doing these surveys.

BRAVE NEW WORLD

What is different today is that nearly one-half of the in-house counsel surveyed last year by FGI and Greenfield/Belser reported Internet sites as a source of information either "often" or "sometimes." Again, that contradicts the studied indifference to online purchasing that many in-house counsel profess. Of course, some of these responses may only refer to perfunctory online research. However, the survey also asked, "How frequently do you go online to seek for legal services? Would you say daily, weekly, monthly or never?" According to Greene, the respondents were from large corporations. About half the participants were at companies that bill over $100 million annually. Some bill over $500 million. Nor are we talking about occasional experiments. An impressive 13% go online on a daily basis, whereas 32% said they did weekly searches and 18% monthly. Only 37% never search online.

Predictably, these numbers represent a dramatic rise over a two- or three-year period. In the mid-1990s, only miniscule numbers of in-house lawyers told survey personnel that they search online. Yet what may be especially significant is that, according to Greene, a large percentage of respondents wrote in their survey responses some sort of favorable allusion to the legal exchanges without being prompted to do so. Again, the differences between what many buyers acknowledge when they're filling in not-for-attribution survey forms, and what they're willing to verbally admit, are palpable. The future may well reside in the subtexts of surveys.

There's also a subtext to the increased usage of the legal exchanges that may actually be more important than the exchanges themselves. The scoffing among in-house buyers is justified to the extent that innovations such as the exchanges are seen not just as "impersonal," but ultimately as merely quick ways to find law firms and to drive down costs. In that sense, they would represent a degradation of the inside/outside dynamic. Yet David Briscoe, a consultant at Altman Weil—which has sponsored a new exchange called iBidLaw that was scheduled to go public in 2001—points to a larger significance. Briscoe says that, "Overwhelmingly, the corporations that are interested in participating on the exchanges say the Number One thing they are after is to get to know other law firms" besides the ones they're using. "Who else is out there? What kind of qualifications do they have? What is their expertise?"

Any downward pressure on costs because of the exchanges is an ancillary, not driving, benefit. In one sense, online vetting speaks to the "inertia" that Flook describes. Users recognize that there is such inertia, and that this inertia is sometimes acceptable, but sometimes not. iBidLaw or eLawForum is a cost-effective way to test the waters without time-consuming RFPs or beauty contests. Those contests can come later, at a more serious stage in the negotiations, when they'll actually be worth the time of both the buyers and sellers.

Law firms are recognizing the same thing, according to Kay Ellen Consolver, Chief Operating Officer of eLawForum, which opened for business in February 2000. There are sixty-four corporations and over 600 law firms using the service world-wide as of this writing. "They want to come to the attention of corporate counsel," says Consolver. "They want to be considered for new work, to build the new relationships." For in-house counsel, she adds, it is a way "to cut through the names of the firms and find the talented individuals who work there." To that extent, it does not supplant the "personal," but actually paves the way for it.

Consolver confirms Briscoe's pronouncement on costs. The in-house lawyers who use eLawForum or other exchanges are not necessarily choosing the lowest bidder. As in all higher-level buying and selling of professional services, the name of the game is value, not price. To be sure, we will be looking in later chapters at any number of corporations, from Genentech to DoubleClick, that insist on, and get, volume discounts. But it's never bargain-basement shopping. And the real revolutionaries among the in-house buyers, including those at DuPont, eschew simple rate discounts in favor of sophisticated risk-sharing or other arrangements designed to create value first and foremost. In that sense, the legal exchanges are continuing a tradition, not diverting it.

Other survey data also confirm the ongoing automation of legal services purchasing. Fifteen percent of participating in-house counsel expect e-mail to replace telephone calls and hard copies. Nine percent "often" visit law firm web sites; 39% "sometimes" do so; 39% "rarely"; and only 13% "never" bother. Information portals are used often by 17%; sometimes by 31%; rarely by 23%; and never by 29%. "All of this, of course, would have been complete nonsense just a couple of years ago," comments Greene.

These online services are not merely specifically tailored to the buying needs of in-house lawyers. Even were there no such thing as portals, corporate legal purchasing would be increasingly technological. For example, 44% of the FGI/Greenfield/Belser respondents often perform a key word search using engines such as Yahoo to help them find legal services providers; 29% do so sometimes; 16% rarely; and 11% never. The low percentile for the "never" category is consistent for purchasers who disdain online resources as well.

The survey asked, "Have you ever used a law firm extranet?" The definition given respondents was a password-protected system, with client-specific or matter-specific content, set up by a law firm to contain and provide voluminous documents. Only 12% said they had done so. According to Greene, however, a significant number of respondents inserted gratuitous comments such as, "No, but wouldn't that be great!" Or, "I didn't know such things existed." Or, "If I see one, I'll use it." At the same time, we may, in future studies, find a further decrease in the use of extranets or of key word searches even as most or all of the information that those resources provide is incorporated into the legal exchanges.

It should also be noted that there is still much confusion over terms: a "forum" versus an "exchange," a "Web site" versus an "extranet." "If you ask several different counsel, you will get several different answers as to what those things are," confirms Greene. "So usage in general is up, but what exactly is going on is still a bit difficult to tease out." Clearly, not all lawyers are equally familiar with computer terminology and usage, and some older, more seasoned attorneys may in fact be computer-illiterate, which can complicate any proposed Internet or extranet protocol.

The foregoing data should also be measured against a theme that we'll see recur throughout this book: the insistence by in-house lawyers that they are impervious to *all* law firm marketing. They ostensibly make their decisions based on their comprehensive referral networks, and their own sense of the prospective lawyer or law firm. Such an attitude is pure posture in many cases, understandable in the sense that it keeps unwanted salesmen from banging on the door. It's also self-serving in that there's an implicit suggestion by the buyers that they are so well-hooked into the market, and can take care of themselves so well, that there's simply no need to go shopping. For law firms, the most daunting question as they confront their markets is how in-house counsel really do make purchasing decisions. The reason surveys such as the FGI/Greenfield/Belser survey, and books like this one, exist is simply because, when you get right down to it, in-house counsel are reluctant to be honest.

That being the case, Greene is probably quite right in suggesting that the percentages of respondents willing to admit being influenced by what they see online is a most impressive number indeed. Greene figures that the 18% of in-house respondents who reported that they don't think the provision of legal services will be changed by the Internet must be close to retirement, or at least "I hope they are."

There are a number of other ways in which the survey encapsulates the market developments of the late 1990s while allowing glimpses into what the new millennium holds in store. One of the signal developments of recent years was the emergence abroad of multidisciplinary practices (MDPs), in particular the large accounting firms now offering legal services in many global jurisdictions and, as a result, threatening the global advance of major law firms. They are continuing to capture market share and lure partners, especially tax practitioners, from law firms.

The survey data on the MDPs relate directly to the data on Internet usage, Greene believes, because these global behemoths are "quite sophisticated" in their online resources. As to the level of competition these technologically advanced firms are liable to offer in the next few years, the survey provides fairly bad news for traditional law firm practices. Only about 30% of the respondents expressed negative views about the capacity of the Big Five and other MDPs to provide credible legal services. About one-fifth of the survey participants were generally positive in their assessment of this global service option.

"BRAIN DIVIDED IN TWO"

So where does this data take us? It suggests, as we noted, that there are discrepancies between how in-house counsel buy and how they say they buy, which is Headache Number One for the seller, who is looking for some reliable guidepost. Headache Number Two is that, whatever the reality has been over the last fifteen years of market boom and bust and boom again, it's changing.

We've emphasized the technology findings in the FGI/Greenfield/Belser survey because those sorts of changes are concrete and immediately understandable. In later chapters we'll see how major corporations have changed in other fundamental ways, actually revamping their entire strategies in terms of the numbers and types of law firms they allow on their short lists. The dichotomy noted above—between the search for lawyers who are true business partners and overall counselors, on the one hand, and erudite sub-specialists, on the other—includes the additionally confusing context in which these strategic changes on the buyer's end have occurred.

When the survey data were presented at the 2000 ACCA meeting, we[4] used it as a framework to elicit responses from discussion participants regarding the sort of professional future they envision. These participants included a number of in-house counsel as well as consultants and journalists. If nothing else, the survey statistics confirm the reality of change, and that the inside/outside selling dynamic in the first and second decades of the twenty-first century probably won't resemble much of what we saw in the 1980s and 1990s. With such change in mind, the question was posed: *"What is it that you want law firms to know in terms of selling to you that will make your jobs easier?"*

Any answer to a seller who asks such a question is adumbrated by the massive consolidation in the sellers' industry, which features, for example, the kind of transatlantic law firm mergers that as late as 1996 and 1997 were deemed unthinkable. Part of the rationale behind such mergers is that the one-stop shopping they allow does in fact "make the buyer's life easier." For the global buyers gathered in Barcelona in 2000, that issue was obviously of direct interest.

Susie Flook was recently asked by one multinational firm, Baker & McKenzie, how the global firms in general are doing. "Not very well," she informed that firm's worldwide conference. "The trend toward these great global multinational law firms is not

---

[4] Levick Strategic Communications, the Washington, D.C.-based firm in which the author is a senior partner.

going to work at the end of the day," she says. "What you need in a particular place is somebody local who knows what is going on locally." It may be positive when a lawyer at a global law firm in New York has been primed on Swedish law, because the client is as multinational as the law firm. But, when push comes to shove, Flook argues that "it is the local guy who has to give the advice." The issue then becomes the inevitability of a global firm having to be weak *somewhere*. All the client can do is cross his or her fingers and hope it's not in Sweden.

Michel Cloes, Paris-based European counsel for the Dana Corporation, is another case in point of a buyer with significant reservations about the current scene. His company is an Old Economy automotive industry giant, a $13 billion multinational. For Cloes, emphasis on "personal judgment" as distinguished from measurable performance standards, or targeted marketing pitches, or law firm brand names, is naturally resonant. He adds, "I like to think we have come to a degree of sophistication in understanding our own business and our own needs for legal services [so that we can] focus almost equally on the management part of service delivery. . . . I always have my brain divided into two: how is [the service] being managed from the legal services provider, as compared to the ideal I have developed over the years?"

When FGI first started surveying in-house counsel fifteen years ago, most in-house buyers probably didn't have any such "ideal." (Coincidentally, it was fifteen years ago that ACCA was first founded in Washington, D.C., which seems to further suggest 1986 through 2001 as an appropriate historical time frame for any study of the evolving inside/outside dynamic.) Yet the management concerns that are so important to Cloes—and, as we'll see in later chapters, to in-house buyers world-wide—transcend current hot button topics such as Internet purchasing. The increased oversight of outside counsel by inside managers has also become a marketing issue as well since so much of the "personal chemistry" that GCs talk about often boils down to the perceived willingness of prospective law firms to collaborate as equals with their in-house counterparts. Back in 1986 corporate counsel seldom asked for control over outside cost and performance, and outside counsel seldom offered. Today, "I end up talking management issues with my outside counsel much more than before," confirms Cloes.

Can we say to what extent Cloes' "ideal" is served or disserved by the profession-wide consolidation? Law firms posit that such consolidation would not be occurring were not their clients themselves consolidating. So it would stand to reason that, at some level, the global and national law firm mega-mergers must be making clients' lives easier in some fundamental way.

Yet there are any number of subtle variables driving the consolidation that may have nothing whatsoever to do with efficiency or client service. As Flook points out, for example, U.S.-based GCs running the law departments of multinational American corporations often have a controlling influence, or last sign-off, on law firms hired in Europe. Their European counsel are reluctant to refer smaller European firms. To some extent, this approach is an IBM-style safety purchase: "I'll hire someone in Europe that my American manager has heard of, so I'll be safe whatever happens." This dynamic drives the buyer to multinational sellers, but it seems a purely political dynamic, with no guaranteed benefits to the buyer.

At Dana, in contrast, hiring is a totally "regional call," according to Cloes. We'll see in later chapters how other U.S. corporations—Caterpillar, Inc. is a good example—similarly empower overseas counsel. Eschewing the "devil-you-know" strategy, Cloes says Dana "proactively" searches for better service on a continuous basis, and that search, for all the efforts by merging law firms to impose the one-stop shopping solution, is invariably a search for "alternatives to the big firms." This approach is additionally noteworthy since it would be so much easier to encompass all Dana's legal needs in Europe under one law firm flag. But easier is not necessarily better, and Cloes has formalized a review of outside counsel, with an eye toward shifting the balance of Dana's weight from the megafirms to smaller firms and boutiques.

Cloes summarizes his discomfort with mega-consolidation for two reasons. First, it results in a deleterious focus by big firms on big deals and big clients. This size- or volume-oriented approach subtly or not so subtly erodes the service-provision sensibility and, in the long run, hurts everybody. Second, the megafirms simply aren't organized to allow for a client-centered focus. For example, training and mentoring in such contexts are deficient, and the staffing of legal teams too volatile by half.

In Flook's experience, there have often been smaller matters that came up outside the U.S. that larger firms wouldn't handle for the client at a reasonable rate. Often the megafirms did not have the expertise to deal with such matters, mainly because the legal area involved wasn't important enough for them to have ever developed the appropriate expertise. According to Flook, the GC wouldn't care where she'd go for these jobs. On the big matters, though, "he'd say, 'You have to use somebody that makes me comfortable.'"

For Dan Fitz, the big firm/small firm issue similarly devolves around the importance of the matter. On the big ones, "we will always go with the people we know," says Fitz, who's GC of Cable and Wireless PLC, a UK-based data and Internet company with operations in seventy countries.[5] Fitz is more amenable to relying on large firms than Cloes because Fitz feels the quality service issue can actually be better negotiated with a larger firm, provided the company is giving that law firm enough business. But quality is not simply a question of size or breadth. Amid the ongoing consolidation among outside counsel, the crux for Cable and Wireless is, "Who's doing the expanding? Is it our firm or the firm that just acquired our firm?"

If its own firm is driving the merger, this is seen as a win-win development for the client, especially since Cable and Wireless is another example of a major purchaser that's been consolidating

---

[5] Dan Fitz was also an ACCA vice president for the year 2001.

the number of firms on its approved list. Part of the philosophy driving that "convergence" trend is the idea that the more work you give a law firm, the more of the firm's concerned attention you can garner in the future. Suddenly, because it's "your" law firm that acquired another law firm, or was the driving force in a multinational merger, the company discovers new-found clout in cities where it had much less leverage before.

"You can use your relationship partner as your referral to stand behind the person in the Paris office or the Frankfurt office," explains Fitz. There's now less risk in buying legal services in Paris or Frankfurt because the client's total fees on a firm-wide basis are enough to engender real commitment everywhere.

Fitz knows "my relationship partner would die rather than let the quality of service suffer. That gives me a great deal of comfort when I am branching out in a new jurisdiction, particularly if it is an important matter." If it is an important matter, the relatively greater cost of using the merged firm becomes less important. In M&A, the tax benefits of doing it right outweigh by far the bump up in legal fees. (With "operational legal matters," which come out of an annual budget, the cost factors are naturally of more concern. Cable and Wireless will shop those matters around and concentrate the work with firms that know how to stay within budget.)

The overriding need for law firms to think more like businesses is "terribly applicable to this issue of large versus small [and] of the mergers of law firms," adds Gabe Shawn Varges, in-house counsel at Zurich Financial Services, an insurance and financial company with about 70,000 employees in sixty countries world-wide.[6] To that extent, Varges is suggesting that clients scrutinize mergers on an individual basis. The smart mergers will serve client interests. The mega-mishaps won't.

---

[6] Varges served as ACCA's president in 2001.

As buyers like Varges suggest, there are three points that companies ought to scrutinize when their legal services providers consolidate:

First, are the mergers well-integrated deals fitting culturally like-minded vendors together into a cohesive whole? Will the people at these reconstituted firms work well together on the client's behalf?

Second, are the resources leveraged right? "It does not make sense for law firms to merge if they are going to remain totally independent of each other," says Varges. Theoretically, the merger should decrease upward pressures on cost, since higher-volume "commodity" work can be delivered more efficiently. At least, the "commodity"-type work that institutional buyers such as Zurich require on a continuous basis ought to be more cost-efficiently leveraged, according to this view. But Varges also warns that "duplicative" resources—two time-keepers in separate offices doing more or less the same work—result in equal or greater cost pressures, which in turn means higher fees.

Finally, are merged firms what Varges calls "learning organizations"? In this regard we need to revisit Cloes' skepticism about the organization of large, multinational law firms, and whether such organizations promote multinational partner-to-partner collaboration on substantive matters in such a way that one lawyer's expertise complements another's. For Varges, it is, again, a case-by-case proposition. He himself is an alumnus of New York-based Shearman & Sterling when it was not nearly the global player that it is today. Varges believes that that firm has indeed been successful in fusing a relatively seamless cross-border firm.

"The New York lawyers are working closer with the Frankfurt lawyers and the Paris lawyers," says Varges, "and those New York lawyers are [developing] much more sensitivity to French law and German law than they were in the past, when they simply used corresponding law firms" in different foreign jurisdictions.

Yet Varges' choice of Shearman & Sterling as an example is itself telling. Shearman has grown apace internally and through lateral hiring in all its target markets—and, in each of those geographic markets—the firm has paid supreme attention to the integration factor, to the collaborative potential of lawyers who would be on the same teams but in different countries. These homogenized teams have become something of a branding tool for the firm as it seeks to differentiate itself from others doing business globally. Shearman partners in New York, Frankfurt, or Paris all sound dutifully signed on to this institutional message when you ask them to talk about their firm. Each of them makes the same salient point about how and why the firm is succeeding internationally. But Shearman has not undergone a large-scale merger with another law firm. Nor, as Varges says, does it rely on affiliations with other law firms overseas, or bank on memberships in far-flung networks of independent legal services providers. It has grown the old-fashioned way, lateral hire by lateral hire, internally promoted partner by internally promoted partner.

More and more, such firms are insisting that they don't have "home offices." They are trying to emphasize how integrated their practices are on a global basis, that they don't think in terms of branch offices or outposts, and that, in response to the concerns of buyers like Cloes, their teams provide clients with seamless counsel around the world. Thus, Morgan, Lewis & Bockius, which used to be identified as a Philadelphia firm, now declines to be so described. Ditto, Mayer, Brown & Platt, which doesn't want to be called a Chicago law firm any more. Consultant Gerry Riskin, one of the founders of Edmonton-based The Edge Group, which works globally (mostly with law firms on governance and client service issues), cites one Australian firm that really makes this an issue. If its lawyers even mention the city in which they practice, they pay a fine on the spot. That, says Riskin, "is an enlightened law firm."

In turn, Riskin suggests that an enlightened in-house department is one that consciously probes the law firms it's using, or is thinking of using, for signs of whether or not they're "learning organizations."

"Get specific," Riskin advises in-house counsel. If the firm is structured around practice groups, find out if the groups meet as a whole to review client matters, and how often. Specifically inquire as to their internal training resources. Some firms take internal training seriously enough to have non-practicing lawyers oversee the programs. Some firms have internal client relations skills training as well that could directly affect the buyer. In some cases, clients participate in these programs. Don't be afraid to ask what the law firm's associate turnover rate is. That rate should also be broken down to include the specific practice areas or partner-led legal teams pertinent to the client. If the rates are too high, find out why, and talk about how such turnover could affect the work.

The in-house part of the equation, says Riskin, is to start asking these questions when "all other things are close to equal, and there are some fine decisions to make" among prospective vendors. The information that surfaces, current and historical, can be decisive. One law firm in San Francisco, the former Thelen, Marrin, Johnson & Bridges, underwent economic distress during the last recession, particularly since it was heavily invested in construction law. The firm fired a number of lawyers it could no longer sufficiently utilize, but it did not fire an in-house training director even though, since she didn't bill out any time, she was a cost-center and not a profit-center. That was a pretty strong statement about the professional quality of the firm. As an example of the survival of such values in this age of law firm mergers, this firm eventually combined with a New York firm to create Thelen Reid & Priest. An "enlightened in-house department" would want to know the extent to which the old Thelen firm's priorities still predominate.

In "learning organizations" such as Shearman & Sterling, as Varges describes them, lawyers don't suddenly say, "That is a German law issue. I have no responsibility for German law issues." Instead, the partner in New York who refers the matter to Paris or Frankfurt shows a crucial "degree of learning" even as he or she stays within jurisdictional limits. This lawyer says, "Sure, I am a New York-admitted lawyer, and I am not going to opine on foreign law. But I do like to feel informed, and if somebody calls me and wants a basic question answered, I will have some competence on that subject, and I will confirm it with my local expert who is part of my law firm." We may see such lawyers on the ground today at Shearman or similarly integrated global institutions. But will we also be finding them in the globally merged law firms?

The very fact that the question is so obvious requires a further restatement: Why do firms go the merger route rather than pursue the steady build-up that has served Shearman so well? From the buyer's perspective, doesn't the very fact of such a global law firm merger raise red flags that could give a Shearman & Sterling an enviable competitive advantage? Why should a global bank or a global manufacturer take a chance on a firm merged across the Big Pond when it has other alternatives?

As Patrick Wilkins observes, the management deficiencies observed by Cloes and by Riskin further suggest that, indeed, buyers should not be taking that chance. Wilkins, editor of *European Lawyer* (with something of a reputation for championing single-jurisdiction law firms),[7] says that, "I think everyone agrees that law firms are not very well managed today. So why do they continue to consolidate into megafirms when they know that they are never going to be able to manage them?"

Good question.

The apparent reason is *fear*. Firms feel that they have to maintain a pace of growth to match the competitive market. Riskin says he gets calls every day from regional firms wanting to know if they should dare stay regional, or national firms worried about the consequences of not going global. The MDPs add to the consternation, of course. They may serve up a second-rate legal product today, but the Arthur Andersens of the world have shown a historical proclivity to trade up fast, whatever they're doing. So, despite the impossible management challenges of a mega-merger

---

[7] Prior to the May 2000 founding of European Lawyer, Wilkins served as Executive Editor of The Commercial Lawyer, a U.K. publication.

or the resultant client service deficiencies, it is commonly perceived that firms simply must merge to survive.

Such fear is often grounded in ignorance. As Riskin points out, many good law firms simply don't know what their clients think about issues such as the global consolidation of legal services. (One Edge Group survey disclosed that less than 5% of responding attorneys even knew what trade or industry publications their clients read, much less how those clients view the future of the legal profession.) "They sit around and speculate," says Riskin, "but they're afraid to ask what their clients think because they may not hear what they want to hear. Or they are not sure what is the best way to ask: Should you ask on paper or in person, and who should ask?"

Thus, the notorious aversion among law firms to formal audits of their clients as to what they think and what their satisfactions or dissatisfactions are with the quality of a firm's work. The Catch-22 is that these audits are often justly cited as the best way to solidify a relationship—and to relieve the very fear about client opinion that keeps the lawyer from performing the audits.

So lawyers' fear of losing clients is often what increases the chances that they will in fact lose them. On the one hand, the assumption that clients will immediately send all their work to the largest firm they can find entices them to roll the dice with often unwieldy mergers. On the other hand, this fear allows existing service problems to simmer. Back in the 1970s one great law firm discovered serious problems in its relationship with its main banking client only because a new managing partner, as part of his incoming agenda, decided to formally audit that client even though he had no idea the relationship was at risk. His initiative saved the client and probably the firm.

These days the situation hasn't changed. It's both typical and highly significant that, at the Dana Corporation, Michel Cloes will spend up to a year firing a client after the relationship gets into trouble. That means many relationships are in trouble without outside counsel knowing it. However, it also means there's time for outside counsel to remedy a situation. Dana even convenes groups of law firms on a regional basis, as many as fifteen at a time, including boutiques and larger firms. The company is virtually inviting these firms to solidify the relationship. Presumably, some take advantage of the opportunity to talk to this client, and some do not.

Mark Greene observes that Dana's twelve-month disengagement is actually "more precipitous" than the gradual termination that is typical with most corporations. Given such periods of protracted deterioration, it stands to reason that, as Greene adds, law firms usually "have no idea of how they lose clients." Presumably, the problems fester unnoticed. Yet it is extraordinary that the one most conspicuous index of client satisfaction—total annual fees—doesn't necessarily send a warning sign to the vendor. A drop from billings of $2 million to $500,000 might be attributed to happenstance, a change in the client's situation, and/or management lapses into either willful ignorance or ignorant bliss about shifts in the buyer's use of outside counsel. The key question is, "What percentage of this company's legal business do we have?" Many firms couldn't possibly be asking that question directly, much less taking prophylactic steps.

As Greene puts it, "Firms just sit there, and sooner or later it is gone; they can't figure out why." Or, they panic and marry the first or second merger prospect that comes their way.

Observers such as Riskin and Greene are painting with a fairly broad brush. In future chapters, we'll qualify their observations with examples of how large mergers have been helpful to the core clients of one or both merging firms—in part because the participating firms undertook thorough due diligence to determine how their clients thought the prospective consolidations would affect their interests. Yet global buyers still cite systemic issues which, from their point of view, inevitably exacerbate the inherent disadvantages of larger law firms.

The day-to-day protocol is upset post-merger. "The best partners now have to manage other partners," observes Patrick

Wilkins. "You do not get the benefits of the legal advice that you previously got from them," not while they're busy trying to fuse new multicultural legal teams and at the same time worrying about the formidable new capital thresholds that will be required to support their newly constituted law firm.

For Cloes, "the current market situation has [indeed] gotten a little bit fuzzier" because of the wholesale mergers. The transatlantic aspect only makes it worse. Cloes certainly agrees with Wilkins' prognosis, that the client's relationship with the "best partners" at the firms they've been using is imperiled. "Even our trusted long-time senior partners are not in a position to talk to us frankly because they are still evaluating [the merger situation] themselves," Cloes says. In some cases, the logistics of the merger take the relationship partners out of the picture altogether once they're reassigned as "transition partners" to help integrate the newly created law firm. "You just can't talk to them any longer," laments Cloes.

Yet "client service" remains the mantra repeated by every law firm manager who is attempting to justify a large law firm merger.

A "THIRD WAY"?

The impact of consolidation on how global corporations buy legal services is further complicated because it is not merely a choice between merged megafirms (Clifford Chance Rogers & Wells) or global giants that have grown instead through steady internal promotion and lateral recruitment (Shearman & Sterling). There is also a plethora of "alliances" and "networks" to choose from.

This "third way," as it were, is nothing new. In the 1980s large law firms such as Weil, Gotshal & Manges were experimenting with close affiliations with European firms. Other U.S. law firms banded together in networks that would provide members with referrals and shared resources. It was an especially popular strategy among mid-sized firms that wanted to protect their clients from the larger national and international practices. For example, the treasured client of a Minneapolis firm might have legal needs in Brussels. The threat to the firm was that once the client hired a global firm to handle those far-flung needs, it would give that big firm a chance to win over more and more of the client's work everywhere, including Minneapolis.

By joining a network of like-minded firms with similar interests, the mid-sized Minneapolis firm shielded its share of the business from the Goliaths by referring the client's other work to its trusted network co-members. Often, these firms were also tied closely together because of common practice areas or client industries. In one network, for instance, the member firms were all targeting technology work. In another, it was state lobbying work, so the network had a small or mid-sized member based in each of the fifty state capitals.

With the global consolidation in the 1990s, mega-networks such as Commercial Law Affiliates ("CLA") that sponsored hundreds of member firms around the world grew and prospered. Global consolidations not only increase referrals, but they ostensibly heighten client service levels as well. A CLA firm in South Carolina can call another member firm in Hong Kong to clarify an esoteric point of Chinese trade law and deliver the needed information to a bedazzled client in Charleston or Greenville. In such situations, the global affiliations, with their umbrella organizations and thousands of lawyers spread around the world, are oddly comparable to the legal exchanges discussed earlier. In both cases, a client may need something recondite. The client's lawyer in Greenville might call a network co-member firm in Hong Kong in the same way as the client might go online to find someone in Hong Kong who can deliver what's needed.

We will explore law firm networks in greater depth in Chapter 3. At this point we must understand consolidation as simultaneously propelling legal services in two seemingly mutually exclusive directions: Toward both the formation of vast networks, on the one hand, and the simple click of a mouse in the client's office, on the other. For the consumer, the common advantage in both cases is, as Kay Ellen Consolver points out, that the law firm can go on to show "how [it will] continue to learn to serve you."

Affiliations and networks have also been first steps toward a merger. Most notably, UK giant Linklaters & Paines formed Linklaters & Alliance with leading firms in other European countries. The result was something tighter than a network, but not as risky—especially at this enormous scale—as a full-blown merger.

The large national and international firms typically argue that quality control is a persistent concern for clients who rely on these networks. If buyers such as Cloes have issues with consistency among dozens of single-firm offices, how much more critical the potential problem when the offices aren't even part of the same firm? Network managers such as CLA's Wendy Horn aver that failure to meet the network's inflexibly high standards can cause, and has caused, immediate expulsion.

For law firms, such strategic partnerships would, in some instances, "make sense," says Gabe Varges. But the quality challenge remains the networks' biggest marketing issue. "From a consumer's perspective, if two companies have an alliance in, say, the airline industry, I won't care . . . if they lead my business in the direction of their alliance partners, as long as the quality stays the same," he adds.

So why must the best firms merge with other large firms? Moreover, why must the best firms join networks or affiliations? Of course, many terrific ones have done so, for whatever strategic or defensive reasons. Yet, as Mark Greene points out, although hundreds of mid-sized firms scurry to elude the perennially anticipated "death of the mid-sized firm," a new generation of firms in that size category—anywhere from fifty to 500 lawyers, depending on your definition—seems to somehow thrive as well as survive. From the buyer's standpoint, offers Greene, this might suggest that some firms in this tier are continuing to offer a successful business-like approach to client matters, and to their own internal staff management, with "top-down leadership" that ensures consistent quality.

It is at least a caveat to all the best-laid marketing and strategic plans when terrifically successful mid-sized firms such as San Francisco's Farella, Braun & Martel or Los Angeles' Munger, Tolles & Olson continue to go their quietly profitable ways. These mid-sized firms prosper year in and year out, often on the strength of bet-the-company cases that buyers prone to a "safe sell" mentality might instinctively prefer to send to a 1,000-lawyer multi-jurisdictional behemoth. Apparently, for the Farellas and Mungers, there are enough companies that are not slavishly tied to that mentality.

Dan Fitz sounds a conclusive theme that we will be repeating frequently in these pages, an oft-repeated point hammered home by successive waves of in-house counsel: "When I deal with big firms, I deal with individuals within that firm. It comes down to the personal relationship I have with certain key partners. I work with small- and medium-sized firms on the same basis." There is simply no way to write about the changing nature of the inside/outside relationship without periodic tribute to this recurrent truism.

Envision the entire subject of how businesses buy legal services divided into two mighty halves. One half is the marketing, the branding, the online purchasing, the seminars, the client audits, the beauty contests, the mergers, the alliances, the lateral hiring. The other half is wholly taken up with the cliché that, "Clients hire lawyers, not law firms." Ignore that tiresome cliché at your peril—especially in a law firm merger situation when buyers such as Cloes bewail the disappearance of relationship partners who are now suddenly taken up with their roles as "transition partners."

"The big firms have a lot of natural advantages in terms of geographical spread, but at the end of the day it still comes down to whether they look you in the eye and tell you the truth about the . . . deliverability of the product and service," says Fitz.

Further, law firm depth concerns how many quality partners and how many quality relationships over a broad geographic span or array of practice areas an institution can deliver to a multi-jurisdictional purchaser. The laws of nature dictate that big law firms must inevitably be weak somewhere, but the great ones can often cross-sell longer without hitting those inevitable weak spots. As Fitz points out, some of the bigger firms consciously "introduce new people over time, so that their links into my company go deeper. They also try to meet people outside the legal department as well to bind up the [whole] relationship."

Cable and Wireless has not, like Dana Corporation, embarked on a search for alternatives to the global megafirms, yet the current consolidation does worry Fitz in some ways too. "My biggest concern is that the mega-mergers make the quest for profit much greater at these firms," he says. "I don't feel as if they have yet become less professional as a result, but I do sense an urgency to get more business that perhaps was not there before," he adds. "It could just be the Americanization of UK and European practice, but I suspect that there are real economic pressures to make more money to make these mergers work."

These buyers do not necessarily believe that such economic pressure encourages better service. As Susie Flook puts it, "I begin to wonder if I am getting the full attention and the best possible legal advice and service, or if I'm being dealt with as expeditiously as possible so they can get their money and move on to somebody else's business."

The color of money causes a quirky dynamic, evident in many professions but nowhere more insidiously than in the legal profession. On the one hand, there is the need to show off success, to create among clients the comfort that comes with knowing that the people you're hiring are good enough to be very successful. On the other hand, lawyers, more so than most professionals, have been historically reluctant to engage in expensive marketing, to decorate their offices too extravagantly, or to vaunt their prized Picassos for fear of what their clients would think.

The wealthiest firms in the world solved the problem rather nimbly. They pretended not to market their services at all. They were too good to market. And they wouldn't waste your money doing so in any event!

A QUESTION OF VALUE

What law firms may have missed over the years is the perception among their clients that the marketing of legal services by outside counsel is a *healthy* thing—despite the fact that those clients might simultaneously affect some imperviousness to that marketing. As Gabe Varges puts it, this feigned imperviousness is, if nothing else, a welcome sign of increased competition. "As consumers of legal services, we want the most favorable ratio of value to cost," says Varges. This value curve "connects to the issue of the mergers. If the mergers lead to a much more favorable ratio for consumers, then they are a good thing."

As a counterpoint to the accelerated demand for more money to support the mergers, law firm marketing in the wake of a merger should therefore result in an increased effort among the firms to justify their rates. And the firms have to be much more willing to negotiate those rates. As Varges points out, marketing may sometimes be improper, and it may even border on crass—"but that is a different issue." The first issue is "that they have to compete, just like other industries, for the goodwill of consumers. And that is a favorable development."

In this context, the online legal exchanges that turn up so intriguingly in the survey data are once again instructive. Here, after all, law firms simply traipse onto a computer screen and participate in a bidding contest. "They're establishing the commercial value of the work at hand," explains Kay Ellen Consolver at eLawForum. No matter that some firms have existing relationships with the in-house counsel who are shopping the Web; those firms must still reiterate that "value," and show those existing clients how valuable their work is to them.

It's reminiscent of silly old domestic dramas where wives, feeling taken for granted, hatch plots to make their husbands jealous. "We are seeing dramatic negotiations," says Consolver, herself a former in-house lawyer at Mobil Oil Corporation (Mobil's former GC Samuel Gillespie also became eLawForum's CEO).

As part of the cost/value negotiation, the exchanges provide a good forum to pursue a discussion of value versus hourly billing. In later chapters we will review the alternative billing, volume discounts, and risk-based compensation schemes that have motivated so many excruciating beauty contests over the last ten years. But there's another perspective to the value equation: As Greene points out, some corporations will admit, readily or not, that the cost of legal services just does not matter. Nor is it only in the obvious cases, like bet-the-company litigation, that cost is ultimately unimportant. One cannot, in fact, grasp the full inside/outside dynamic without understanding how and why the cost of legal services can fall off the corporate radar screen in diverse other circumstances.

Often the issue is, who actually pays? In project finance, for example, one might expect the enormity of the work itself to dwarf fee considerations. How much could a law firm's bill matter when you're electrifying half of Malaysia? But as Varges points out, the legal price tag in such matters is often extremely sensitive because the party engaging the lawyers is not necessarily the one paying them. It may be the lender who engages, but the borrower who pays, and the borrower "cares very much that you have tried to negotiate the best price possible. These are huge, huge amounts" in any event.

In M&A, by contrast, equally large or larger legal fees cause less concern. Yet if there are such areas where total costs never seem to tip the value lever, Varges worries that the residual effects on the buying and selling of legal services profession-wide are potentially negative. "I think it would be the wrong message to send to law firms that [their fee structures] can ever be inflexible," he warns. "In fact, I would predict, even in those contexts like

M&A—particularly when companies are being made to justify why they made a particular acquisition, and to justify the [total] cost—that the cost of legal fees will be a significant item that will be scrutinized."

In this context the issue of hourly rates becomes especially important. The pressure to find alternatives to the billable hour has not abated since the discussion went into high gear in the mid-1980s. At the low end, there's the pressure to put a cap on the cost of commodity work, or to price it on a volume rather than time basis. At the high end, there are risk rewards, premiums, and percentage bonuses that buyers are willing to pay, often based on profits per share results, that are astronomically higher than any sum of inflated hourly rates could possibly yield the seller. As a result, both sides of the table are palpably impatient with the billable hour. Yet, profession-wide, the billable hour persists withal. Who in the next year or so might we expect to push most effectively for the next move toward value billing?

Gerry Riskin expects that, considering the management malaise that besets most law firms, only new DuPont-type initiatives, whereby creative fee arrangements are one absolute prerequisite to staying on the company's list of approved vendors, will drive prospects for value billing further along. Dan Fitz agrees that "it has to be the consumer" taking the initiative. Cable and Wireless has experimented with negotiated fee projects and risk-sharing arrangements and, presumably, will continue to do so.

Such companies naturally find that certain matters are better suited to negotiated fees than others. For example, Fitz says that commodity work, staggered bilateral loan agreements, or certain kinds of commercial contracts that must be standardized are ideally suited to flat fees. In one sense, this price negotiation recalls older approaches where, beyond the set fee for the bulk project, buyer and seller agree on additional compensation for future consultations on, say, the fine points of the boilerplates written for the loan agreements or contracts.

In contrast, Fitz warns that flat fees are ill-advised, particularly where a matter can better be negotiated on a success basis. Significantly, though, Fitz would discourage many value-based fee alternatives for M&A work, even though this is the one area where lavish premiums are most often deemed appropriate. Hourly rates befit transactional work as a matter of professional ethics. According to Fitz, "If, at the eleventh hour, [outside counsel] feel the deal is wrong for the company, they know they're still going to get 90% of their billable hours. They're more likely to raise their hands and say, 'Hang on a minute, let's think twice before approving this transaction.'" The hourly rate is a vital check and balance on the investment bankers who get nothing if the deal does not go through, and who are therefore less likely to caution the Board.

Fitz' point—especially hearing it from the client side—is also interesting since charging by billable hours is usually blamed for inefficiency and dishonesty that law firms have allegedly imposed on clients. Fear of the unknown, or inertia, or comparison rate shopping is usually the response to the question why inside counsel aren't more aggressive in their insistence on non-hourly alternatives. Here, though, hourly rates are seen as an ethical safeguard.

WHAT "KNOWING" MEANS

Yet M&A lawyers expect and certainly get premiums. It's a badly kept little secret that they often do have a vested interest in pushing deals forward. Of course a lot of clients don't think like Fitz. One reason they don't is that a lot of clients aren't lawyers.

We're not just talking about companies that, for whatever reason, don't have in-house departments. Such companies would include smaller traditional companies, New Economy start-ups, and even some larger concerns where a decision was made early on to minimize fixed overhead on legal services by not having attorneys on staff inside. In addition to these, we're also talking about companies with very large in-house legal contingents that nonetheless make diffuse buying decisions. Here, the GC or Associate GC is just one part of the equation. This decision-making becomes increasingly diffuse as the companies grow more complex and more global. They add more autonomous operating units and independent managers who like to hire and fire their own vendors, including legal vendors.

Thus, completely new "client knowledge" is required of outside counsel. What Riskin and Greene mean when they talk about "knowing the client" is the need for insight into the predictable tastes and buying habits of a very limited buying population, namely, in-house counsel. It is, of course, essential for law firms to have that knowledge; they must know who their in-house counterparts are, and they must know how the business operations of the client affect the company's legal needs that are overseen by the law department.

Yet even within the law department the rules are changing. As we'll see, many of the GCs interviewed for this book insist that they no longer care a fig about hiring law firms. That job is really delegated to the Associate and Deputy GCs who can do it better anyway because they're the ones who are actually in the trenches with outside counsel.

In the meantime, "client knowledge" as an ideal may be unachievable, as Gabe Shawn Varges points out. It is, he advises, a "Herculean" task for clients to "know their clients sufficiently." There are changes affecting clients as a result of cross-border alliances and mergers that make any sort of in-depth understanding elusive, even with regard to the basic logistics of the buying and selling process. "You may not even know who is going to be the decision-maker next month," says Varges, or whether he or she will be a lawyer.

In such an environment, the way to begin "knowing" the client is by establishing discrete relationships with discrete client segments. Varges advises law firms to follow the example of the great consulting firms such as McKinsey or Bain, that typically carve out just such highly differentiated pieces of the client landscape.

"They realize they have to have a multi-point approach," explains Varges. It is not enough to say, "I know the head of IT," or "I know the Chief Financial Officer," or even that "I know the CEO." Instead, the consultants learn to "know" the client by knowing the head of the e-commerce business. In the insurance area, it is similarly best for law firms to know the person who runs the Claims Department, because that is where a lot of the legal spending actually takes place. Is this a client with a separate M&A department? If so, is it as important, or more important, for outside counsel to "know" the executive who is driving that department rather than the in-house lawyers who may have much less sense of the real value of the deals they'll be working on?

The model is thrown even farther afield from the law department when, as Varges observes, the "levels of interaction" criss-cross and any number of managers influence retention decisions. He cites e-commerce as an example of an area where law departments have not typically driven the hiring. The young product VPs and engineers are looking for a law firm they can relate to. That may be a radically different law firm than the one the in-house lawyer across the hall finds amenable. One may tremble indeed for the law firms that, as Riskin and Greene observed, are too fearful to even learn what other lawyers, who happen to work in-house, think of them. How can they now go about "auditing" the profoundly different sensibilities of the nonlawyers who populate the e-com, M&A, and HR departments? Lawyers who know so little about their own kind are suddenly being required to think like McKinsey or Bain in order to survive.

Most people think that lawyers have at least taken a first step toward "knowing" their clients. Otherwise, the Riskins and Greenes wouldn't have the strong voice in professional discussions that they often do. Indeed, the MDPs may be the best thing that ever happened to outside counsel, in the sense that Japan was the best thing that ever happened to Detroit. This is the positive side of fear. If fear sometimes leads law firms into inexplicable strategic cul-de-sacs, it also prompts them to do market research, undertake marketing and sales training seminars, and launch strategic communications initiatives.

Yet the final outcome may be that, to serve their clients as their clients increasingly demand, law firms will have to alter themselves beyond recognition. Fitz, for example, believes that the partnership structure is "an old-fashioned way of doing business." Example after example of successful law firms—the ones that can "know" and can relate to their clients—are, by contrast, observably top-down in their structure. "Unless partners in firms are willing to delegate authority up to their management committees, and unless the management committee seizes the reins and behaves like a Board of Directors, it is going to be very hard for law firms to meet our aspirations for them," says Fitz.

In Riskin's view, this more corporate structure, with strong leadership, "gets you halfway there." The other half, Riskin reminds us, is the McKinsey model cited by Varges—and that is a very different kind of creature than the organizations run by corporate bosses like Jack Welch. This corporate/McKinsey model relies on collaboration as the fundamental cultural glue. "God help you in McKinsey if you are not collaborative," quips Riskin.

The law firm paradigm toward which these commentators are groping thus synthesizes opposites. The kind of "learning organization" described by Varges emerges mainly from a true partnership. On the other side of the equation, efficiency and direction come from strong leaders and managers. This paradigm isn't just something for law firms to ponder as they mull over their futures vis-à-vis the MDPs (many of which have for years been moving toward just such a balance of leadership and collaboration). This is an in-house issue as well because clients, insofar as they want to help foster ideal service levels, can play major roles in changing outside counsel for the better.

Following is an example. As Riskin observes, the great law firms should be willing to toss out a bumptious, uncooperative partner even if he or she bills many millions of dollars. That's a risky move, of course, however admirable. But the firms that can win their clients' support at such moments, not just with tea and sympathy, but with real commitments of future business, are the ones that can create a relationship of lasting value for themselves and the businesses they serve. The scenario doesn't have to be quite so dire. Commonly, managing partners still hang on to their personal clients despite the fact that the demands on law firm management in this day and age are prepossessing. It would seem that clients have a key role to play in encouraging change among outside counsel if, for example, they can take a collaborative role helping managing partners and/or originating partners pass the service baton on to someone else.

THEIR LOOMING SHADOW

McKinsey is always a comfortable paradigm for the professional services because it is unique, and neither could nor would compete with a law firm. The MDPs are less palatable as models for obvious reasons. They have now proven their ability to expand into legal services. Arthur Andersen is the biggest law firm in France and, in the UK and Spain, the accounting giants are also legal giants. In the United States, they may soon be given equal room to mount an assault on corporate legal business. Yet even without such an assault, law firms are losing talent, especially good tax attorneys, to these ubiquitous competitors.

The MDPs are relevant in this context for two reasons. The first is because they offer something akin to the organizational paragon described by Varges and Riskin. Like Varges' "learning organizations," they can be wondrously homogenous in the services they provide across borders. Like the consulting firm paragons, they are "multi-point." They lock in relationships, not just at the obvious points, but at more strategically segmented levels as well. And, like Riskin's collaborative endeavors, whereas the MDPs may have their share of 900-pound gorillas in their partnership ranks, they're not torn culturally asunder by the dominance of these revenue-generators—who, at many law firms, use their books of business to rule the roost without necessarily even bringing in profits.

Second, the MDPs pose a threat to the conventional inside/outside legal services relationship for reasons directly related to the client-service issues we've mentioned. The organizational coherence of the MDPs poses a striking contrast in the minds of many corporate buyers to what observers like Fitz perceive to be the growing obsolescence of law firm partnership structures. Clients may, as we suggested above, help law firms change. In the meantime, the PricewaterhouseCoopers and Arthur Andersens offer a global alternative that is not quite so frustrating to work with. They are more user-friendly organizations for clients who'd rather not have to be concerned about partnership politics that they often worry about when dealing with law firms. If nothing else, the Big Five are easier to work with because, on a day-to-day basis, they're more predictable.

The MDPs are indeed global, and big, which intensifies the fear among law firms that they must merge with other law firms or else they'll be outsized and discarded. Yet, despite their expanse, the MDPs have parlayed client service into what many observers see as their real trump card. As we've noted, in-house counsel worry that, as they expand, law firms will ruin the client relationship. The MDPs, no matter how big they get, are simply not perceived that way. Whether this rosier perception of these behemoths is justified or not is irrelevant. In the marketplace, of course, perception is reality.

"They're always *there*," remarks one partner at a mid-sized law firm in the Midwest, by which he means that the MDPs can build better relationships with his clients because they're constantly in the client's presence, selling this or selling that, handling this issue or managing that one. Their incursion into law firm profits in the U.S. is already tangible regardless of the prohibition on their practice of law in the U.S. Once upon a time, says this lawyer, associates at his firm would spend twenty billable hours preparing a document. Now, the MDPs hand some piece of boilerplate to the client and say, "Have the lawyers approve this. It shouldn't take them more than one hour."

It would seem that, with all that's been written about the MDPs in the late 1990s, the attitude of the buyers has either been ignored or been difficult to ferret out. "Provided they are not our company's auditors, I look at an MDP as a law firm with integrated services," says Michel Cloes, adding, however, that the MDPs still need to prove to him that they can offer superior levels of legal management. Interestingly, Cloes is not very interested in the wider range of non-legal services that the Big Five provide. "I look at them as law firms," he says. Their "integrated services" don't necessarily represent a one-stop shopping scheme any better than what some traditional law firms customarily provide with their deep referral networks reaching into other professions.

Cloes is speaking as an in-house legal manager, but that's not where the MDPs forge their significant relationships. Other GCs who do not view MDPs as law firms, but as multifaceted hybrids, could find themselves obliged or pressured to buy legal services from them anyway. As such, these gargantuan clones represent some threat to in-house counsel as well. Cloes may be able to disqualify a Big-Five law firm if it happens to also be the company's auditor, but at other companies the legal managers might not have that option.

Auditing is not the main non-legal service provided by the MDPs in any event. (Andersen, of course, has already stopped auditing.) There are also the consulting services, the corporate financial advice, and right sizing, to name just a few. No doubt general counsel have had law firms foisted on them by interested CEOs or CFOs in the past. But, with all that the MDPs now have to offer corporate buyers, their presence in the executive suites will be ever more constant and ever more powerful in the years ahead.

Will conflicts abound? Apparently, they already do, and in-house managers such as Flook cannot see any resolution. According to Fitz, Cable and Wireless hired a Big Five for right-size consulting, only to find out that its allegedly independent lawyers were advising on the right size of the Legal Department. Fitz sees that as a conflict of interest at a very personal level. But once companies dutifully start disqualifying services—in a conflict checking process that would be both comprehensive and continuous—they mitigate the very advantages that drew them to the MDPs in the first place. Once you disqualify your own auditors, asks Fitz, what value-added does a Big Five law firm bring to the table?

According to Andersen Legal spokespersons, the answer has a lot to do with how buyers such as Cloes view the marketplace. Arthur Andersen in Paris, or Arthur Andersen in Madrid, is a law firm that should be judged as a law firm, period. "I don't know what the other Big Five have as a strategy," says Andersen's Blake Redding (who previously worked in-house as well). "But [ours] is a philosophy that, if you want to come to us, come to us because we are good lawyers. Don't come to us because we have these other things that you can get." Sure, Andersen can provide you with access to abundant and diverse resources, but legal services come first if that is what you are specifically intending to buy. The other services get added if and when you want them. Whether such a tack was implicit in the Andersen strategy from the beginning, or evolved in response to the conflict problem that ACCA and other in-house powers happened to take quite seriously, is a matter of conjecture. Right now, though, the Andersen or Price or KPMG law firm *qua* law firm will, Redding feels, "make or break" the MDPs in this area.

However, there is another way to look at the value question that has a lot to do with full services, including non-legal services. As the survey data suggest, the buyers are saying, "We want our relationship firms; we want our firms to understand our companies." Regardless of whether Andersen might now want to present itself as a discrete legal entity, the broader multidisciplinary services that the MDPs can provide have a direct impact on that kind of understanding. The more you can give the client, the better you get to know the client.

"It's the degree to which there are more and more hooks," explains Greene. "If they are providing IT consulting, they know where [the client] is on that. If they are providing some litigation support, they understand how much infrastructure [the client has] to support the litigation." The issues are training, efficiency, money, and not having to bring somebody up to speed every time.

Greene's last example is additionally suggestive. It is well known that the Big Five don't litigate and probably never will. Yet when it comes to litigation support, they've been doing it longer and stronger than just about anybody. At the very least, they will partner with the attorneys, in-house or outside, who handle the actual discovery and trial work. Law firms that ignore the role the MDPs could play in the litigation arena are living in a fool's paradise.

For all the reservations of in-house counsel, and Andersen's efforts to assuage them, the good news for the MDPs is that the conflict wall won't stand up against efficiencies that clients themselves demand. This supposition is especially supportable since, at a fundamental level, all legal ethics, at least in the American canons, are strongly influenced by concern with client choice. (That is why, despite the insights of in-house managers like Dan Fitz, clients give big premiums to lawyers who make their deals happen.)

Here, Redding's emphasis on the crucial question of whether an MDP is a good law firm—all other considerations aside—makes potent sense. By "good" he means not just the ability to render a sound opinion on a tax question, but the overall suitability of the firm to represent the company. "We can talk about the ethical rules all day," says Redding, "but, at the end of the day, the clients are going to make the decision, rightly or wrongly, if there is a conflict. If you think there is a conflict of interest, you are not coming to us. It is that simple."

Ditto the confidentiality issue. Patrick Wilkins is no doubt correct in pointing out that MDPs were born from an accounting culture based on public disclosure, and that there's a strong likelihood such a cultural predilection won't change even if these accounting firms continue to de-emphasize auditing in favor of consulting and law.

"I would be thinking that the [MDPs] are passing on my secrets all over the place," says Wilkins. Redding's response is that the MDPs are fully aware that there are such fearful perceptions in the marketplace. The "challenge" for the MDPs is to convince the world that they "can keep a secret as well as anybody else," and that they are as professional in the rendering of legal services as competitor law firms. In fact, adds Redding, there are "internal rules" at Andersen, strictly imposed, with which the firm hopes to familiarize clients and prospects in the months and years ahead. On that point, the MDPs will either succeed in the marketplace or not.

Observers such as Wilkins sense disingenuousness in market-based explanations like Redding's. In the United States, points out Wilkins, Andersen would simply be disqualified by a court of law. However, a quick look at the politics of the American Bar Association shows that there are forces marshalling in support of change. As of this writing, tax lawyers in key ABA positions favor greater leeway for the MDPs. In the face of potential market demand, the ABA rules seem antiquated, and there is movement at local levels to lessen restrictions.

Nor are the conflict or other ethical issues for global buyers necessarily any worse with the MDPs than the problems that might arise at global law firms in the wake of large mergers. If "client choice" is the ethical linchpin, some law firm mergers have produced ethical quagmires. The Dana Corporation lost its outside counsel in Germany after a merger, reports Cloes. In other instances, the company has had to ask for legal fees to be returned because the value of past work already billed and paid for was vitiated when a law firm joined with another law firm.

The view that either the MDPs or the mega-mergers have resulted in an "antiquated" ethical canon continues to greatly bother observers such as Wilkins. "If those rules become antiquated," he argues, "then you rip out the entire ethical core of the legal profession. You are basically saying that a lawyer no longer will need to keep confidences with his client, and [can] give advice based on the things that he has learned from a competitor client."

But Wilkins isn't just lamenting a deterioration of standards. He is warning both the buyers and sellers that this diminution of standards will cause a backlash. In Europe, the results for the buyer will be sufficiently vexatious that tighter American-type ethics standards will be imposed there. The MDPs may be an unintentional long-term invitation to stricter guidelines in the inside/outside process, not ultimately the liberating force they want to be.

Buyers such as Varges envision a middle-ground scenario. "The rules will have to [be] . . . adapt[ed]," he says. Some conflict rules protect the integrity of the client relationship. Others are simply "protectionist" and make clients' lives more cumbersome, not safer. Varges uses the example of a married couple wanting to use the same lawyer to end their relationship amicably, and less expensively. The conflict rules would not be "consumer-friendly" in this situation.

Of course, a profession has to avoid conflicts "to do its job," and it is not enough for the seller to simply say that it has internal controls in place. In other ways, though, Varges does echo Redding: That the selling point for MDPs is to show clients and prospects *how*, as their representatives, those controls will be ensured. We're far beyond the ABA Code of Professional Ethics in any event, and the notion of that Code as "antiquated" may still be inevitable. Conflict and confidentiality become, as it were, free market commodities: "We—Andersen or Clifford Chance or KPMG or Shearman & Sterling—will better guard your vital interests than the other MDP or the other law firm down the street. We sell confidence along with service and expertise."

Wilkins and others continue to point out that case law in the United States just doesn't support this notion of a Chinese Wall as something that's saleable on a situation-by-situation basis. Yet the growth of MDPs speaks for itself. By all accounts, they should really have washed out of the legal business at this stage of the game. Some clients have loudly complained about the quality of the legal services they've gotten from MDPs. Lawyers who've left law firms to join MDPs have returned, often in disgust because there were quality issues and management issues that they, as former partners in a law firm, could not abide. Indeed, their complaints pointedly belie the pretensions of the MDPs to being the sort of paradigmatic professional services organizations that Cloes, Varges, and Riskin envision.

For all their real and pervasive problems, however, the expansion of the MDPs continues, sometimes in fits and starts, but onward and upward in any event.

CONCLUSION: BABY TIGER

The interface of the MDPs and the legal exchanges punctuate the importance of both, and further exemplify the mega-changes roiling the inside/outside dynamic. Kay Ellen Consolver observes that that interface is naturally significant outside the U.S. where the MDPs are not constrained from practicing law. The price issue may not be dispositive but it does have some impact since the MDPs are often cheaper than law firms, especially in the high-volume commodity areas such as tax that they feature. The comparison-shopping that the exchanges provide online would therefore be one more reason the Big Five or other MDPs would want to sell this way.

We've seen how directly or indirectly related the legal exchanges are to most of the issues we've touched on in this first chapter. The exchanges are a part of the intensively new automated approach taken by some buyers. They pertain directly to cost as a determinant as to which firms will get hired. They help define the commoditization of the legal market, and are therefore of great potential interest to the MDPs as a selling mechanism, and as part of the whole sea change that the MDPs represent. They punctuate the "personal" nature of the inside/outside dynamic by abetting referral networks or, conversely, by offering some users a less personal, more mechanistic alternative. They typify a fundamental principle: That buyers often don't admit to how they buy. And they even relate to the global client service potential that the vast international networks and affiliations have been set up to exploit; like those networks, they offer quick access to increasingly specialized fields of hard-to-get expertise.

Whether or not the legal exchanges actually presage an important future for in-house buyers, their multilateral significance is thus of undeniable substantive interest. Some additional commentary from both the exchanges themselves and their potential users seems an appropriate way to conclude this initial discussion.

David Briscoe at iBidLaw acknowledges that the exchanges are "really a market in its infancy." He tends to think the pundits "always overestimate" the extent and speed of the change directly ahead. As one of the pioneers in this new legal technology, Briscoe prefers to "manage expectations" regarding the exchanges. In fact, he's "taken aback" by the FGI data suggesting such meteoric ascendancy among buyers and sellers. In contrast, he predicts that the "tremendous impact" that lies ahead will occur over what he estimates to be a ten-year period, rather than a much shorter time.

"Our experience has been that the commodity legal services are what is coming to us initially," he says. It's still the kind of work where the buyer's "knowledge" of the lawyer or firm is of somewhat less consequence.

"The legal exchanges are going to start at the bottom of the pyramid, which is where a large part of legal work actually is," adds Briscoe. But "it will move up that pyramid. The Internet accelerates the commoditization of services in general, not just legal services, because it [helps] a buyer and a seller find each other much more easily." Later in the game, however, the dialogue may change or the work itself may expand. "What we define today as commodity work might be very, very different in five years," Briscoe concludes.

At eLawForum, which had the benefit in the 2000-2001 period of considerable publicity (as well as the support of respected figures such as Sam Gillespie), Consolver reports that migration upward has already begun. That migration was a direct function of repeat buyer-to-seller activity using the exchange. Consolver says that patent infringement litigation, for example, is now being staffed online through eLawForum.

In some ways the survey data, although it shows strong proclivities among in-house buyers to use the Internet in one capacity or another, does support Briscoe's depiction of the exchanges as an industry in its infancy. Twenty-eight percent of the survey respondents say that the exchanges will change the legal profession. But that doesn't mean those respondents are themselves using the exchanges or have any intention of ever doing so. Of the 13% who search the Web for legal services on a daily basis, there is, further, no indication how much of that searching is via exchanges such as iBidLaw or eLawForum.

Although Greene reports that there were unsolicited favorable comments about the exchanges, there were pointedly negative interjections as well. Greene's belief in any event is that the exchanges "may really take off." Yet he doesn't think their growth will be "client-driven"—a fairly unusual observation to make about a marketplace that is inundated with the rhetoric of client-driven service. An industry leader such as Consolver would certainly disagree.

Greene isn't suggesting that the clients will be collectively resistant but, rather, that they won't be proactive. "It is going to be pushed by the law firms rather than pulled by the clients," he explains. At this point, the buyers don't yet see the need. Only after they're up and running at full speed will they see the "utility." Even then, he suggests, demand won't outstrip supply.

Yet Cloes wonders who would really be interested other than a "first time purchaser of service. . . . We have years of experience personally, but we also belong to global multinational groups that [provide] contacts everywhere. It is very rare that somebody from one of my corporate groups says, 'Oh, we are missing a link in Hungary.'"

Were there such a missing link, buyers such as Cloes and Fitz would still think primarily in terms of existing referral networks to fill the gap. Further due diligence after a solid referral is simply easier than starting from scratch. For now, as Fitz puts it, "it's all about what other people I know and trust have said about a firm. The classical values are still the most important values."

For now. By tomorrow, one of Gerry Riskin's recent experiences may turn out to be predictive. Riskin was asked by the in-house department of a railroad company to help outsource a "staggering" volume of legal work. Despite the 150 years that the railroads have been in business, and the innumerable lawyers they've employed, Riskin now found it difficult to locate outside counsel with sufficient in-depth knowledge of the industry. (Old Economy counsel—for really Old Economy industries like the railroads—may be as difficult to find these days as cutting-edge New Economy counsel.) Add to that the likely desire of the smarter railroad clients to gather together a network of outside attorneys with talent and legal knowledge, and you have a recipe for *en masse* legal services purchasing.

A single referral may turn up a single lawyer. But that community of outside experts will still have to be assembled if the client in this particular industry is to be best served. For such a global task, how could online searching, especially under the structured aegis of a formal exchange, not be valuable?

Fitz acknowledges that Cable and Wireless has already done such searching with extranets, using one law firm in Sydney and another in London on a major project. He points out, though, that this approach was successful because the two firms put out their own feelers, tapping their own already established relationships, much as they could have done without benefit of advanced technology. "The Internet is an imperfect medium still," says Fitz. It still lacks the requisite "touch and feel," whether you're hiring one lawyer or building a network of outside firms.

"I am not saying it can't work without the face-to-face meetings, and working side-by-side for weeks, but all that sure does help," adds Fitz.

Yet Fitz has a final suggestion as to where the legal exchanges might go and, in so doing, render significant benefits to in-house counsel. What if the 600-plus firms on exchanges like eLawForum, as a condition to selling their services on the exchange, sign on to rules of behavior, conflict controls, confidentiality agreements, and competency guarantees above and beyond their ABA or Law Society requirements?

This would not merely be an additional reassurance to the buyers that the potential ethics issues with the megafirms and MDPs that we discussed earlier can be effectively addressed. In a global economy, this would also be a matter of enormous convenience, since in-house counsel in England won't necessarily have close knowledge of the rules in Brazil. Or perhaps the rules of one country are deficient by the standards of a client in another. The exchanges could create their own rules and thereby make a meaningful attempt to achieve more professional consistency wherever the client does business. It could be a powerful selling tool as well, motivating corporate buyers to proactively support this emerging technology.

It may well be that the exchanges will thus develop well beyond a buying mechanism, and that the eLawForums could be on to something bigger than they imagine. In the 1980s and 1990s the inside/outside dynamic was clouded with distrust: What, for example, were law firms doing with the increasingly high fees they were charging? Gabe Shawn Varges sees the exchanges as a way to achieve greater transparency. He cites the insurance industry as a salutary example of how buyers can now go online not only to ascertain comparative costs, but also to actually see in some instances where their premium dollars go. There are numbers available on how much the insurers spend for administrative purposes, how much they spend for client services, etc.

Varges envisions law firms gaining a competitive advantage by exploiting the potential of the legal exchanges in order to do more or less the same thing. Making controlled disclosure is not immediately likely, but it's not unthinkable either. Some law firms are already allowing unprecedented client access to such information over their extranets. As we'll see in Chapter 5, two UK firms, Walker Morris and DJ Freeman, already provide clients online information about their unbilled time. It is a provocative way to head off incipient fee disputes since the buyer can respond to the billing data before they get billed. As an alternative to extranets, the exchanges are a promising venue for such disclosure on a turnkey, user-by-user basis.

Most important, this minimal unfettered access by clients to their own case information is just one more example of the as yet imponderable surprises that lie ahead.

APPENDIX *

How General Counsels Buy and Will Buy Legal Services

The Fundamental Process

STEP ONE: *Finding Qualified Service Providers: Creating the Short List*

♦ Inertia the greatest force of all
   Very high credibility

♦ Seek referrals
   High credibility

♦ Check directories/Web search
   Some credibility

♦ Often unacknowledged: advertising/brand image

♦ Objective criteria key to making short list

---

* Presented by Dr. Mark T. Greene, FGI Customer Research and Quality Consulting, by permission of FGI, Inc. and Greenfield/Belser Ltd.

STEP TWO: *Choosing from the Short List*

♦ Objective measures less important than subjective
   Fine differences in objective criteria
      Difficult for buyers to evaluate
      Relatively unimportant to buyers

♦ Firm image/brand matters (50% admitted in 2000 survey)
   Safe choice (especially international matters)
   Scare opposition

♦ Personal contact sought
   Face-to-face
   Seminars
   Articles, white papers

♦ Individual lawyers sought/evaluated
   Liking, personal chemistry
   Innovative thinking
   Trust

With Specialty Services, Expertise Is Very Important

♦ 1994: Reputation/expertise top criterion

♦ 1996: In-house counsel significantly more likely to evaluate expertise than executives

   Fastest-growing companies more likely to be concerned with relationships

♦ 1999: Firm's expertise and nature of relationship most highly correlated to likelihood of using a firm

♦ 2000: Expertise factor is much more important to emerging biotech/infotech companies (56%) than to decision-makers in large corporations (23%)

Sources of Information

♦ Opinions of colleagues and other counsel are still the primary source of information about outside attorneys and firms.

♦ Recently, a third of counsel mentioned Internet sites as one source of information.

HOW WILL PROVISION OF LEGAL SERVICES BE CHANGED BY THE INTERNET?

TABLE 1

Non-Internet Tactics Still Effective

Tactics	Percentage of Counsel
Referrals/Word of Mouth	60
Newsletters/Updates	19
Brochures	16
Call/Visit Me	13
Seminars	12
Established Relationships	11
Networking	11
Personal Experience	5
Representative Matters	5
Portals	4
Articles	3

TABLE 2

Frequency of Searching Online
for Legal Services

Mean = 2.8, N = 98

Frequency	Percentage of Counsel
Daily	13
Weekly	32
Monthly	18
Never	37

TABLE 3

Visiting a Law Firm Website
to Search for Services

Mean = 2.6, N = 70

Frequency	Percentage of Counsel
Often	9
Sometimes	39
Rarely	39
Never	13

TABLE 4

Using a Legal Portal
to Search for Services

Mean = 2.6, N = 70

Frequency	Percentage of Counsel
Often	17
Sometimes	31
Rarely	23
Never	29

TABLE 5

Using a Key Word Search Engine
to Find Services

Mean = 1.9, N = 70

Frequency	Percentage of Counsel
Often	44
Sometimes	29
Rarely	16
Never	11

TABLE 6

Ever Used a Law Firm Extranet?

Mean = 1.9, N = 110

Yes	12%
No	88%

TABLE 7

Likelihood That Decision to Try New Firm Would Be Influenced by Internet Presence

Mean = 4.6, N = 108

Not at All Likely	10%
Extremely Likely	10%

TABLE 8

Can MDSs Provide Legal Services as Effectively as Law Firms?

Mean = 4.1, N = 328

Strongly Disagree	30%
Neither Agree Nor Disagree	22%
Strongly Agree	10%

TABLE 9

How Do You See the Provision of Legal Services Changing Because of the Internet?

More efficient due to the speed of the Internet	36%
Ability to communicate more via e-mail and webcast	23%
Exchange documents quicker and easier	21%
Access research information easier	8%
Ordinary people will have more access to the information	8%
Information that is free	6%
Have the ability to get the most up-to-date information	4%
More electronic transfers	4%
Still need human contact	3%
Handle legal disputes online	1%
Cost of the firm will decrease	1%
Keep people informed on the status of situations	1%

TABLE 10

What Do You Think Will Happen in the Next Two Years?

More e-mails exchanged	15%
Exchange documents quicker and easier	11%
Ability to communicate more via e-mail and webcast	6%
More information in general will be available	6%
Paper documents will become rare	5%
Firms will consolidate	5%
More electronic transfers	4%
Geography of firm will become less important	4%
Billing electronically	4%
Cost of the firm will decrease	3%
Access research information easier	3%
Still need human contact	2%
More competition between firms	2%
Handle legal disputes online	1%
Share intellectual knowledge between firms	1%
Easy access to legal forms	1%
Ability to identify legal counsel	1%

TABLE 11

What Would You Like to See Happen?

Cost of the service will be affected	6%
Be able to work on document in real time	5%
Exchange documents quicker and easier	3%
Ability to communicate more via e-mail and webcast	3%
Court filings online	3%
See all lawyers go away	3%
Access research information easier	3%
Billing electronically	3%
Still need human contact	2%
Information that is free	2%
Easy access to legal forms	2%
Webcast/video conferencing	2%
Security on the web	2%
Access from anywhere	2%
More websites and portals	1%
Task-based billing	1%
Quicker responses from lawyers	1%
Be able to closely monitor the status of lawyer	1%

Table 12

How Do You See This Changing as a Result of Legal Exchanges?

I would not use it	20%
Clients have more resources to examine	18%
Get recommendations/referrals/word-of-mouth reference from	12%
Established relationships	8%
Sounds interesting	7%
Use to facilitate research, but not chose firm	7%
Want human contact	6%
Help narrow the field without having to call or meet the lawyer	5%
Have a broader pool of lawyers to choose from	5%
Cost of the law firm will decrease	4%
More competition between firms	4%
Lawyer's expertise/experience	4%
Could be a positive thing	3%
Hire more in-house lawyers	3%
Rely on personal knowledge of the lawyer	3%
Webcast/video conferencing will increase	2%
Geography of the firm will become less important	2%
Practice area information/expertise	2%
Use a bidding process	1%

Solving the Global Puzzle: Are Yesterday's Megafirms Tomorrow's Answer?

L
istening to buyers such as Michel Cloes, Gabe Varges, and Susie Flook, one hears many of the same themes that come up in discussions of how legal services are best bought on a national or regional basis echoed on a global scale. Here too, for instance, the most "local" of considerations is determinative, i.e., is there a strong individual partner with whom you, as the client, can regularly deal? Will that partner oversee the work? Will that partner be ultimately responsible for the law firm's responsiveness and performance even if he or she is removed from the day-to-day activities?

Indeed, when Harold Barron was a partner at the Chicago firm Seyfarth Shaw, he would sometimes "upset" his partners by continuing to "watch over" the cases of clients he had developed or with whom he had close relationships. When Barron became general counsel of Unisys Corporation, he looked to outside counsel for that same oversight—"a partner who had clout," someone he knew and could "rely on" to be answerable for the firm's performance. As Unisys matters became increasingly global, there was no reason to alter that approach. Wherever the legal matter occurs, the personal element is paramount.[1]

There's another somewhat related, very salient message that such buyers offer, at least implicitly. For all the talk of global

---

[1] Barron is now the Vice Chairman of Unisys. Nancy Sundheim replaced him as GC.

markets, and how law firms must re-strategize to tap those markets, there are many situations where globalization has *not* had a decisive impact on inside purchasing habits.

In part, that's because companies like Unisys are already set up to buy local legal services overseas as they might have fifteen years ago. Unisys, for one, does business in 100 or more countries. There are a dozen or so in-house lawyers in Western European offices, a few more than that in Latin America, and in-house counsel in Asia and Australia. All these lawyers report directly to the GC, but they select outside counsel in the same way that Unisys lawyers might in Detroit, Michigan, or Norcross, Georgia. They bring their local market knowledge to bear, and they match appropriate outside counsel to the matter at hand and the budget in force. If additional law firms are needed, the Unisys GC, as well as her deputies, continues to rely on informal networks of corporate buyers and on associations such as ACCA.

It's therefore significant, but not particularly surprising, that Hal Barron, for one, does not seem to have strong opinions about the global consolidation of law firms, at least not how that consolidation directly affects the servicing of his own company on a global basis. Nor are global law firm networks or affiliations at the top of any list of concerns for Barron to be pondering.

In other words, glib assumptions about new opportunities generated by globalization must be modified somewhat when the needs of large corporate buyers do not necessarily demand exponentially increased global resources. Not every company has a Daimler/Chrysler deal in the offing. Not every overseas transaction requires any significant change in the usual retention process, particularly when there are strong in-house contingents on the ground in far-flung locales.

Oracle Corporation may be the best case in point. That company does business in 160 countries, and forty of its approximately 105 lawyers are based overseas in regional operating units in Asia, Japan, Europe/Africa, Latin America, and Canada. The regional GCs in these units report to GC Daniel

SOLVING THE GLOBAL PUZZLE:
ARE YESTERDAY'S MEGAFIRMS TOMORROW'S ANSWER?

67

Cooperman, who has final approval of all retention decisions. Those decisions are naturally made by the managing counsel in the regional units. They have determined the legal issues and designated the local firms that can handle them.

Cooperman does suggest that, for companies with high-volume litigation and transactions, the big global firms have resources that they "can move around," presumably to provide comprehensive, even cost-efficient services. He worries that the big firms will encounter conflicts, which "we take very seriously." In fact, Cooperman personally signs off on every conflicts waiver. Conflicts are never automatically assumed to be merely "technical."

However, at Oracle there just isn't that much outside work to be assigned overseas. According to Cooperman, the "vast majority" of Oracle's legal matters involve customer "out-licensing" when other companies use Oracle systems. These matters are not simple, but involve "tricky issues" with challenging variations from one national venue to another. No outside law firm can possibly do this work better, or with more intimate familiarity of the specific facts relevant to specific Oracle products, than Oracle's own lawyers. Outside counsel, by contrast, are brought in on a limited basis, typically in anomalous situations. There's not much, if any, product liability work, for example, and other types of lawsuits also arise fairly infrequently.

It's especially interesting that Oracle's use of global counsel has not tilted toward outside law firms even during the period since 1998—when Cooperman became GC—after which the company very consciously adjusted its legal services strategy from a region-by-region approach to a more cohesive global configuration. As Cooperman explains, it was his mission to ensure that the regional GCs began reporting directly to him. Before that, they reported to their regional general managers.

This centralization coincides with the rise of e-business, adds Cooperman. Oracle's risky but historically momentous corporate shift in that direction mandated worldwide standardization. After all, people in Brazil were buying the same products online as folks in Beijing. Prices were standardized. Contracts were standardized. Legal problems might vary from region to region, but the same customer protection guarantees would apply regardless of venue. And, to legally oversee that single regimen, the only efficient approach would necessarily be in-house.

This strategy has become more viable since the dot.com crash of 2000. Even in the immediate aftermath of that crash, Cooperman had trouble finding enough new lawyers to provide staff at ideal in-house levels. Now, with the slowdown in venture technology continuing through 2001, his telephone rings off the hook and candidates line up outside Oracle's door.

The attraction for these lawyers is powerful. First, they get to stay in the technology area, which was where they mapped out their careers, either practicing at high-tech law firms with venture capital pull, or working at dot.coms. The latter are gone, and, as of mid-2001, the cutting-edge firms in Silicon Valley and the other high-tech corridors were making fewer job offers and rescinding their notoriously lavish bonuses.

Second, new Oracle in-house counsel get to work for a powerful, established company (subject to the layoffs and restructuring that all corporations may face as the economy remains at a slow- or no-growth pace). And third, the new in-house counsel need not develop business in an economy where business development is an excruciatingly formidable challenge even for lawyers who enjoy it.

When Oracle must hire law firms overseas, Cooperman relies on his own local lawyers. As at Unisys, they know their local markets. They know who's good there, and they have enough relationships in place to hire effectively. That is a major advantage of having corporate counsel practicing worldwide. Again, why worry about what's happening to law firms? Why worry about big New York firms merging with big London firms? Why bother with global law firm networks that provide referrals to attorneys in Singapore or Toronto with whom your own people are already personally familiar?

SOLVING THE GLOBAL PUZZLE:
ARE YESTERDAY'S MEGAFIRMS TOMORROW'S ANSWER?

69

GLOBAL OPENINGS

The comments of both Barron and Cooperman are thus significant
for a couple of reasons. They remind us that not every global
corporation is a cornucopia of burgeoning legal business for law
firms. By the same token, these in-house managers may also be
giving us a clue about where some global openings exist. Those
openings are multifarious. They're not just a by-product of mega-
events where, say, mergers of global corporate giants necessarily
require squadrons of outside attorneys in New York, London,
Paris, or Hong Kong.

We might even extrapolate a somewhat novel idea from the
comments of Barron and Cooperman: That a large law firm can
actually be the most cost-effective way to serve corporations on a
global basis. Unisys, for one, will often dispatch lawyers for a week
or two to oversee outside counsel in a foreign jurisdiction. One
reason is control. As Barron puts it, "We won't necessarily want to
settle a case in London just because some law firm there advises us
to." Having a Unisys lawyer close at hand allows the company to
make a more informed—and controlled—decision.

We then must ask: Why can't a relationship partner at a
global megafirm—the kind of "partner with clout" that Barron
describes—serve some of that same advisory function?
Presumably it is in the interests of both the client and the law firm
for a senior partner to play such a controlling role. At times it will
still be necessary to send over a company lawyer to monitor the
work, but in some situations it could save considerable in-house
time and money were the company to have a senior relationship
partner, at a large law firm with which it does business around the
world, to advise that a settlement is appropriate, etc.

The second reason Unisys sends its in-house attorneys
overseas is cost, especially in pricey markets such as London. UK
rates are sky-high, says Barron. UK firms charge the same rates in
pounds that the top U.S. firms charge in dollars. So we must next
ask: Can a U.S.-based megafirm do the work for less even when its

rates in England are the same as those of British firms? Ostensibly, global teams could be using blended rates, higher than the average U.S. fees, perhaps, but lower than the average in the UK. Alternatively, the U.S. members of the team might charge lower U.S. rates, which would bring down the total per-matter cost.

We're in fairly uncharted territory here. The supposition among most observers, and among many in-house buyers as well, is that large law firms are by definition the most expensive source of legal work. That's often true. The current wave of law firm mergers has made many clients nervous about who's going to pay for the extraordinary costs of those combinations. Even where there are no such new costs to pass on, large firms are, of course, highly leveraged. Clients pay for extravagantly staffed teams of timekeepers billing market rates and sometimes higher.

How, then, can a megafirm be cost-effective, especially on a global basis where the legal teams are often large, and where ancillary costs and disbursements climb higher and higher? There seem to be bottomless money pits for hapless global corporations to stumble into. The solution may lie in what these megafirms bring to the table in addition to sheer size.

Let's briefly review the options for in-house buyers that have legal needs in different countries:

1. You have a staff abroad large enough to handle work best done in-house. These local lawyers know their legal communities well enough to hire local counsel if and when they're needed. Indeed, if you're Oracle, you may not even need to read the next four options.

2. You depend on referrals, including referrals from the main law firms you use on your home turf. This approach is probably the most common and it may be quite adequate for many companies. However, you may (a) not really be exploring all your options, (b) be missing out on the best outside counsel that your money can buy, or (c) be overlooking significant efficiencies if you use a single full-service source to handle your matters everywhere.

SOLVING THE GLOBAL PUZZLE:
ARE YESTERDAY'S MEGAFIRMS TOMORROW'S ANSWER?

71

3. You depend on a law firm network that can supply member firms on a global basis. Commercial Law Affiliates is a multi-national case in point. Such entities stress quality control, and swear that they terminate relationships with member firms that don't continue to perform well. But you'll still have your eggs in a lot of baskets, and you might still be wondering if you would be better off paying more for a single-source global provider.

4. You hire a multi-office law firm, with a presence everywhere from São Paulo to St. Paul. But quality control is a problem in Brazil because that São Paulo office is an entirely different creature than the St. Paul office. You'd probably be better off with a network since the network has to oversee quality to some extent to survive. In contrast, the multi-office law firms often get away with a lemon of an office in this city or that.

5. You hire a more fully integrated name-brand law firm that can, as Cooperman says, shift resources around. They do good work, but my, how those costs build up!

An ideal creature would likely be the fully integrated law firm that has not recently merged and does not, therefore, have the troublesome cultural and economic baggage that accompanies most large mergers. Like Shearman & Sterling, such a creature feeds on organic growth and careful lateral hiring. Most important, such a creature has had a system in place for years that facilitates the sharing of resources so that, as Gabe Varges suggested in Chapter 1, a member of the firm can call a Frankfurt partner on a New York matter knowing that that lawyer will nimbly turn to his partner in New York to get the answer.

At some law firms the system is cultural in the sense that the partner just knows by instinct to pick up the telephone and call New York for help on a client matter. At other firms—and there aren't many of these—the total global practice is organized to maximize seamless teamwork. These organizations are built so that it is almost impossible for one arm of the firm not to be informed by the other, no matter where in the world the work is being done.

The costs for such service may not always be as high as they seem, considering the nature of the work—its scope, complexity, and importance. In fact, if there is a real sharing of resources, and not just a shuttling of paper and files, this approach is, by definition, the most cost-effective approach possible simply because there isn't much waste.

"If you don't have the structure, you have increased costs," says David Clossey, head of the international practice of Jones, Day, Reavis & Pogue. "You have entropy." Jones, Day, to be sure, has structure galore.

WHEELS IN GEAR

Jones, Day may not have a better international practice *per se* than firms such as Shearman & Sterling or White & Case. At the same time, for in-house buyers planning a global legal services purchasing strategy, Jones, Day is a firm that's worth focusing on for several reasons.

First and most important, Jones, Day shows the value of a past, of having had something to bring to the table before the globalization of the 1990s even began. One thing it always brought was size. Jones, Day was already very big when it decided to embark on a global strategy. Throughout the late 1980s and 1990s, it was perennially one of the three largest U.S. law firms. The other two were Baker & McKenzie and Skadden, Arps, Slate, Meagher & Flom. The former incarnates the multi-office approach to global expansion, and quality control has been a problem for Baker & McKenzie in some of its offices, as the firm itself has had to acknowledge from time to time. Skadden features a strong global practice, but the firm is more intimately reliant for its core work on the capital markets. Jones, Day covers both fronts more expansively. The firm will do work for The B. F. Goodrich Company overseas as well as represent Goldman, Sachs abroad.

With the advantage of size, Jones, Day has been able to hire laterally in foreign markets because the firm could show a

SOLVING THE GLOBAL PUZZLE:
ARE YESTERDAY'S MEGAFIRMS TOMORROW'S ANSWER?

73

formidable menu of existing resources. It offered a "platform"—i.e., the opportunity to expand a lawyer's personal practice exponentially and immediately—to choice candidates. It didn't need to merge with anyone in order to grow. The firm could let the natural cycles move apace, internationally as well as in the United States, and both laterally and organically. Other law firms had to scramble to serve clients with legal needs in Europe or Asia. They hired quickly, transferred partners, and often took big economic hits on leaseholds and other costs. They were being compelled more than they were choosing, i.e., chase the clients to Europe or lose them to someone else who can do the work abroad and, worst of all, start representing them domestically as their relationship develops. If the firms did set up overseas to serve the client, there often was little chance of then attracting additional significant business from new buyers to further justify the trouble and cost of the office.

In other words, smaller firms, even including many in the 500-to-600 lawyer tiers, went abroad defensively. In contrast, the larger firms such as Jones, Day could grow enough at will to keep B. F. Goodrich close and attract additional clients as well.

Yet size alone was by no means a sufficient head start on globalization. Some firms have the will and the desire to be global. Others do not. Los Angeles-based Gibson, Dunn & Crutcher, for example, has struggled to achieve an international presence. But the partnership itself was historically divided on the subject. A Hong Kong defection to Shearman & Sterling some years ago underscored the deep internal rift. Gibson, Dunn even tried to confer premature partner status on the lawyers who remained in Hong Kong, but to no avail. Morgan, Lewis & Bockius is another enormous law firm with an international strategy that has cratered, which was evident when its Brussels head joined Jones, Day. Meanwhile, Morgan, Lewis' London office is well under the growth rates achieved by other U.S. firms in the UK, and its practices in Frankfurt and Hong Kong continue to be small.

Jones, Day has a strategic advantage that sets it apart from most of the other firms that have also succeeded globally: It is not as dependent on a consensus of thirty or forty, or 100 or 200, powerful partners. The firm has a top-down management style that is most unusual, if not unique among mainstream corporate law firms. There are real bosses at Jones, Day. The current managing partner in Cleveland, Patrick McCartan, has extraordinary power, as did his predecessors Allen Holmes and Richard Pogue.

For in-house buyers, this management culture is relevant for several reasons. First, it mirrors how the clients themselves operate, certainly to a greater extent than the flat, owner-operated law firms that they're accustomed to hiring. Second, a top-down style guarantees that the reporting relationships and team responsibilities that are assigned will be enforced, and that the firm's complex organizational apparatus, which is designed to maximize team interaction, will not bog down in bureaucracy. In essence, such a management culture ensures that the firm will do what it promises to do, simply because its commitment has been blessed from on high. The in-house buyer won't have to change horses midstream because partners in the firm decided, much against the will of its managers, to abandon the race.

Specifically, Jones, Day's global practice structure is a matrix embracing twenty-six offices, including fourteen overseas. There is an interweaving of practices and practitioners that ostensibly ensures faster and better lawyer training as well as the kind of knowledge management, technological and otherwise, that buyers like Varges dote on.

The matrix revolves around both geographic and practice area axes. The geographic axis includes Europe, Asia, and Latin America, as well as North America. A regional chairman presides over each geographic area; that chairman is also the managing partner of one of the offices in the region. (All offices have their own managing partners.) Thus, the managing partner in Paris is regional chairman in Europe; the Tokyo managing partner chairs the Asian regional group. There are no offices in Latin America, so that practice is headed up by a partner based in New York.

SOLVING THE GLOBAL PUZZLE:
ARE YESTERDAY'S MEGAFIRMS TOMORROW'S ANSWER?

75

Clossey says the practice group axis is even more important to the overall strategy, presumably because it is more directly related to the day-to-day legal issues facing clients. There are four umbrella practice groups: litigation, business practice, government regulation, and tax. Many law firms used to divide themselves something along these lines but, as their clientele and legal business grew more variegated, they abandoned these larger groups in favor of the many narrower practice areas that are commonplace today among most firms. The transformation proved a mixed blessing. More focus was achieved, but often at the cost of firm unity. Practice groups went off on their own and competed with other practice groups. More and more often, they'd just pick up and leave their firms.

Jones, Day's structure aims to achieve the best of both worlds. Although the umbrella categories are naturally broken down into numerous, more specialized practices, the latter still report to the heads of the four main groups. The woof and warp is completed as lawyers also organize by industry groups: energy, financial institutions, technology, and real estate. Whoever you are at Jones, Day, you're dealing with a full complement of other lawyers in other disciplines and other parts of the world.

An historic significance of the Jones, Day model is that it's probably the most conspicuous example of how, by starting off big, and with a history of internal tough-mindedness, a law firm created a global entity that others are now trying to create via merger, or via formal affiliations and networks. From the standpoint of the in-house buyer, law firms seem to be living in two different universes when it comes to global strategy. The Jones, Days and Shearman & Sterlings have worked, with relative degrees of success, to globally integrate their own lawyers. When Linklaters creates a European alliance, or Clifford Chance merges with a large New York firm, they are trying to globally integrate *somebody else's lawyers*.

In later chapters we'll hear from corporate buyers about how helpful some of these mergers have been, including the epochal combination of Clifford Chance with Rogers & Wells. It brought rich new client opportunities to both the merging firms—and, according to companies like Prudential, tangible benefits for clients as well. Indeed, there are no simple answers to the questions general counsel must ask themselves. Some big mergers work, period. Jones, Day itself grew in the United States via mergers with major mid-sized firms such as Surrey & Morse in Washington, D.C., and Hansell & Post in Atlanta.

At the same time, Jones, Day is an example of why it makes good sense to rely on services providers that are already dealing from strength and have been for some time.

FAST ACTION

As examples of how these behemoths function overseas, let's take a look at a couple of Jones, Day deals. They offer important lessons for in-house buyers because they are pointedly illustrative of the resources that Cooperman mentions, and the cost-effectiveness that—despite the proverbial criticisms of their high-cost leverage structures—the multinational law firm behemoths can provide.

One deal, on behalf of Abbott Laboratories, was well-publicized, including a feature in *The American Lawyer*.[2] In December 2000, M&A partner Libby Kitslaar completed a thirty-day, non-stop negotiation of Abbott's $6.9 billion bid for Knoll Pharmaceuticals, the pharmaceutical unit of German conglomerate BASF AG. It is significant that, in the reporting of this and similar transactions, *The American Lawyer* customarily details the size of the troop strength and how the troops were deployed. Here, a Chicago-based partner "mobilized and managed" over thirty Jones, Day lawyers from ten offices, representing seven countries and three continents.

Kitslaar had four days to assemble a team of lawyers to handle the due diligence.

---

[2] "Big Deals," The American Lawyer (Feb. 2001).

SOLVING THE GLOBAL PUZZLE:
ARE YESTERDAY'S MEGAFIRMS TOMORROW'S ANSWER?

77

She tapped attorneys in Jones, Day's London office and was even able to include a German-speaking associate from the Chicago office. Kitslaar then needed more lawyers to prepare the bid. Since Knoll had subsidiaries in Japan, India, and Pakistan, along with operations in Germany, Britain, France, and Spain, Kitslaar needed input from colleagues who were knowledgeable about the law in all those places. She got just that.

"Local counsel are not always as responsive as your own people," Kitslaar told *The American Lawyer*. This is the kind of modest observation that entire inside/outside relationships can be built on. Yes, you can hire from law firm networks, and use referral sources, and try any number of novel lawyer combinations and configurations—but, in the end, those lawyers are just not as responsive to your immediate crucial needs as a single law firm's "own people."

The fact that corporate counsel see this truism reinforced on a daily basis in deals such as Abbott's Knoll acquisition no doubt explains why the established global law firms still dominate the inside/outside dynamic in the world's major legal marketplaces. When the legal concepts are new, and must be refined on a cross-border basis, the appeal of a megafirm that can provide immediate multi-jurisdictional counsel increases proportionately among in-house decision-makers. A case in point was when Jones, Day's Paris partner Edward Nalbantian represented J. P. Morgan and Société Générale in the financing of Groupe Pernod Ricard's joint acquisition, with Diageo plc, of the Seagrams spirits and wine business from Vivendi Universal.

In this case, an innovative collateralization based on trademarks was devised. As more business gets done online, companies have fewer tangible assets such as real estate or office equipment to offer as collateral for a loan or line of credit. In the Groupe Pernod Ricard/Diageo transaction, the lender bank holds the consolidated borrower's trademarks and has the right to retain them if the company defaults on a loan. The benefits for both parties are obvious: Protection for one, new capital for the other. It is a potent fillip to M&A activity, and a real mother lode for marketing departments—since the more branded a trademark becomes, the more pure cash value it will have for companies that may want to re-capitalize failed ventures or raise money for new ones.

Any good lawyer might have thought up the notion of trademark securitization, but corporate legal buyers are looking for more than mere innovative thinking. The laws affecting such new instruments vary from country to country. In fact, in its representation of J. P. Morgan and Société Générale, Jones, Day counseled its clients on the governing law in eight jurisdictions, including the United States, Australia, France, Japan, and Spain. In-house buyers cannot now rely on their own legal staffs, or on smaller firms or law firm networks, for such comprehensive advice in such a recondite area. Chances are, they never will.

In a global market, innovation thus favors established providers. The more advanced their businesses become, the more nervously will corporate counsel lean on the mighty, and the more eagerly will they be opting for the ever-popular safety buy.

THE LAY OF THE LAND

Jones, Day's development from an enormous national law firm with imminent global potential to a full-scale global powerhouse offers both legal services buyers and providers a coherent picture of how international firms have developed over the last two decades, and of the specific country-by-country impediments they have surmounted.

According to Clossey, a firm must have strength in the UK, France, Germany, Spain, Brussels, and Italy in order to be credible in Europe. As of this writing, Clossey is in Milan as Jones, Day moves toward a final decision on whether to open an office in that city. But for all intents and purposes, "We have achieved our objectives" abroad, says Clossey. On the practice area side, the one last remaining missing piece in Europe is an international arbitration practice. The firm is now building one.

SOLVING THE GLOBAL PUZZLE:
ARE YESTERDAY'S MEGAFIRMS TOMORROW'S ANSWER?

79

Like other global firms, Jones, Day has transformed its foreign offices from outposts staffed by American lawyers to indigenous legal practices with native practitioners. For example, the firm had inherited a small Paris office when it merged with Surrey & Morse, and in 1990, there was only one French attorney in that office. Today the partners in the Paris office are mainly French.

The debate that persisted into the early 1990s is now over. Firms such as Sullivan & Cromwell did not want to practice foreign law because it might jeopardize the quality control they could maintain on a firm-wide basis. But the White & Cases saw much more value for the client, and obviously more growth potential, in actually doing legal work for clients wherever they might open an office.

The Sullivan & Cromwell approach was essentially a business development model, designed to capture foreign work heading into the United States, or help U.S. clients find suitable representation overseas. Globalization has made this model fairly obsolescent. Meanwhile, the seamless international practice that the Jones, Days envisioned was, at their size, eminently achievable. The biggest stumbling block would be local restrictions on foreign lawyers. Particularly in Spain and Italy, the bars have fought back on behalf of local practitioners who are now consolidating (especially in Italy) as a hedge against the Americanization and Anglicization of their legal markets. By contrast, the French acceded fairly quickly, mainly because French lawyers were eager to participate in the mega-deals on which the Americans and Brits were feasting. (A major event for Jones, Day in France was its representation of the oil giant Total in two successive acquisitions.)

In the UK, firms such as Jones, Day have been fortunate in being able to take advantage of the London tradition of excluding many very good lawyers who will never practice at London's elite "Magic Circle" firms or even be considered for a job in any of those firms. Hence, in spite of widespread resentment of the American interlopers, these talented London lawyers find Jones, Day, Shearman & Sterling, or Cleary Gottlieb Hamilton & Steen to be an attractive alternative to the second-tier UK firms. The fall from the storied heights of Slaughter & May isn't quite so Miltonic if you can land at Cleary.

Jones, Day grew rapidly in the early 1990s in Germany because tough local restrictions—particularly a single-office regulation limiting law firm growth—were lifted in one signal deregulatory moment. As a result, the legal marketplace was left in a state of complete shock. No-one knew how to react at first, but then the consolidations began. Suddenly, large new German firms were being created overnight, while Shearman & Sterling was opening offices in Düsseldorf as well as Frankfurt.

Germany's banking and capital markets are centered in Frankfurt. The industrial Ruhr Valley is already an important market for Jones, Day, and Berlin is getting to be one. Munich is also very much on the firm's radar screen as a high-tech growth corridor. (It is the home of the European Patent Office.) Indeed, what was once an airtight marketplace has been pried wide open by globalization. In-house legal and other corporate buyers are certainly cognizant of which firms work within these new arenas, and which firms do not. The ability of a large law firm like Jones, Day to strategically target so many developing areas, and to situate attorneys there faster than other firms, is a formidable advantage that it will continue to exploit in its business development efforts.

THE RISING SUN

In the Far East Jones, Day has offices in Tokyo, Taipei, Shanghai, Hong Kong, India, and Sidney. The work in Japan is both outbound and inbound—again, a measure of how a foreign market that was once highly restrictive is continuing to loosen up. United States firms have had numerous offices in Tokyo dating back to the 1970s which all followed the Sullivan & Cromwell model: They were all business development outposts. Not so anymore in this brave new world!

SOLVING THE GLOBAL PUZZLE:
ARE YESTERDAY'S MEGAFIRMS TOMORROW'S ANSWER?

81

Jones, Day is the only western firm with offices in India; they're in New Delhi and Mumbai. The benefits of being in India apparently justify the bureaucratic maze that foreign businesses (or native ones, for that matter) must perambulate in order to simply exist. India is, for all its problems, a treasure trove of high-tech businesses, resources, and people. If nothing else, Jones, Day's interest in India is presumably paying off for the firm's technology practice worldwide.

According to Clossey, the firm will open in Beijing in two years. Again, such commitment to a difficult market is more than just an example of a law firm prospecting for gold. It is also meant to send a message to the buyers about commitment and about the willingness to take risk. For the client, the payoff will be reliable legal service in an unreliable environment. The implicit conclusion for the client is that the global megafirms are uniquely positioned to provide long-term commitment in such areas.

The risk incurred is by the law firm, since it is guaranteeing the work of all its lawyers in these pioneer markets. A firm such as Jones, Day is telling you, the client, that it absolutely eschews formal alliances with indigenous firms, that it will not incur responsibility for the failures of other law firms. Others tap unexplored markets with less risk by formalizing alliances with those indigenous firms.

To get work done in the People's Republic of China, however, a foreign law firm must develop local alliances simply because, at this juncture, there is some legal work that foreign attorneys are not permitted to do. Jones, Day's response in China has been painstaking. There are thick internal logs describing the firm's experiences with and impressions of local counsel.

The firm opened in Shanghai in November 1999. (It has been in Hong Kong since the mid-1980s.) For buyers, a well-integrated organizational structure such as that of Jones, Day has to be a crucial asset in this culture, since developments in Taipei might have a direct bearing on Shanghai, or Shanghai events may directly affect client interests in Hong Kong. Looser law firm confederations or practice group fiefdoms in a place like China are worse than useless to clients doing business there.

As of this writing, the PRC was in the process of phasing out a one-office rule governing professional services. Heretofore it's been necessary for the U.S. and UK firms opening in Big China to make an initial strategic decision where to locate their offices. Some chose Beijing because it is the political heart of the country, and the center of the approval process for various foreign enterprises. But Jones, Day chose Shanghai because it is the commercial heart of the country. When the Jones, Day lawyers there need something approved, they travel to Beijing.

Big corporations with lots of money to invest in a booming city are typical Jones, Day clients, which means that Shanghai is a typical Jones, Day city. At the same time, bureaucratic blockages throughout the PRC may be relatively short-lived. Volatility is a problem, but it is also an advantage of pioneer markets in contrast to, say, Tokyo. In Tokyo, foreign firms must still battle decades of entrenched protectionism. In China, anything can happen sooner as well as later, for better or for worse.

Large law firms can often untangle such bureaucracies more expeditiously than other kinds of service providers simply because they have so many people worldwide who might be able to help. For example, Jones, Day's global ranks include Lord Geoffrey Howe, who endeared himself to the Chinese when he opposed Margaret Thatcher on the Hong Kong consolidation. As a result, official approval for Jones, Day's Shanghai opening was obtained in one year. It's supposed to take three or four.

THE GLOBAL TWELVE

If the global giants like Jones, Day do have a decisive advantage when global buyers hire law firms, it will only mean further legal industry consolidation ahead. Of course, smaller firms won't entirely disappear from the international scene. Regional clients

SOLVING THE GLOBAL PUZZLE:
ARE YESTERDAY'S MEGAFIRMS TOMORROW'S ANSWER?

83

can still turn to regional law firms that have some global breadth;
Minneapolis' Dorsey & Whitney typifies such firms. Even smaller
global players such as Boston's Brown, Rudnick, Freed & Gesmer
have been carving out choice niches for themselves and will
probably continue to do so.

By and large, however, a dozen law firms will be
identified—"branded," if you will—as the prototypical global
players. This is the "Global Twelve Model" cited by lawyers such
as Clossey. We should expect four of the five firms that comprise
London's Magic Circle to be part of this new paradigm: Linklaters,
Freshfields, Allen & Overy, and Clifford Chance Rogers & Wells.

Slaughter & May, the last of the five Magic Circle firms, is
too small. Its position is similar to the prestigious Wall Street
corporate and capital markets law firms that will continue to do
significant business throughout the world well into the twenty-first
century, but not by offering the kind of critical mass to diversified
Fortune 500 companies that the Jones, Days feature. Theirs will be
a lucrative but more confined practice. They will represent issuers
and underwriters, buyers and sellers, but they will not be
arbitrating too many disputes in Stockholm or spending much
time researching trademark securitization law in Australia.

For the Global Twelve, along with the four UK giants, add
these Americans: Jones, Day; White & Case; and Shearman &
Sterling. On the probable list: Cleary Gottlieb; and Weil, Gotshal
& Manges. Skadden hasn't quite made the total commitment to
global depth that Jones, Day made a decade ago. It might still tilt
back, despite its great size, toward the elite capital markets tier, in
company with Slaughter & May; Wachtell, Lipton, Rosen & Katz;
Cravath, Swaine & Moore; Davis Polk & Wardwell; and Simpson
Thacher & Bartlett. In California, Latham & Watkins and
O'Melveny & Myers may succeed where Gibson, Dunn failed, and
join ranks with the dazzling dozen.

These predictions are conjectural, of course. Strong firms
have been known to switch strategic gears altogether. The fact that,
in the late 1990s, Davis Polk would even discuss merging with

Freshfields suggests how fast an institutional identity can change in the face of impending global trends, no matter how profitable and reputable the institution. In any event, who the players will be is less important than that the game is going to occur. The consolidation is by no means over. It may just be beginning.

What will this further marketplace consolidation mean for in-house buyers? As we've suggested, the buyers themselves are the ones who caused it. As their businesses globalize, they increasingly depend on the kind of services that the megafirms provide. So, to that extent, the effect on them will be salutary because they will have been matched to the legal services they require. Such is the rhetoric with which the megafirms have marketed themselves in the past and will continue to do so in the future. And there is much substance to their rhetoric, no matter how much nostalgia we may harbor for young David facing mighty Goliath.

The Jones, Days and Shearman & Sterlings have taken great pains to feature a "one-firm culture." In Jones, Day's case, that claim of global homogeneity, in terms of professional firm-wide standards, is buttressed by a complex weave of practice groups, industry groups, and regional divisions and subdivisions. Some in-house counsel may continue to insist that they hire "lawyers, not law firms." Other in-house counsel are pointedly interested in firms' total resources and how they're delivered. For both buyers, the megafirm sales pitch is that much more powerful when it includes a supportable claim of international consistency.

In a market predictably dominated by twelve law firms, the problem, even for powerful and persuasive corporations, will be to remain important. In later chapters, we'll see what happened to New Economy companies when the law firms that had helped create them suddenly forgot them. That's not likely to happen to Daimler or Novartis or The Walt Disney Company, not in this life. Yet that "partner with clout," as Harold Barron describes him or her, may yet become more important in the years ahead as buyers navigate an increasingly limited pool of sellers.

Law Firm Networks: For the Right In-House Buyers, a Persistent National and Global Solution

The picture we drew in the previous chapter isn't quite complete. Global buyers find it hard to refute the claim of global law firms that the latter provide the best-integrated, most in-depth services on the widest possible platform. Yet not every buyer is a Fortune 100 or even a Fortune 500 company. There are small and mid-sized companies with occasional national or global needs.

There are also companies for which those needs are more frequent and on-going, and that therefore continue to rely on regional or local firms to serve their legal needs abroad. We discussed law firms such as Dorsey & Whitney in Minneapolis and Brown, Rudnick, Freed & Gesmer in Boston that, with a few overseas offices in select cities, show every sign of continuing to flourish on a global scale despite the apparent emergence of the branded "Global Twelve" international providers.

However, in an age of consolidation we must ask how such firms can ensure their future survival. In spite of the recent prosperity, the future is naturally replete with inevitable downturns and unforeseen client needs to which they may or may not be able to respond. The larger firms are building structures designed to be impervious to almost all such changes. Whatever new legal issue arises in whatever far-flung jurisdiction, they intend to have the solution.

For in-house counsel at multinational companies the corollary question is: What benefits if any justify continuing loyalty to law firms that aren't Jones, Day, Shearman & Sterling, or White & Case? Especially if price is *not* the name of the game— and many fifty-lawyer and 300-lawyer firms charge as much per hour as the megafirms—how can buyers be confident that the sellers will continue to grow along with them?

Law firm networks offer corporate and other legal services buyers a significant alternative to either very large firms or merely big firms. To understand why, let's revisit and expand a few of the key points about the current legal market that we touched on in the first two chapters.

THE HEAT IS ON

Law firm managers such as Francis Burch, Chairman of Piper Marbury Rudnick & Wolfe, intend to prove that a quality law firm can keep pace in the presumably heady growth periods ahead. For Burch, on-going expansion is an imperative. The only alternative to attaining critical mass is to be small—very small and very specialized. The market prognosis is that you're either full-service or you're not. And full service has to be just that. The so-called mid-sized firm is the proverbially endangered species. In 1999, Burch pointed out to this writer that a 500-lawyer law firm is now actually "mid-sized." A decade earlier, a "mid-sized" firm had up to 150 lawyers.

Burch's comments were in defense of his firm's merger, the combination of the Baltimore and Washington, D.C. firm Piper & Marbury (where Burch was Chair) and Chicago's Rudnick & Wolfe. In 1999 the new entity had nearly 700 lawyers, but it certainly wasn't avoiding additional growth. As of mid-2001, intensive merger talks with another 300-plus lawyer firm, San Francisco's McCutchen, Doyle, Brown & Enersen, had just broken off. Presumably, Piper is now in search of other merger partners.

To some extent even the boutiques are in danger as the larger firms grow. Recently a trademark firm could claim to have among its members the focused expertise that made it a natural buy for clients that needed specific esoteric legal work. Yet to a great extent the larger firms are eroding that independent soil as well. How many trademark experts can surpass what Jones, Day brought to bear in the trademark securitization matter discussed in Chapter 2? Even if their local expertise compares to the big firms, can the boutique firms also provide that expertise simultaneously on three or four continents?

To be sure, the death of the mid-sized firm has been predicted since the mid-1980s, and it hasn't quite happened. The good news about a vibrant economy is that, despite downturns, it is inevitably producing new growth at every level. Entrepreneurial companies often spring up and buy legal services from smaller law firms. As those clients grow, they become mid-sized companies and provide a burgeoning client source for mid-sized law firms.

The key issue is relationship. A mid-sized firm will have trouble selling itself to strangers. All things being equal, there's no reason for a company with problems in three different countries to hire a 300-lawyer law firm with offices in two countries—unless it already knows and trusts that firm. The "Marketing 101" lesson— that the vast percentage of new business comes from existing business—therefore is especially applicable to mid-sized law firms. A Minneapolis company that has a longstanding relationship with Dorsey & Whitney, or a New England company that has a longstanding relationship with Brown, Rudnick, will *want* to maintain that relationship if it can. Such companies are used to being treated well by these firms. They know they're important to the partners. They are confident that they can get the best legal service from their friends, or at least they won't be taking a chance that, by retaining somebody new, they'll sooner or later fall off the larger firm's radar screen of client priorities.

The big "if" then becomes, can our friends help us in Australia or, for that matter, Florida or Oregon? If not, companies have no choice but to find someone else who can, and a new law firm may eventually develop its own trusted relationship with the client. Then it's a dog fight. All bets are off as to who will become the client's main outside legal services provider. The new firm, as it develops trust with the client, continues to grab bigger and bigger pieces of the budget: a class action law suit here, an acquisition there. This is precisely the scenario that keeps partners at mid-sized and small firms awake at night. And it's why decisions to open marginally profitable branch offices are made. It's called "chasing" your clients or "guarding" your clients. And it's a totally defensive growth mode.

Law firm networks become vitally significant players in the current marketplace precisely at this key juncture where relationships must be backed up by resources. As mentioned in Chapter 1, these networks are formal structures in which member law firms pledge to share resources and referrals. Not surprisingly, they arose, both domestically and internationally, during the mid-1980s when large full-service firms really began to dominate the domestic and international markets.

Wendy Horn, executive director of Commercial Law Affiliates (CLA), the world's largest global network, has articulated four best practices for corporate legal buyers pondering the law firm network option:

♦ *First, how does a firm become a member?* Simply paying for a membership should never be sufficient. In fact, the due diligence and selection process by a law firm network considering a new member should be comparable to the process your own law firm department follows to select outside counsel.

♦ *Second, does the network monitor client satisfaction and member firm performance?* Such oversight should be ongoing. There should also be programs sponsored by the network to help member firms maintain high quality. These programs show commitment by the network—that they're actually in the business of providing service to clients rather than just serving as a forum where law firms can meet each other. The network should also establish specific procedures that enable clients to air grievances about member firm performance.

♦ *Third, what is the geographical breadth of the network?* Make sure the network has member firms in locations where it may not be easy to find local representation. Otherwise, you gain little by enlisting the network as a service provider.

♦ *Fourth, how many and what sort of collaborative projects have member firms worked on?* These projects may be legal matters handled for clients, or they may be various joint marketing efforts. Your purpose in making these inquiries is to ascertain just how well the law firms get along and work together. Just because they're members of the same network doesn't mean you'd gain anything by having them all involved with your affairs.

For new clients, however, the networks can still face a hard sell. Who needs to worry about whether or not two or more law firms get along! Quality control is a persistent issue as well, despite the insistence by network managers such as Horn that they monitor the performance of member firms (and eliminate firms that underperform) more closely than some large firms do their own branch offices. Also, for a company that is choosing a new services provider, it is simpler to approach providers directly than negotiate with a network. Anyone who has ever sold anything knows that the less you have to explain, the better.

In some ways, the networks are also bucking a market trend toward fewer and fewer outside providers. As we will see in Chapter 7, corporate America has been "converging" since the mid-1990s, in search of a reduced number of law firms that will provide better services and lower costs in exchange for guaranteed volume. Smaller companies are equally resolved to keep their buying approach as contained and manageable as possible. One or two law firms, with one or two trusted "relationship partners"—

that's the ticket, not a wholesale referral network full of law firms these companies have never heard of, will never meet, and don't particularly want to even think about. Of course, the networks can make the opposite argument that, precisely because they do deliver hundreds of legal service providers in one fell swoop, and guarantee their performance, they are in fact answering the client need for the most compact buying process possible.

One advantage for networks is that their formal structures can add to client comfort levels. Imagine a company that wants to maintain an existing relationship with a favored law firm. The relationship part already exists. As for resources, it's easy for the trusted relationship partner at the firm to advise the client not to worry about finding somebody to handle a law suit in Seattle: "We can provide a firm in Seattle. It's not just another law firm that we've heard good things about, but a law firm with which we have a close and formal relationship. We can guarantee that the job will be done right. There's no need to run to a big firm just because it happens to have an office in Seattle and twenty other cities as well."

In this scenario, using the network is also a defensive strategy, but an effective one, and a lot less expensive than trying to guard the client from competitors by opening a satellite office in Seattle. However, the networks also offer palpable service benefits. Maybe that Seattle situation doesn't involve a full-blown law suit. Maybe it's just a question involving a local statute. The network member calls his or her network colleague in Seattle, gets the point clarified, and passes the information directly to the client, within twenty-four hours, and looking very capable in the process!

Being part of a network is more than a theoretical advantage. One general counsel at a $50 million company (speaking not for attribution) offers a good example. His company sells toys around the country. For ten years a 200-lawyer firm based in the same city has handled 80% of the company's work. (The other 20% involves employment and ERISA law, which is handled by an employment firm that also has a long-term relationship with the client.) After NAFTA, the company tripled sales to Mexico. According to this GC, its main firm does not have a track record for doing much of anything involving Mexico.

"Under most circumstances, I would have first asked [that primary law firm] for a referral," he says. "I might have gotten a good referral, and that would have been that. But I might also have shopped around. I would probably have called Baker & McKenzie."

It would have been a natural call to make since Baker & McKenzie has five offices in five different cities in Mexico. The GC's business might also have wound up at Baker Botts, a Houston megafirm with significant ties and broad experience in Mexico. Either one of those law firms could then have encroached on more of the company's legal business in other parts of the country. But the company's original firm was part of a network that included a San Diego member with a track record handling cross-border deals. The client now uses that firm on a regular basis.

It is significant that the client did not contact the Baker & McKenzies and Baker Bottses in these circumstances. As the GC confirms, the San Diego firm provided both convenience and legitimacy. Work sent to San Diego wasn't just another referral. If this arrangement wasn't exactly like dealing with a single law firm, it was close enough for the GC's needs.

"I felt taken care of," the GC says. His word choice is important, including the word "felt." At their best, the networks give clients something of a sense of closure, and that they're being provided the seamless legal counsel that the megafirms, at their best, provide.

A VARIEGATED LOT

The survival of these networks speaks for itself. In some instances, they've existed for over fifteen years. On the one hand, that survival may not be anything special since, in some cases, network memberships are relatively low-maintenance propositions. The investment in time and money is not always significant.

Moreover, in some cases law firms may really be continuing their membership rather indifferently. In particular, some megafirms take a "might as well" approach toward networks. Morrison & Foerster has been for many years one of the largest firms in Lex Mundi, an international network, even though it has branches in the very cities where other member firms are located. A MoFo partner simply shrugged his shoulders when we asked him why, as if to say, "Why not?" Some megafirms cover all the bases. At one point, Dechert had a branch office in Brussels and a formal affiliation with a Brussels firm, and was part of a network that had a member firm there.

On the other hand, megafirms aren't the typical network members. Most network members are mid-sized or smaller because those are the firms that need to be members, often as a matter of survival. Also, most networks don't admit law firms that have branch offices in the same cities where other members are based. (Just about all networks have only one member firm in any given city as well.)

To further understand the complex strategic issues involved, note that typical member firms can't afford a desultory approach to network membership—because, for many of them, there's some real risk involved in committing to a network. In particular, law firms need to worry about their existing referral relationships. Talk to many law firm network members, and the constant burning question on their minds is: "If we are committed to providing referrals to a network member in Dallas, are there other referral sources in Dallas that might dry up as a result, because they no longer trust us to send them the choice local assignments that cross our desks?"

It's a Catch-22. Without some exclusivity, the power of the network to provide a consistent stream of work is vitiated. As a result, motivation to join a network often must be strong enough for member firms to willingly run the risk of losing referrals from other firms outside the network. Again, that motivation is all about shielding important clients from competitors. Firms ought to have made a decision to sacrifice some new business in order to protect core business. They need to join a network with their eyes wide open and weigh the risks against the benefits.

Firms that join networks expecting a flood of new referrals often withdraw rather quickly. A case in point was Hillary Clinton's controversial firm in Little Rock, The Rose Law Firm, which dropped out of Lex Mundi in the late 1980s because the referral stream from other member firms was too small. It sounded like a fairly short-sighted reaction when then-managing partner Bill Kennedy described his firm's reasoning to this writer, especially for a firm in Arkansas that had major corporate clients that might have been susceptible to a sales pitch from big global law firms.

The variety of law firm networks suggests that they've targeted some very specific niches. A network has to market itself just like a law firm. It has to target a specific clientele and play to that clientele. By doing so, a network increases the comfort of buyers like the toy company described above. That buyer wanted something very specific: Confidence that a particular kind of cross-border business would be handled with maximum expertise. In that case, fortunately for outside counsel, there was a law firm in the network that fit the bill. But how much more powerful would a network have been that was specializing in the client's industry, or in a practice area directly related to his legal needs?

Over the past fifteen years we've seen a plethora of networks, domestic and global, that are both general in scope as well as very niched. As with all strategic marketing, the more defined the network, the better. Immigration and intellectual property firms are prominent among boutiques that have networked to share referrals so that they don't compete for the same clients. A good example of how networks can offer clients a concrete alternative is the State Capital Law Firm Group, which has fifty members, one in each state capital. The purpose of the SCLFG is to provide any client with local lobbying anywhere in the country. State Law Resources is another such network with lobbying resources throughout the United States.

From the client's standpoint, such precise niche marketing may be especially significant because, in the SCLFG instance, it goes beyond what most megafirms can nimbly provide. Even though large law firms may have some strong local legal/lobbying practices, none of them have one in every single state. If a corporate client must lobby a legislator in Cheyenne, Wyoming, a megafirm based in New York will not dispatch someone to Cheyenne, but will try to refer to a Cheyenne attorney who knows his or her way around the capital, and who usually knows the lawmakers personally.

This is very much like trying a law suit: You don't want to send a hot-shot New York litigator into a small-town courthouse who may misinterpret or offend the local judges, jurors, and general public. However, it is tough for a big New York law firm to find an often scarce local lobbyist, whose skills aren't as commonplace as trial skills. The State Capital Law Firm Group ostensibly has the special manpower on hand and the kind of connections that no other legal services entity can provide.

Clearly, it is fundamental and, perhaps, the strategic conclusion for many boutiques and other small firms to find an area of practice that is both so narrow that the megafirms either can't handle it or don't want to and yet so basic that, like statehouse lobbying, it will provide a strong, steady flow of work. A network such as the State Capital Law Firm Group doesn't have to justify itself to the client. Its benefits are obvious.

In contrast, the generalist networks have enjoyed much less of a strategic foothold. One of the early networks, now defunct, was Unilaw. It typified the *modus operandi* of all networks: Mid-sized firms in different cities banded together to protect their clients and themselves from the tentacles of the multinational firms. But the network had no other real focus. One of its founding firms, Philadelphia's Mesirov Gelman Jaffe Cramer & Jamieson, left the network and eventually merged with Schnader Harrison Segal & Lewis.

Schnader itself once proposed setting up a global law firm network in which it would be the only large member. The other members would all be small firms or even solos. The network was short-lived, but at least Schnader's thinking was closer to the kind of focused strategy that, like law firms, law firm networks require. The small firms would have been referral sources for Schnader, and would help Schnader serve its clients. For the small firms, the promise of being on the receiving end in a relationship with a relatively big referral source must have been very attractive, at least initially.

As one former member in Europe now reflects, the sum total of client business "that we were able to do didn't amount to all that much. And there was squabbling. You know, it can be a challenge to mesh an English approach to doing business with a Spanish one."

As with law firms, it's not easy for a law firm network to define what constitutes a viable "niche." The success of the Houston-based Lex Mundi suggests that a global focus, without a more specific industry or practice area definition, might suffice as a differentiating foundation. When Lex Mundi was founded in the 1980s, law firms were just beginning to explore their global potential. At the time, therefore, Lex Mundi enabled these firms to fulfill a pressing need to connect with colleagues in other parts of the world.

The network, which now has over 158 members encompassing 14,000 attorneys in ninety countries, marketed itself aggressively and developed something of a brand name reputation. Whether it might do as well just starting off in the current environment—at a time when so many firms have already implemented global strategies, and don't have as great a need for a supporting network—is anyone's guess.

Lex Mundi's statement of purpose doesn't even mention referrals. It emphasizes instead "the exchange of professional information about the local and global practice and development of law facilitating . . . the members' abilities to serve the needs of their respective clients." Further, in the second paragraph of this two-paragraph mission statement, Lex Mundi disclaims any right to exclusivity, and guarantees all members the right to join whatever other organizations they please.

This non-exclusivity is a key point that differentiates Lex Mundi from other networks. Lex Mundi does not hold itself out to corporate buyers as a global alternative to the megafirms. That's why it can include a megafirm like Morrison & Foerster in its ranks. The fundamental purpose of Lex Mundi is informational, and referrals might even be considered gravy by some of the member firms.

It is therefore a mistake to think of Lex Mundi and Commercial Law Affiliates as direct competitors. The latter is very much in the business of being a legal services provider, not just a resource center—and on the most global scale imaginable.

A Test Case

CLA may indeed be the network to watch and an important ongoing entity because it has directly challenged the megafirms for a portion of their global market share. To be sure, it faces formidable strategic obstacles. For example, CLA is niched, but only to the extent that "international" is a niche. Unlike the State Capital Law Firm Group, the 200 CLA firms in seventy countries together offer a full-service global capability. It is open to question as to whether a network of law firms, or any other legal service entity, can compete on that basis with the multinational firms.

Clients that have used CLA firms include billion-dollar corporations like Lubrizol, Inc., along with smaller public and private companies. A list of companies that have retained three or more CLA firms includes Microsoft Corporation and McDonald's, although, with 200 member firms, there's no way to vet the list and determine how extensively such corporations used the CLA members.

Quality control and efficiency are watchwords. The network is constantly reminding the market that it rescinds its affiliation with member firms that don't perform well or comply with its non-negotiable standards. As articulated by CLA, those standards include an obligation to:

♦ Respond to all communications within twenty-four hours.

♦ Provide clear, initial information about the firm and working procedures.

♦ Provide clients with Alternative Dispute Resolution options when appropriate.

♦ Provide initial fee estimates and seek prior approval before proceeding with work that exceeds estimates. The fee estimates will, if the client requests, describe the basis for the fee (hourly or otherwise), the personnel working on the matter, the range of disbursement charges, and the currency for payment.

♦ Use technology to expedite work, including direct e-mail to attorneys and both Word and WordPerfect capabilities.

♦ Provide detailed, understandable billing. Separate matters are to be billed separately. Frequency of bills will be determined by client need. Disbursements will be itemized and the basis for each charge will be detailed.

♦ Discuss the clients' requirements for status reporting on legal matters, including frequency and format, at the beginning of the relationship.

♦ Have a back-up plan for key lawyers in place for CLA clients during those lawyers' absences from the office.

♦ Undergo a re-certification process that requires the member firm to be AV-rated in *Martindale-Hubbell* where available.

♦ Have a conflict avoidance procedure in place.

♦ Carry professional liability coverage in a sufficient amount where available.

- Maintain a docket control system.

- Meet Continuing Legal Education requirements.

- Have an English-speaking receptionist and an after-hours message system.

By enumerating its requirements with so much specificity, CLA has added something new and quite welcome to the inside/outside dialogue. After all, how many large law firms make such guarantees? In a marketplace where "partnering" and "client responsiveness" are shibboleths, CLA at least deserves serious mention because it has added substantive meat to the rhetorical bone. Here's a thought for in-house counsel: Take the CLA standards guarantees and use them as a negotiating tool with all outside counsel. A few of these standards, such as docket control and CLE requirements, won't be a problem. But twenty-four-hour response deadlines, initial fee estimates, and back-up plans for absent lawyers just might.

However, these service guarantees aren't going to dislodge corporate dollars from the Jones, Days and White & Cases in and of themselves. To do that, CLA must define a client base that is not currently controlled by the megafirms. It will have to remain organized so that in-house counsel and other buyers immediately recognize it as a cost-efficient—not just quality-controlled—way of delivering top-notch services.

Finally, to reiterate the concern we addressed earlier in this chapter, buyers need a reason for choosing a network rather than a large law firm. The guarantees listed above comprise a good start toward providing that reason. But the network, and its member firms, are up against the biggest and the best. They will have to go further in their marketing, and in continuously refurbishing their infrastructure.

Toward that end, CLA is revamping itself with a new strategic plan that provides for a branding campaign to launch in 2001 and continue through 2003. The overall goal is to ensure closer cooperation among members. If it is insufficient for CLA to be merely a resource center, being a referral clearinghouse is also inadequate—which is how CLA began life in 1990. The best strategy is to implement new procedures at the local and regional levels while allowing member firms to maintain autonomy. The North American membership will be particularly affected, but because North American members represent 75% of the total population, changes in how these members operate, or market themselves, will therefore be decisive for the entire organization.

The outcome of this plan should send a strong message about what lies ahead for all but the most shrewdly niched networks. If the outcome is uncertain, corporate buyers and potential law firm members will avoid future efforts to found global networks, assuming such efforts will even seem worth the effort. If the plan proves to be a triumph, CLA may spawn imitators and help diversify global legal markets for buyers and sellers alike.

Part of the impetus behind the new plan was pressure from member firms. They want to see bottom-line improvement in their own practices, and they expect CLA to play a big role in helping them achieve that. The new plan draws on initiatives already begun in Europe, Canada, Australia, and the western U.S. region where member firms have been particularly eager to maximize their deliverables and their profits. These disparate initiatives have been ongoing for the last few years. Common goals include continuing the independence of member firms while at the same time doing more to leverage the strengths of the organization. Those strengths include size, depth, quality control, and what CLA describes in its 2001 business plan report as a common service culture and a "history of shared client work." Priorities include decreasing operational costs as well as increasing revenues.

CLA's plan explicitly acknowledges the forces that are reshaping the business of law:

♦ client consolidation,
♦ globalization,

♦   new evolving technology,

♦   the ongoing scramble for both legal and support talent, and

♦   the continuing threat of the accounting firms and other worldwide MDPs.

CLA members have certainly not been exempt from evolving forces that often scuttle law firms trying to navigate cross-border shoals. According to the business plan report, CLA firms are finding that their profits have shrunk even as their revenues have increased. The local competition is tough, client demands are equally tough, and the costs of associate recruitment and retention are ever higher.

CLA has gone back to the drawing-board with great urgency because, within the last two years, twenty-two law firms have left CLA either because they went out of business or were acquired by other firms. Not counting the firms that were ousted for bad performance, that's more than the combined total number of firms that were lost during the 1990s. Surviving members continue to face the proverbial choice of exponentially increasing the scale of their practice or becoming boutiques.

In its business plan report, CLA identifies five reasons why member firms left the network and joined larger firms (both regional and national):

♦   *First, the need for greater size and mass to achieve economies of scale and cover operational expenses.* "Economy of scale" has long been the bugaboo of mid-sized firms. The more they grow, the more expense they take on because they're just not growing fast enough or big enough. The alternative is to scale back and only accept premium work that these firms can bill out at premium rates. That's what the consultants have been telling them to do for over a decade—fire unprofitable clients, raise your rates, minimize the commodity work, improve your realization—but some actions easily recommended by consultants are difficult to implement, especially in the flat environment of a law firm.

♦ *Second, having enough financial resources to acquire and maintain a "brand name."* Marketing can be an uncertain investment, especially when it comes to branding. In a later chapter, we'll look at whether the high-priced marketing investments that firms have made have paid off.

♦ *Third, somewhat related to branding, convincing clients that CLE is a "safe" choice.* Quality often has nothing to do with the safety sell. Clients are attracted instead to the mega-resources that the big law firms can provide, especially in litigation.

♦ *Fourth, the costs of recruitment and retention.* It's risky for the best new graduates to join a firm that doesn't have its name up in lights. Why should they, when Skadden or Clifford Chance is desperate for their attention as well? Meanwhile, more firms are measuring the actual costs of attrition. Even the wealthiest are shocked to learn how much money they've wasted training associates who don't stay very long.

♦ *Fifth, proving depth of practice or industry expertise to client prospects without having hundreds of lawyers on staff.*

To lose members because of these problems seems especially serious since the whole point of CLA is providing critical mass to solve them. CLA's collective size is larger than the three largest global law firms combined. Yet that did not achieve economies of scale for the firms themselves. Their operational costs were still problematic. Nor do the global resources of CLA firms necessarily afford buyers that warm and fuzzy feeling of being "safe" in the embrace of a multinational giant.

CLA firms share a wealth of client experience and worldwide reputations. Yet, acknowledges the business plan, "most firms do not display their link with CLA in any consistent way."

THE BRANDING CHALLENGE

So the dilemma consists of a very specific marketing problem: If former member firms felt deprived for want of a "brand," so too does the network itself. Recruits don't join or stay at CLA firms because they're CLA firms. They are indifferent. Some clients may appreciate the breadth and depth of the resources they gain by hiring a CLA firm, but the message is not reinforced by the firms themselves. The advantage of using a CLA firm may be duly noted by clients, but that is then tucked away in the recesses of their memories. Nothing saleable results. The fact that many CLA firms simply weren't bothering to deliver the message is especially frustrating. Often their clients didn't even know they were members.

The core of CLA's plan is, therefore, to create a bankable global brand name for itself and its members. But this is easier said than done. Branding is serious business. One issue CLA had to first address was the scope of the campaign. To brand a large organization worldwide, and nearly from scratch, requires millions of dollars. Another issue was consensus. Too aggressive a campaign, or one that is driven top-down by the network's central office managers, could alienate member firms. The last thing CLA wanted, in the middle of a campaign to brand itself as rich in multinational legal services, would be to lose more members.

The solution was a branding initiative based on measured evolution, with marketing resources (described below) made available to all member firms. Presumably, even those firms that won't support a full-scale branding campaign can utilize these resources. The initial member firms to be included in the effort are located in the larger U.S. cities; this "Alliance," as CLA calls it, will include at least thirty-five law firms, which represent 80% of the CLA firms in U.S. cities with a population over 1 million.

All U.S. firms that are members of CLA can participate in the Alliance if they choose. Firms that initially decline to participate but choose to do so later will likely be charged an initiation fee, since they'll be benefiting from the effort and investment of other member firms. Actual fees are the least part of the cost in any event, since the campaign will require that a good deal of partner time be devoted to planned CLA branding initiatives.

Meanwhile, non-U.S. firms already pursuing a CLA branding initiative independently can continue to do so, subject, of course, to oversight by the network, particularly to ensure that these efforts are consistent with the efforts of the Alliance in the United States. The final step will be phasing in the brand on a network-wide basis.

This is no small chore, to be sure! There are many skeptics, including a number of law firm marketing consultants, who believe that achieving consensus on a branding campaign within a single law firm is next to impossible. Here, we have wheels spinning within wheels. CLA firms in Canada, Europe, Australia, and New Zealand are already pursuing separate branding campaigns. Further, as the business plan report informs us, members in Asia Pacific and Latin America "do not support global branding in their regions, mostly because they view themselves as inbound markets and get a majority of their work from non-CLA firms."

Again, many network members worry that they might be alienating their own referral sources as a result of being in a network. The problem isn't resolved once the decision to join is made. As is evident, the concern can still have a dampening effect on a network's overall marketing commitment.

Yet CLA may be wise to at least start a branding initiative, and wiser yet to do so on behalf of an "Alliance" of American members. These firms are CLA's leaders in recorded referrals and generate much of the network's operating budget. The business plan report cites an equally important reason for starting in these major U.S. markets: The CLA firms in those cities are the most sought-after merger partners in the network simply because they are so well-situated geographically. Branding is thus a defensive measure in part, intended to reaffirm the loyalty of those firms that are involved in the effort.

Because of the various problems facing CLA, it's clear the branding initiative must have both internal and external applications. Internally, additional marketing resources will be provided to member firms. Even if the grander branding goal remains elusive, these resources should help achieve organizational goals because they may well increase the chances that member firms will use them to promote the network more than previously.

Among the resources available to CLA network members are:

♦ *Marketing tools that member firms can't afford to develop independently.* Among others, these tools include professionally written monthly newsletters targeted to specific client groups; software and boilerplate for RFPs, including an automated cut-and-paste proposal library; a comprehensive client survey agenda; marketing and sales training customized for each member firm; a database to identify members who can provide introductions to prospects; targeted advertising; and editorial material featuring member firms.

♦ *A database of all CLA lawyers, with qualifications, so that members can more efficiently locate people with specific legal skills or industry expertise.* The network will train members on how to use this database to better serve existing clients or help recruit new ones.

♦ *Internet-based legal, business, and marketing CLE.* The hope here is to reduce member firms' own costs in this area by 40%.

♦ *CLA teams to develop multi-jurisdictional products that are in demand by clients (e.g., a turnkey database of governing law in specific areas such as Blue Sky laws or consumer finance).* These products should help firms compete for business and develop a reputation for specialized expertise.

♦ *Centralized recruitment and other associate-related services on the CLA website.* The firms' websites should feature a recruitment module that emphasizes the added value of a career with a CLA firm as well as associate rotation programs.

♦ *Economically priced technology resources: a website template, client extranets, and a back-office ASP service.* In addition, group buying options to lower member firms' costs on hardware, software, office equipment, etc., should be included.

The second phase of the branding is external. According to the business plan report, that phase should comprise "displaying and marketing a common global identity to ensure that clients understand at a glance how each firm is stronger because of its CLA membership." CLA is working with Ogilvy Public Relations Worldwide on this part of the campaign. Ogilvy was quick to observe that, although CLA firms are confident about the quality of their affiliates, there is no standardized way for them to show their membership on printed materials. As mentioned above, many firms don't indicate their CLA connection at all, which squanders the benefits of being part of the most comprehensive network in the world.

Ogilvy recommended that CLA retain its current logo but rename CLA to ensure greater trademark protection and improve name perception among clients. The new name would be tested in major markets worldwide. There would be separate regional name brands such as "CLA Europe" that differentiate sectors of the organization but still maintain the institutional link. Once a name is selected, member firms will have a limited range of options for featuring it in conjunction with their own names. These options are subject to local restrictions; CLA will explore alternate means to display its co-brand with firms in states that don't allow law firms to use trade names.

CLA's plan then calls for focus marketing that targets key client groups through trade shows, conferences, e-mail newsletters, joint printed materials, and a sales effort geared toward prospects. According to the report, "[W]e will require Alliance firms to proactively communicate the brand via meetings with their own clients and contacts, and through integration of the brand in all levels of their existing marketing programs." Presumably, the Alliance firms are sufficiently committed to the campaign, and will have found the resources listed above valuable enough, to readily comply with these directives.

The campaign is significant for additional reasons. As we've suggested, it may tell us whether the networks themselves are viable, or at least those networks that are full-service providers. In addition, as a window on the inside/outside dynamic, the campaign may speak volumes about the efficacy of branding, and the susceptibility of in-house buyers and other legal services decision-makers to respond to or ignore an evolving brand.

Of course, in this instance branding is a particularly monumental task since it involves not just many strong-minded partners within a single law firm, but many different law firms as well. If this campaign works, it should encourage law firms to look more seriously at branding, despite the costs. However, CLA may have an advantage because it has something that is tangibly brandable: The notion of quality control tied to immense size. If it's difficult for Clifford Chance to differentiate itself from Freshfields, for example, it may be less difficult for a legal services entity such as CLA to differentiate itself from just about any other organization in the world. In other words, it helps to be unique when you launch a branding campaign.

Finally, in-house counsel will be observing how CLA handles the issues of conflicts and vicarious liability. As the business plan report notes, those risks multiply when organizations like CLA "present themselves publicly as though they were offices of a single firm." One tactic CLA will likely use is a common engagement letter. The letter will stipulate that engaging a CLA firm does not give access to the lawyers and expertise of other member firms except by specific engagement. Confidentiality guarantees will be repeated. Fee-splitting is prohibited except in joint engagements.

If, as a result of these safeguards, there is no need for global conflict checking, the risk of a successful assertion by a disgruntled client of vicarious liability against CLA (except for an action against individual participants in a joint representation) is similarly minimized. Yet CLA is now looking at other ways to avoid such claims. Chances are, the network can purchase separate liability insurance policies that do not require its members to change their carriers. It seems that, in an era of consolidation, the CLA model is no more subject to these potential professional problems than large law firms that are undergoing massive mergers or formally affiliating with other large law firms.

CHAPTER 4

Value Selling:
How Law Firm Marketing
Helps Legal Services Buyers

I mplicit in our first three chapters, there are generally two forms of marketing by outside counsel to inside counsel. First, law firms simply endeavor to place a value on their services to clients and prospective clients. They buttress the message with demographics to indicate how the number and type of lawyers they've situated in such-and-such a place may support specific client business goals and solve client legal problems. Like Jones, Day, they can make a convincing argument that their large global clients enjoy seamless legal services. Or, like an intellectual property or other boutique, they impress clients with the sheer concentration of expertise and experience they can assemble in one important given area.

There's nothing wrong with this generic selling. It's how most professional firms develop business. It's a "Try us, you'll like us" approach that's more useful than most advertising because it's backed up by evidence, by demonstrable past successes, and by referrals and recommendations. Yet, from a buyer's standpoint, there's a second, even better way for professional services firms to both market and sell themselves. (By *marketing*, we mean how firms get found by buyers, become a part of their consciousness, and get on the buyers' short list. By *selling*, we mean how these firms actually get hired by the buyers.)

What defines this second, superior business development mode, and what, in fact, makes it superior, is the delivery of value to the buyer. In other words, superior marketing and selling occur when the buyer is *better off* because of the experience, regardless of whether the seller ever makes a sale. Often, in these pages, general counsel and associate general counsel say that the marketing they like best is often a good substantive seminar where a law firm gets to show off its expertise, and its desirability as a potential hire, and where the attendees learn something about the law that they can take back to their offices and put to good use.

Of course, the two "modes" are not in opposition. To the contrary, a complete marketing campaign by a law firm would tell the buyer why it ought to hire the firm and offer useful substantive material, at no fee, in order to back up the firm's argument.

With this value-based touchstone in mind, let's take a look at two major events in the recent history of law firm marketing and how they affect the in-house client.

Don't "Just Do It": Branding

The first is branding.

There have been reams of articles in the legal press about law firms launching branding campaigns, attention generated in part because a few of those campaigns are relatively aggressive. San Francisco-based Brobeck Phleger & Harrison has spent a reported $7 million to promote its brand name with print and even television ads. Such campaigns also typically include targeted media efforts along with logos, websites, and recurring message points intended to reinforce a desirable, saleable institutional identity. At one large New York firm that had plans to unveil its branding campaign in late 2001, a member of the marketing staff refers to these diverse components as "identity supporters."

Law firm branding has also attracted media attention because the tactic is rather aggressive for a profession that's only acknowledged within the last fifteen years the appropriateness of any formal public marketing whatsoever. As a result, law firms seem to have gotten clumsily caught up in a public fad. Branding is ancient, but since about 1999 the public has been particularly preoccupied with branding. People from all kinds of firms, from small companies to corporate behemoths, have been talking about branding.

A branding campaign ostensibly creates an immediate, specific point of reference and a selling point for a product or service. For example, you think Michelin tires, you think safety. You think Ivory soap, you think purity.

You think Brobeck Phleger, you think . . . what?

As a result of sufficient and prolonged exposure to Brobeck's branding, you might think of high-tech legal practice when you think of this law firm. Yet there is a synapse between the manufacturing world and the world of professional services that vitiates the effectiveness of branding by law firms, accounting firms, and consulting firms. In fact, one might question the fundamental integrity of branding in professional services.

Consultant William Flannery, of the WJF Institute in Austin, Texas, comments on what that gaping synapse entails. In manufacturing, a brand is integrity-based to the extent that it guarantees the consistent quality of the product, no matter where it's purchased and no matter who purchases it. "A Sony TV operates the same in Singapore as it does in Duluth," says Flannery. But no major law firm can make that claim nor should it try to do so. There are, naturally, differences in style and quality within the organization. In fact, a law firm's deliverables *ought* to vary from lawyer to lawyer—not to mention from office to office—because human beings are involved, and human beings behave differently no matter what firm-wide standards are supposed to govern their work.

Sometimes this is a quality issue. One lawyer is simply better than another. One office is simply more efficient than another. Other times, the quality may be equal, but the personal styles still vary because the professional services require individualized approaches to widely different client needs. In a dark and critical moment for the client, a lawyer or consultant will apply his or her own personality and instincts to the situation, not a scripted or formally defined "Brobeck approach," "Arthur Andersen approach," or even "McKinsey approach." Since that's really the way services ought to be provided, we're back to the old saw among in-house legal clients, that "We hire lawyers, not law firms." This is the persistent truism that belies institutional branding and will likely outlive it.

In the last chapter we saw how concerted branding does indeed fit with the fundamental goals of the Commercial Law Affiliates. But we're tempted in these pages to give branding conspicuously short shrift for several reasons. First, marketers point out that branding is still a fairly mythical concept among law firms. With the exception of Brobeck and a handful of others, law firms have not made the financial or time commitment that a real branding campaign requires. So why talk about it now?

Second, branding doesn't really seem to bring any value to the buyer, except a certain ease of identifiability, i.e., that Brobeck is a firm you want to think about if you've got venture capital projects, especially in high-tech industries. Yet such branding doesn't really tell the buyer much about the firm's deliverables compared, say, to how a Jones, Day, without slick subliminal association techniques or sundry self-serving shibboleths, can ably articulate its own critical depth on a global basis and explain, with examples, why that depth makes for seamless service delivery. Nor, certainly, does branding provide substantive legal help to a prospect. In-house buyers benefit more from a seminar on Title VII that costs $5,000 to produce than they possibly can from a $7 million branding initiative replete with bells, whistles, and logos.

We're also tempted to dismiss branding, and quickly move on to the next topic, because this would make a sharp statement about the irrelevance of such efforts to in-house counsel. In response to all the articles being written, and all the money being spent, the briefest possible back-of-the-hand treatment would send a salutary message.

Yet, exploring the subject a little more fully, we may still find that we gain a better overall understanding of the inside/outside dynamic if only as a negative example. There are reasons in addition to cost why so few law firms have launched branding campaigns.

Prominent among those reasons is the internal politics of branding. You can't just brand an entire firm, at least not a large one. You have to pick specific areas—an industry specialization such as high-tech, or practice specializations such as IP or capital markets—and make those the vanguard of your campaign. However, this invites institutional disruption. Practice groups that are not included in the initiative feel deracinated. Are you willing to send the message to some partners that they are not in the first rank of the firm's future? Are you prepared to see them leave once you do? Can you even muster sufficient internal support for a branding campaign if you exclude too many partners?

Hale and Dorr in Boston has been quietly but resolutely pursuing a high-tech brand and letting the chips fall where they may as far as other practice areas are concerned. Most firms can't do that either because they're unwilling to alienate some sectors or because their partnership procedures may require a majority approval for a major investment that isn't logistically possible when they exclude entire practice groups. As a partner in a media/marketing consulting firm, this writer has found that such exclusion can be a political problem in some instances even when a client firm contemplates a relatively modest project to benefit one or two practice groups. Other practice groups might balk. And such a project isn't even close to the dramatic commitment required in full-scale branding.

The very fact that such inner conflict exists casts doubt on the truthfulness of a branding message. By definition, law firms that are not boutiques—that claim to be full-service—are in a contradictory position: They're branding themselves as one thing, yet they contain practice groups and partners who aren't a part of that one thing, and are likely to have grave misgivings about a brand identity that doesn't include them.

In contrast, a boutique that brands itself for its IP practice or its FDA practice isn't really "branding" at all. It is merely doing the same sort of niche marketing that boutiques have always done. In other words, "differentiation" is not branding. Differentiation in the marketplace often occurs naturally, even among the largest law firms, without a formalized strategic program. Skadden, Arps, Slate, Meager & Flom is the best example. To some extent, Skadden is already branded as a preeminent M&A powerhouse. So significant is Skadden's brand that clients with substantial M&A needs wouldn't dream of excluding the firm from its short list of potential outside counsel if possible.

Skadden's brand was achieved decades ago before "branding" was something that most firms in the professional services thought about consciously. The fact that many clients were retaining Skadden without actually using the firm, but simply paying a retainer fee to make sure that Mr. Flom and his colleagues wouldn't represent opposing parties, powerfully affirmed the brand. Yet there was no formal branding campaign at Skadden. The firm's great legal work simply influenced how buyers thought about their retention options in the marketplace.

In fact, at the height of its M&A "brand," Flom and his lieutenant, Peter Mullen, went in the opposite direction by diversifying. The firm built great bankruptcy, environmental, and antitrust practices. Sheila Birnbaum's product liability practice offers a particularly good example of how Skadden avoided the traps that now ensnare law firms when they spend millions to affirm a narrower identity. Flom had no particular strategic reason for hiring Birnbaum other than that he greatly admired her talents. Product liability had nothing to do with what Skadden had achieved for itself by way of a "brand name" on Wall Street. But Birnbaum was wildly successful and her practice wildly profitable. If anything, she naturally developed her own "brand name" even as Skadden's primary identity as a strong M&A practice continued to be undiluted and undiminished.

Even in the manufacturing sector, and in the marketing of products, the value of branding to the buyer is questionable. "Just Do It" sells a lot of shoes, but there is nothing in Nike's campaign that ensures the value of its products. Even if one doesn't really believe that Michelin tires are safer than Goodyear's, at least there's some assurance of value in Michelin tires. Not so with Nike; the company's classic branding approach does not elevate the product over the competition. In the professional services, selling by slogan doesn't work in any event, yet law firms are even adopting tag lines to blithely anoint themselves with instant marketplace recognizability.

The "cutest" tag line is that of Greenberg Traurig, a Miami-based firm with strong technology practices in a number of markets. Their line: "We Get IT." In Toronto, one firm's tag line is "The Hard Working Lawyers." Presumably, that differentiates this firm from all the other law firms where lazy partners encourage wheel spinning among their associates. If any of this sloganeering speaks to the across-the-board uniformity that Bill Flannery defines as the essential purpose of branding in the manufacturing world, it does so only in the blandest, least persuasive way.

Once again, observes Flannery, law firms have been beguiled by marketing strategies that apply to the manufacturing world but not to professional services. The most recent other instance of a misapplied marketing strategy was "total quality management" ("TQM"), a corporate system of performance and productivity measures that includes objective criteria that cannot be applied to the subtler dynamics of legal counseling. Law firms soon realized that and jettisoned their TQM initiatives. But branding seems to be fooling them longer.

Interestingly, there has been no plethora of derisive commentary in the press or at conferences from in-house counsel, perhaps because the press and in-house counsel are members of corporate cultures where branding plays such a large, permanent role in the marketing and sales processes.

However, one early, instructive response to law firm branding came in 1999 from William Lytton, GC at International Paper Company. Brand names "have no effect on me in making a decision or coming up with a short list," Lytton told *Of Counsel* magazine.[1]

What was particularly interesting about Lytton's comment was that, at the time (1999), Washington, D.C's Howrey Simon Arnold & White was pioneering a branding effort (replete with the tagline, "In Court Every Day"). Howrey was one of the law firms that Lytton relied on often for outside legal services. Howrey is a law firm that Lytton greatly respects. Yet Lytton said then he had never seen or heard of the firm's brand development campaign.

EXCISE THE SELLER

Measured against our value-based paradigm—that the delivery of value to the buyer is crucial to the integrity and efficacy of law firm marketing regardless of whether the buyer actually buys— branding would thus seem a specious "event." From the in-house buyer's perspective, it offers little of substance that the buyer can extract from all the high-priced hoopla.

Another "event," so to speak, in the development of law firm marketing and sales strategies provides a fundamental contrast. That is, consultants such as Flannery, and Michael O'Horo, principal of Sales Results, Inc. in Arlington, Virginia, have been providing law firms with sales training instruction for the past fifteen years. The approach may vary from one sales trainer to another, but the good ones share common fundamental assumptions.

Sales training does not merely provide corporate buyers with useful legal information in a seminar or newsletter that they

---

[1] Tripoli, "Law Firms Rush to Embrace 'Branding' Strategies," 18:6 Of Counsel 10 (Mar. 15, 1999).

can take home and apply to an existing legal problem. Rather, the procedure comprises a complete sales process designed to help the buyers better define their business problems as well as their legal problems. As such, the selling process itself becomes a consultation. Because the dialogue helps crystallize what the buyers need, both for their companies and for themselves, the experience is one that prospective clients will *want* to have. It's in the self-interest of prospective clients to participate, not simply a favor to the law firm or whoever might have referred them to the law firm.

As O'Horo describes it, the more usual approach in today's marketplace is for a law firm's "gang of four" to beleaguer prospective buyers "with what the buyers already know." The four or so partners describe their qualifications, and talk about how smart their associates are and how efficient their paralegals. Traditionally, in-house counsel haven't known any better. They just sit and listen even though, at many companies, their own sales forces utilize far more sophisticated sales techniques than this sort of purgatorial didacticism. Unfortunately, in-house departments can themselves be alienated from their clients, so they may never learn from them that there is indeed a better way.

However, we should bear in mind that the New Economy in its incipient days during the 1980s brought with it a savvier breed of legal services buyers. "Supply chain management" became the byword: "As your client, you help me help my client. You help me cut through to the real issue I'm facing, and help me understand how you might address it. In the process, you make me look good."

It is the nature of these consultative dialogues to vary significantly from situation to situation; indeed, such flexibility is a virtue of any "sales approach" that goes beyond the conventional reiteration of bona fides and self-plaudits. Different sales trainers might similarly draw up different dialogue models to characterize a typical consultation.

The following model of a law firm discussing an impending transaction with a prospective client was created by the author, but it carefully followed examples and language used by Michael

O'Horo as training tools in other sales situations. It may at least offer some notion of how these dialogues evolve and, implicitly, why they add value beyond the conventional sales pitch.

DIALOGUE MODEL

Sales Function	Question	Effect
Introduce yourself or reconnect if you have previously met.		Establish comfort level, receptivity to relationship.
Test for *Demand Trigger* business problem.	♦ *Foundation:* "There's a lot of uncertainty in this market. Businesses identify desirable acquisition targets, maybe even crucial acquisition targets. But in this environment, any sign of a problem creates a lot more caution than might have been the case two years ago. You suggested to me on the telephone that there are a number of deals where you've laid a groundwork for going forward, but that there are legal concerns that are now causing	Bridge from rapport-building "schmooze" dialogue to potentially compelling business purpose.

Sales Function	Question	Effect
	unanticipated resistance on the executive team." ◆ *Question:* "Would you say that's true in the NovaSolutions deal?" [If the answer is "no," ask the person to elaborate more on the comments he made on the telephone, and why he made them. Upon reconsideration, he or she may better define what the legal or business issue is in the NovaSolutions matter that's of concern.]	
Test for importance, scale, criticality of problem: ◆ "Size the problem."	"NovaSolutions is a $20 million company and $16 million in debt. If you were to draw a revenue and debt chart, where would NovaSolutions fall compared to your other acquisitions since 1999?"	Determine whether the problem is big enough to justify meaningful investment in a solution. If not, the sales investigation ends. If it's big enough, you have the beginnings of a basis for projecting the actual amount that the prospective client stands to gain or lose.

Sales Function	Question	Effect
◆ Current negative effects or consequences due to the problem.	"What negative strategic or operational effects do you see from this opportunity-conversion problem?" [You may have to prime the pump with some common examples, e.g., their competitor acquires NovaSolutions, stockholders are upset because the deal was tabled, etc.]	Establishes objective, observable, measurable consequences. This is an early test of whether the problem is a true imperative or merely an irritant. It is the beginning of defining the *Cost of Doing Nothing*.
◆ Expected positive effects or consequences if the problem is solved.	"What positive strategic or operational effects would you expect if the problem were solved?"	The mirror image affirms the previous negative response, and often yields one or two additional items not considered during the first go-round.
◆ Personal effect.	This depends on whether the respondent considers himself as one who suffers from the problem, or is in a leadership position and is concerned with those who do. "How does it affect you [or other executives] personally?" [Answers should be emotional effects, e.g., frustration, embar-	This determines whether the respondent [or others] is [are] personally invested in the problem or merely engaging in intellectual analysis. Only those with a personal stake in the game are motivated to be reliable advocates, and have reason to take risks and resist the

Sales Function	Question	Effect
	rassment, anxiety re: compensation, status, loss of face among stockholders, etc.]	inevitable decision-avoidance forces.
♦ Economic impact.	"If the legal problems identifiable with NovaSolutions were to be solved, what economic impact would that have on your company?"	This begins the process of defining the tangible dollars associated with doing nothing.
	The first response will be a demurral, e.g., "Oh, that's hard to say. It will depend on X or Y or Z."	This merely reveals that the respondent hasn't thought of the problem in such specific monetary terms before. Now he has.
	Be empathetic: "I understand, but what's your gut feel for the economic impact?"	Simplify the task. You're not looking for detailed analysis, just a sense of scale.
	This response will likely be qualitative, e.g., "Oh, it would be very significant."	He acknowledges that the amount, when defined, will be a large one.
	"By 'significant,' are we talking $100 or $1 billion?"	Create a numeric framework for response, defining the two poles of the numeric continuum with absurd extremes.

Sales Function	Question	Effect
		This allows the prospect to probe where his instinct leads him. Final response will be a specific amount, e.g., "$X million."
Conclusion/ Alignment.	If the number is as large as we suspect, "Why do you think the resistance to solving the legal problems at NovaSolutions, and going ahead with an offer, is so great?"	This identifies additional barriers that we wouldn't have explored, and sets up an ensuing discussion of internal sponsorship and championship.
Sponsorship.	*Foundation:* "In most of these situations, if a cadre of influential executives gets behind an idea, it happens pretty reliably." *Question:* "What core group of executives' support would make certain that your company would go forward and identify and solve the legal issues at NovaSolutions that are now gumming up the works?"	This defines the number, profile, and possible identities of a critical mass of decision stakeholders.

Sales Function	Question	Effect
Championship.	"Who, besides yourself, is the natural person to really get behind this and champion it inside the firm?"	Identifies the key stakeholder or buying influence.
	If the stakes are too low, you must conclude, "Despite the operational difficulties and personal aggravation, it doesn't sound like there's enough money involved for the company to really feel any urgency to fix the legal problems and buy NovaSolutions. Is that right?"	At worst, you preserve your credibility by acknowledging that it doesn't make sense to pursue the matter. However, many times the prospect will argue forcefully that the operational and emotional effects are sufficiently compelling, e.g., they've been going on for so long that everyone has reached his or her limits. A solution is necessary.
Collaboration.	"How confident are you that you could arrange a meeting [conference call if geographically remote] between the Champion, yourself, and me?"	This is a logical next step, but it also recruits this prospect as a Guide, and challenges his ego to prove his influence by producing the meeting with the Champion. It also eliminates his subconscious fear that our connecting with the Champion would eliminate him from

Sales Function	Question	Effect
		the mix, since we'll be doing it together.
Reiteration.		This is a continuous loop. Repeat this entire sequence with each successive stakeholder or group of stakeholders. Don't assume that the stakeholders are in alignment; they rarely are, so don't take any shortcuts. Be disciplined. Let the buyers do all the work.

This is a rudimentary outline but suggestive enough to differentiate between the traditional law firm selling technique, which is of no value to the client, and a more considered consultative approach.

In the former, the ultimate message is: "Hire us, and we'll write you a beautiful brief detailing all the legal liabilities you'll assume by acquiring NovaSolutions. If you decide to go forward with the deal, we've got the lawyers to handle it, along with any derivative problems that may or may not ensue as a result of the liabilities we outlined."

The more consultative approach allows the buyers to make an *informed* decision based on the importance of the matter and the likelihood of gaining the requisite consensus to then move forward and actually do the deal. As O'Horo points out, in this second selling model the law firm has no predetermined objective. The law firm is inviting the prospect to investigate the situation in order to lead the client to whatever resolution is best. That might very well entail doing nothing.

In fact, this mode of selling *takes the seller out of the picture altogether*. It is instead a platform on which the buyer begins to strategize his next move. There can be no greater value provided to a prospective buyer. At the same time, the law firm has positioned itself well on several grounds. First, if the decision is made to do nothing, the buyer's opinion of the seller has at least become far more favorable. Indeed, the buyer may leave the table feeling indebted to the seller. Second, if the decision to go forward is made, the firm has, for all intents and purposes, already begun working on the case; outside counsel is already a partner, and a sense of inside/outside teamwork has already been established.

O'Horo may be right in his view that too many inside counsel are wedded to the older "talking-heads" approach, but law firms should note that the cannier buyers recognize this consultative approach when they see it, and will respond accordingly. Buyers will immediately recognize in a prospective seller any law firm that purports to become their partner, not merely their vendor. Among sophisticated buyers, the sales medium is the message, and a powerful message indeed!

It's no accident, perhaps, that one of Flannery's first major clients in the legal industry was a corporate law department—not a law firm—and that the department was part of a New Economy company. The in-house lawyers brought in Flannery because they wanted to treat their own clients at the company like business partners. They understood that those clients needed higher-volume sales reports in order "to look good." Their goal was to be perceived by the sales executives as facilitators, not bureaucratic deal-breakers.

Again, the supply chain moves from CEO or CFO or COO to the law department, and from the law department to the law firm. The essence of selling is to make the guy ahead of you look good to the guy ahead of him. No doubt an outside lawyer would be well-advised to use the same sort of consultative approach with a particular company's in-house legal managers as those in-house legal managers have used internally with their own clients. That—not the Gang of Four—is what these buyers have been trained to expect.

The consultative approach encourages delineating the parameters of factors that are pertinent to the inside/outside relationship. As O'Horo's model shows, to maximize value to the buyer, you sell by mainly asking questions. At no point in O'Horo's model does the seller recommend a course of action to the buyer. Now consider pending litigation in which the business issues are already well-defined and the consensus to fight the case well-established. In that situation, the specific terms of retention may come up earlier rather than later. Here, too, asking questions, rather than haggling over those terms, will maximize value for both sides.

As an example, Flannery posits an interview in which the buyer immediately demands a discount on rates. Actually, that kind of a demand is as much an opportunity for outside counsel as it is a challenge. A "yes or no" response, or an equivocation, squanders the opportunity.

Consider instead the following value-based alternative dialogue:

Buyer: I will require a discount from any law firm we hire for this case.

Seller: Why?

Buyer: Why? To save money, of course!

Seller: In what way do you think a discount will save money?

Buyer: Because I'll be paying lower rates, of course.

Seller: But do you think lower rates will save you money?

Buyer: They should.

Seller: Are you concerned that, even with discounted rates, total costs might exceed what we would both want?

Buyer: Well, we'll see. We'll control that.

Seller: Would you like to explore other ways to save money?

Buyer: Such as?

Seller: What if we kept our current rates the same but found a way to share the risk?

Buyer: Such as?

Seller: Let's look at the results we produce at our current rates. If the case goes south, we'll give you a 15% discount on total fees. If we save you money, we'll bill you at our current rates with the expectation of more work on those terms.

Buyer: That's interesting.

Seller: Well, it's just one suggestion. Do you have any others?

As we'll see in Chapter 7, it was their demand for just such "shared risk" that drove companies like DuPont to fire hundreds of law firms and strike deals with a handful of others. In those instances, it was the client that forced the issue, and it was the client that eschewed straight-rate discounts in favor of more innovative arrangements.

In contrast, one effect of asking the right questions is that the seller can also help define the options that may work for both sides. There need not be a *cul de sac* in most cases. For example, if the in-house buyer will not entertain shared risk or alternative billing arrangements, the seller can then ask if there are other, non-monetary considerations that might serve in lieu of rate discounts. Remember, the buyer isn't really trying to save money. One of the questions on O'Horo's chart pertains to "personal effect." That crucial element is in force here too. The buyer mainly wants to look good. A rate discount will help him look good. But something else may do just as well, if not better. Listen hard enough and you'll find out what that is.

The power of value-added selling has created a real cottage industry of sales trainers focusing on the legal profession. Indeed, Flannery's effect has been so powerful among so many firms that the word "Flannerized" has worked its way into the professional parlance. It's anyone's guess, though, how effectively lawyers are actually applying the principles they're taught by the Flannerys and the O'Horos. Again, the in-house buyer is a wild card. When the in-house buyers finally send the clear message, based on their own self-interest, that this is the kind of selling they want, and that this is the kind of selling they will respond to most favorably, the real sea change may occur.

In any event, these two phenomena of law firm marketing and selling haven't, until recently, been compared. But the programmatic branding that has attracted so many large law firms, and the personalized selling that bases itself entirely on the needs of the buyer are, in fact, polar opposites. Our prediction is that "branding" will disappear from the lexicon of law firm marketers by the year 2005 whereas, in that same year, corporate legal buyers will be as familiar with the principles of consultative selling as the law firms trying to learn it now.

The Extracurricular Equation: How Lawyers Who Solve Non-Legal Problems May Revolutionize the Legal Profession

The "value" discussed in the preceding chapters is defined rather narrowly by some corporate legal clients. Often that definition comprises a specific substantive legal insight or practice tip that is useful to the client's business. But some people, among both buyers and sellers, talk so generally about "value-added" that, worse than a shibboleth, the term becomes a catchall that eventually means nothing. Clients can invoke "value-added" to support unreasonable expectations. Law firms can bandy it about in their marketing pitches without ever saying what the "value" they're "adding" really is.

Fortunately, among a growing number of professionals in this field, value-added is at bottom a mindset. At superior law firms, it has become more instinctive to think about how whatever it is that affects the firms—including their own internal workings—affects their clients as well. Sometimes, the instincts of good lawyers can be discerned vividly in the smaller things of life.

Recently, for example, Mayer, Brown & Platt in Chicago found that a section of its attractive library (attractive even by lavish law firm standards) was not, for whatever reason, being fully utilized by the firm's lawyers. The stacks in that section were also something of an aesthetic blemish amid the handsome surroundings. So the firm removed the bookcases there and replaced them with conference tables for client roundtables and receptions. Because the books shelved on those cases were primarily accessible online anyway, moving the hard copy materials would not really inconvenience anyone.

Mayer, Brown then decided to further generate goodwill among clients by taking another step. Because the library is such a design gem, it reasoned, why not offer some of the space for boardroom meetings to organizations with which the firm's partners are associated? It would seem a natural and unremarkable thing to do. Yet the firm is sharing the benefits, not only of the available space, but also of the online technology that allowed it to remove the books. In a client-dominated world, everything is multidimensional.

Ironically, in the actual delivery of legal services, "value-added" frequently has nothing to do with legal services *per se.* To the contrary, the value-added is actually what takes the practitioner beyond his or her own narrowly defined practice. A recurrent theme in our discussions, already touched on in Chapter 1, is the perceived value achieved when lawyers act more like business partners with their clients than just attorneys. In the most basic sense, this means, for example, not charging fees to find a thousand legal reasons why a revenue-generating venture won't be possible but, ultimately, finding ways to help businesses stay within the law and still get their deals done.

It's been a crucial transformation for lawyers, inside and outside. The traditional negative view of lawyers isn't just that a lot of them are crooks. Among corporate buyers, the historical dread has been more that, having just cooked up a whale of a business idea, that idea would now have to be "cleared by legal." So don't hold your breath; it will take the lawyers three months to "clear" the deal and they're bound to sabotage the whole thing anyway.

In contrast, the rosiest future for lawyers entails different perceptions altogether. In this scenario, businesspeople want to send their idea to the legal department or to outside counsel so that they *will* spot the hidden problems and liabilities. Once they do, it means the idea has reached the final launch stage because, having spotted the problems, the lawyers will know how to solve them.

The client/lawyer business partnership goes beyond reacting to problems and solving them. It's also proactive in the most genuine sense possible. The lawyers don't just solve problems facing a business venture. The lawyers help conceive the venture in the first place or, at an early stage, they're instrumental in funding and implementing the project. They persuade capital investors to invest, help identify the best executives to run the project, and contribute their own ideas on the best ways to market the project. As we'll see in Chapter 10, the abiding mystique of the great Silicon Valley law firms wasn't so much that they had good lawyers on staff. It was the naked fact that, if you had a great business idea, these were the law firms that could help get you the venture bucks to make it happen.

CLIENT-CENTRIC SYSTEMS

To a great extent, those law firms, like Wilson, Sonsini, Goodrich & Rosati, or Cooley Godward, always saw themselves operating on a different plane. Equally interesting are the more traditional law firms that, one day, find themselves presented with the opportunity to take client service beyond traditional law-related works—and then jump at the opportunity.

In the two examples we'll look at, such an opportunity arose first as a way to deliver better and more cost-efficient legal services. In both instances, the law firms worked closely with their clients to create technology systems to provide for legal needs. In both instances, it became apparent that the systems had wider uses. And, in both instances, the law firm did not merely say to the client, "Go ahead, run with it." Instead, the firms stuck around. They structured the systems to accommodate non-legal applications and, in so doing, fused exceptionally tight relationships with the clients (that, to be sure, happened to be important clients).

First, Dickinson Wright in Detroit built a document management system for Chrysler Financial Company called the Real Estate Loan Tracking Database that allows online review of the latest information on all loan applications, and enables users to add comments or respond to issues in real time. Similarly, the Texas firm Haynes and Boone created a system called ClientConnect that allows clients to interactively share documents and critical information in real time, not only with the lawyers, but with the clients' other professional service providers as well.

At first blush, neither technology seems extraordinary. Even small companies have systems that allow for multiple users in multiple locations to handle multiple tasks. But there are significant features that distinguish these client-service innovations. First, the systems connect different individuals in different organizations. "Over the past decade, a great deal of effort has been focused on tools for improved collaboration and knowledge sharing within business," explains John Parkinson, National Director of Innovation and Strategy at Ernst & Young. "As valuable as these tools have been in improving operational effectiveness, it's now clear that they have limits, especially when focused on the equally critical and more challenging issue of collaboration between businesses."

"Inside enterprise boundaries, many things can be controlled or mandated," Parkinson continues. "Between enterprises, there are far fewer or no controls, and mandates must at best be negotiated. The more businesses that must participate, the fewer the controls and the harder to negotiate the mandates."

The Dickinson Wright and Haynes and Boone systems provide control because they establish integrated participation in the same technology system from the beginning of a project. The collaboration that's involved in producing a document naturally creates a consensual result. (At the same time, the systems are turnkey so that users can only access what they are specifically permitted to access.)

The technologies are, by definition, also "client-centric" since all service providers must be using the operating system developed by and for the client. In the case of Chrysler, it was a Lotus Notes-based program. ClientConnect, developed by Haynes and Boone in partnership with Archon Group, L.P., is Microsoft-based. (The Archon Group is a global, full-service commercial real estate investment and mortgage loan company.)

"[P]rofessional services providers . . . have tended to approach collaboration on the basis of, 'Here is how we want to do it,' rather than, 'How can we serve you best (or at least better)?'" remarks Parkinson. "Few of the existing corporate collaboration tools can support this transition in viewpoint."

Historically, technology represented an opportunity for some top law firms to further lock in, as it were, their most important clients—to "institutionalize" these relationships. A firm such as King & Spalding could share the same automation systems with a client like The Coca-Cola Company. It no doubt meant faster and better legal services for the client. But it also served the seller most propitiously. It would make it cumbersome, if not prohibitive, for the client to entrust important matters to law firms with which they were not so technologically entwined. It would entail going back to the drawing board and setting up a new system with a new outside provider, meanwhile squandering the time and resources that had been invested in the client's technological partnership with the primary law firm. In the 1980s, Davis Polk & Wardell was, along with King & Spalding, among the cutting-edge firms pursuing this strategy.

Of course, it should be noted that the experience of the clients with these particular law firms made the introduction of such online connectivity attractive. Having been provided second-to-none legal services for many years, these clients viewed investing in a relationship that guaranteed more exclusivity to their top firms as altogether reasonable. King & Spalding and Davis Polk are great law firms, after all. No-one was getting hustled.

But times have changed and the Internet, as well as more flexible operating systems, is now providing other options. How major clients buy legal services from law firms has also changed. For example, the Real Estate Loan Tracking Database evolved after Dickinson Wright won a Chrysler Financial beauty contest in the early 1990s when the company consolidated the number of law firms it would use for real estate work, according to Stephen Dawson, the partner in charge of the law firm's banking/real estate/environmental group.

The Dickinson Wright system is much more localized than ClientConnect. It was set up only for Chrysler Financial; ClientConnect is designed for as many clients as possible, to handle all sorts of projects involving all sorts of practice groups. The Real Estate Loan Tracking Database has a specific single purpose, which is to monitor loans made to car dealers based on their commercial real estate equity, and to complete the loan process online from inception to archive. Chrysler Financial's central legal and credit departments, which are based in Southfield, Michigan, interact with dealers in about fifteen zones. The dealers complete their loan packages and, once they're approved, Dawson and his colleagues prepare the commitment letters and other loan documents. Until Dickinson Wright built the loan tracking database, a daunting paper trail would typically develop.

The database, created for Chrysler Financial by Mike Harnish, Dickinson Wright's chief technology officer in the mid-1990s, includes pending loans, replete with applications and full fact sheets; approved loans, along with the commitment letters prepared by the law firm; canceled loans; and an archive of funded loans. Environmental reports are also part of the database, which is updated three times daily.

The innovation is twofold.

First, the system allows multiple parties—the dealers, the loan officers, the GC's office, and the law firm—to access the contents and add whatever notes or other material they want. Again, collaboration equals control. Not only are the records, showing what was actually agreed to, readily accessible, the chances of future disputes are also decreased because all the parties to the loan will have worked out the details in real time. There are no decisive telephone calls differently interpreted by different parties. Nor are there lost faxes to search for.

Second, much of the work accomplished in this manner, especially during the pre-approval phase, is non-legal. Of course, everything in the database is potentially useful to legal counsel. All pre-approval department-dealer exchanges can be examined by a lawyer for legal reasons if need be, as can the archives. But the utility of the system for Chrysler Financial goes well beyond legal documents or legal prophylaxis. The system allows the company to simply organize its business process better, regardless of whether or not lawyers have occasion to read this or that part of the data.

From an economic standpoint, this better use of technology has real potential for both the buyer and seller. For the seller, it naturally means more efficiency. The waste involved in tracking paper from Southfield to Kalamazoo and back again is incalculable. A system like Dickinson Wright's obviously means fewer billable hours to pay the legal piper as well, since you don't have bunches of lawyers discovering documents and laboriously reworking them.

Moreover, the law firm can lock in a higher hourly rate for a senior partner like Dawson and still save the client money in the long run. Since Dawson is charging higher rates for fewer hours, he estimates a typical dealer loan still runs $5,000 to $7,000 in legal fees. But the client is not swallowing the extraneous costs that run wild in a hard-copy world and the legal fee doesn't include junior associates chasing that hard copy. Meanwhile, Dawson does the whole job faster, since it's automated—and he can then move on to the next job, charging the same higher rate.

The term of art is "realization," which basically means getting the client to pay all of what you've billed. In a highly leveraged firm, inexperienced associates doing high-volume "commodity" work may bill out $200 per hour. But, since the work is so high-volume and often inefficiently performed, the client renegotiates the final amount and the firm writes off time. At the end of the day, the associates are only really earning $100 per hour for the firm, which is a poor realization rate. Technology ought to improve realization. It ought to mean more top partners billing $500 and collecting the full amount without significant overhead or disbursements.

Technology, of course, was supposed to revolutionize legal practice in the 1970s and 1980s by making the billable hour obsolete. A few keystrokes could accomplish just as much as associates researching cases all day long in the library. That didn't happen. The billable hour has been persistently impervious to any such automated flood. Here, though, we have another way in which technology might, if not make the billable hour obsolete, at least change how it affects the buyer/seller relationship. It can decrease the total number of hours billed in favor of fewer, better, and more profitable hours.

Not coincidentally, perhaps, both Dickinson Wright and Haynes and Boone have worked with the same consultant, William Cobb of WCCI in Houston, who for years has been advocating an efficiency billing model in which the law firm gets rid of its lower-end legal work one way or another, either by not accepting it in the first place or by automating it. You charge more money for better senior legal work, and you collect it all. You become more profitable. Your realization rates go through the ceiling.

It's also a good way to separate the wheat from the chaff in terms of quality practitioners. The better senior partners will want to be efficient because they know that, however fast they finish the job, there's another job waiting for them. We are, in fact, talking about a law firm growth model based on quality, not merely utilization and increased lawyer numbers.

ALL HANDS ON DECK

Unlike Dickinson Wright, Haynes and Boone has created a system for all its lawyers and practice groups to plug into. Steve Jenkins, the Haynes and Boone partner who spearheaded ClientConnect, acknowledges some early resistance from lawyers. They hesitated to make status information available to clients on a 24/7 basis.

However, as of this writing, three years later, about half the firm's 400-plus lawyers are using ClientConnect. More than 2,000 client projects have been tracked with ClientConnect.

The breadth of the system is such that each project has its own separate entry space, database, and turnkey pass code. Like Dickinson Wright's database, ClientConnect is as much a forum as a resource, and allows for professionals to work together on matters in real time. Jenkins emphasizes that it is not a case management system of the kind typically used by GCs to, say, monitor budgets on ongoing cases. It is a tool to improve the flow of critical information and accelerate business decisions.

ClientConnect includes a virtual library of documents specific to each project. Users are alerted via e-mail when new drafts are posted, and can hyperlink right to them, avoiding printouts and faxes. The system has sophisticated highlighting, and a Notes section allows for high-volume comments, reminders, and the like. A Status section facilitates direct access to all users' permitted documents, and separate folders for due diligence and other such broad categories can be created. E-mails are automatically generated when users choose to alert others of updated priority content.

As was the case with Dickinson Wright and Chrysler Financial, the willingness of Haynes and Boone to engage in a technological enterprise that would benefit the client on both legal and non-legal fronts turned out to be a real competitive advantage for that law firm in its relationship with Archon. Yet ClientConnect originated in the mid-1990s as a purely internal management tool for two large Real Estate Investment Trusts (REITs) involving two separate clients. REITs are multifaceted and multidisciplinary. As such, the technology that evolved would naturally be friendly to diverse users. "In just a few months, the implications, allowing around-the-clock oversight by clients . . . were readily apparent," says Jenkins.

Ron Barger, Archon's senior vice president and general counsel, recalls that, in the early stages, the system was still oriented toward the law firm's own technology, mainly to enhance the firm's service delivery capability. But, says Barger, Jenkins was soon thinking much more innovatively. Jenkins envisioned a system that would allow clients to include other professional firms and advisors as well as their own people. ClientConnect would be the client's system, not the law firm's.

Archon worked with Haynes and Boone "every step of the way" during the development of the system, says Jenkins. So it was inevitable that ClientConnect would become an inclusive system and involve many other professional firms—including other law firms—since it was in the client's interest that such a wide variety of organizations be potential users.

What ClientConnect has become therefore represents the *opposite* of the strategy pursued in the past by the King & Spaldings and Davis Polks. Far from guaranteeing exclusivity, it guarantees non-exclusivity. A recent Archon beauty contest confirms that concept. According to Barger, in order to survive as one of the company's forty preferred law firm providers, contestants had to agree to use ClientConnect. At this point, adds Jenkins, Archon is even bringing on a system administrator to manage the elaborate user network encompassing the company itself and the myriad professional services firms retained around the world.

To be sure, the finished product serves Haynes and Boone's direct economic interests as well, and not just higher realization potential that is emphasized by consultants like Bill Cobb. Haynes and Boone has, in fact, profit-centered the system itself and plans on licensing ClientConnect to other professional services organizations that are not connected with Archon. That is why Microsoft is the *lingua franca* here. The Lotus Notes that Dickinson Wright used on behalf of Chrysler Financial was deemed too limiting for the widespread distribution desired by Jenkins.

As of this writing, Haynes and Boone is trying to spin off ClientConnect as a separate business entity worldwide. No lawyer will direct this venture but, rather, businessman Jim Melson will be at the helm. The search for money has been slow due to the 2000-2001 tech downturn, but Jenkins sounds confident that, by early 2002, if not sooner, the venture will be fully capitalized.

Some licensees may want to contract with ClientConnect solely for internal users. Others can deploy it like Archon, including multiple users at diverse other companies and firms. Jenkins figures that competitor law firms are pretty smart too. They'll soon be seeing the need to develop transparent document-sharing systems that provide many of the same benefits as ClientConnect. So why not sell it to them now, at a time when their own efforts to evolve something like ClientConnect are still mainly "rudimentary"?

Jenkins likes the idea of selling to other law firms for a couple of reasons. First, it suggests that those other firms are acknowledging that Haynes and Boone has been well ahead of this particular curve. Second, law firms have terrific distribution channels, so licensing the system to them may publicize and "sell" the innovation very effectively.

Haynes and Boone can exploit its current advantage by permanently, and globally, identifying itself as the developer of a cutting-edge resource that competing law firms and non-client companies have put to effective use. Traditional law firms cannot be differentiated on the basis of what they traditionally do, agrees Jenkins. Most efforts in that direction deteriorate into hollow platitudes. But ClientConnect ostensibly achieves differentiation for its law firm creator because neither the technology itself nor the underlying client-service strategy is at all traditional.

In some instances, being first, or among the first to do something, results in a decisive marketing advantage because it does achieve some differentiation. In other instances, being first is an overrated advantage if it sends no other message besides, "Boy, weren't we clever!" From a marketing standpoint, the substantive message is that being first says something about our ability to better serve our clients. Based on that, Haynes and Boone deserves some mileage for this innovation. If nothing else, the non-exclusivity that defines ClientConnect, as opposed to the very exclusive computer linkages between major firms and their clients in the 1980s, bespeaks a strong client service sensibility. The message is: "We want you, our client, to have all the options that you could possibly need."

The non-exclusivity also bespeaks the changing nature of technology; after all, the Internet is all about open architecture. ClientConnect is a child of the Internet, and the decision three years ago to make this tool Web-based was a forceful, creative decision. It's easy to forget that the Web was real frontier stuff even as late as 1998. Most law firms were way too conservative to want to venture there first.

By doing so, Haynes and Boone was showing that it is, in contrast, a venturesome organization. Jenkins was canny enough to peer into the Internet early on and to see it even then as a client service tool. Now, it's up to Jenkins and his colleagues to follow through on this fairly strong advantage by continuing to remind the world of what Haynes and Boone did and how the presumed benefits have affected professional services.

THE TRANSPARENCY REVOLUTION

Archon's commitment to ClientConnect seems validated by disinterested observers such as John Parkinson at Ernst & Young. "ClientConnect represents one of the few attempts that we have seen to provide a client-centric view of inter-corporate collaboration between and among service providers serving a common client," he offers. "It also represents a rare combination of excellent design factors—process orientation, intuitive operation, flexibility, ease of adoption and use—and operational economics, [including] subscription-based use and external service provider operation."

We've seen how, by relying on technology, a law firm can improve realization and achieve growth based on quality rather than the massing of overpaid timekeepers. There's yet more revolutionary potential in systems like the Real Estate Loan Tracking Database and ClientConnect. Technology can also mandate transparency. In systems like these, the lawyer's work product can be looked at and massaged *as it's being created.* That's one reason Barger, for one, believes that ClientConnect will change the way legal services are delivered. If nothing else, it represents a further diminution of the mystique of lawyers. Their work will be collaborative, and that's a major demystifying sea change for professionals who are accustomed to medieval isolation in the crafting of their intellectual output.

As matters often go in today's world, a lawyer shows up at the bargaining table and presents the fruit of his or her deliberations. An investment banker or an accountant argues with the lawyer. They go back and forth, having come to the table from different places. But what if everyone's final deliberations had been reached collaboratively, with everybody at their work stations plugged into a system that allows concurrent input and feedback on the documents being produced or discussed? As we suggested earlier, transparency produces both control and consensus.

Deborah McMurray, a marketing consultant in Irving, Texas, points out that the extranets being developed for sale these days by law firms aren't really selling. These Web-based resources generally miss the point, however—which is not to provide clients with resources, but to directly engage them in the day-to-day work process.

As we've seen, the client gets to play a decisive role in how ClientConnect is developed. In contrast, extranets are often finished concepts delivered to a client's work station. The client can certainly offer suggestions for improvements and modifications. Yet Barger is clearly talking about a system in which he feels a direct proprietary interest. In fact, Barger is already talking about creating additional matter management applications "on the front end" of ClientConnect that will allow him to compare the cost of one firm's service, and the time it took to perform the service, with that of another firm. The purpose of these comparisons is to "model" the transactions (the sale of a particular kind of real estate holding, for example) and generate performance standards and predictable costs. "On the back end" Barger foresees dramatic enhancements as well, in terms of tracking, processing, and paying the bills for these services.

There's a final transparency frontier that no-one on this side of the Atlantic is discussing yet. This is unbilled time. Here, clients will be able to actually access the hours that a firm has logged before they're finalized. If the clients have questions, or objections, the "transparency" allows them to raise the red flags immediately in order to solve the problem, rather than wait until the bill is processed and a full-scale fee dispute ensues.

Such transparency permits access to the very *sanctum sanctorum* of most law firms. Neither Barger nor Jenkins has any comment on such a possibility. Nor is there any evidence that a single law firm in the United States is ready to traverse this daunting frontier.

Across the Atlantic, however, there are two forward-thinking UK law firms, Walker Morris and DJ Freeman, both in London, that have already offered this service to their clients. Meanwhile, in the U.S., Dixie Peterson, GC at the Illinois Department of Children and Family Services, indicated in an article published by *Of Counsel* that she wouldn't be surprised to see clients start demanding such data as a cost-control strategy.[1]

Ponder the client-centric model and—if you really believe in it—there's no reason to believe such predictions are fanciful. After all, if the client is at the center of the universe, and all the professionals who serve the client are knights loyal to the monarch's abiding self-interest, how could anyone deny a glimpse of his or her logged time?

---

[1] Curriden, "U.K. Firms Let Clients See Billable Time—Before It's Billed," 19 Of Counsel 3 (Oct. 23, 2000).

THE INCREDIBLE SHRINKING LAW FIRM

The presumed marketing advantage for law firms such as Haynes
and Boone that have pioneered client-centric products or services,
is the transformation of the inside/outside relationship from one
where law firms monopolized a client and defined the relationship,
to one where the guiding instinct is to benefit the client by being
as open to new ideas as possible. No doubt, many law firms have
been dragged kicking and screaming into such a brave new world,
but the proverbial writing is on the wall.

In 1999 this writer attended a conference of the College of
Law Practice Management where attendee breakout groups were
literally asked to "draw" the law firm of the future. Not one group
(of some extremely sophisticated lawyers and consultants) drew a
law firm at all. They drew a circle with radiating spokes leading to
other circles. The central circle was called the client. The other
circles were labeled law, accounting, human resources, janitorial
services . . . you name it.

We may indeed be talking about the disappearance of the
professional services firm, not just the law firm, as a discrete entity.
All that will be left is the client and a swarm of busy bees hoping
to suck honey from the blossom. The MDPs discussed in Chapter
1 have no doubt catalyzed this new vision.

What we're seeing among law firms represents an
evolutionary trend that's already old news to the MDPs. They have
been multi-service for years. The Big Five, for example, realized
long ago that auditing could not define the future and they've been
adding ingredients to the full-service stew ever since. The current
debate on whether MDPs should provide legal services may
revolutionize the legal profession. For the Big Five, however, it's
simply a question of whether or not they can garner a new market.

In a sense, law firms are now feeling the same sort of
pressure to expand beyond the law that the Big Five felt with
respect to auditing. Patrick McKenna, a founding principal of the
Edge Group consulting firm, has taken an interesting look at law

firm economics based on the numbers reported in *The American Lawyer* over the years, and he has concluded that leverage and utilization have continued to be the engines that drive real profitability among law firms. The problem is, leverage and utilization have caused the well to run dry. Human beings can only work so many hours. Firms are reaching a point of no return when profitability growth will slow and there will be no other direction to go, numerically, besides down.

McKenna's solution: Law firms must innovate new ways to be profitable that clients will not only tolerate, but welcome. One way may be better technology or shrewder, more discriminating work intake to achieve higher realization rates. Another may be significantly greater transparency in terms of ongoing work, or even unbilled time-in-progress, as a way to win and hold client loyalty.

This, in any event, is the critical juncture where systems like Dickinson Wright's Real Estate Loan Tracking Database and Haynes and Boone's ClientConnect fit in. They may define, not just exemplify, the kind of innovation McKenna is talking about. They typify new ways law firms can make money, serve the client more cost-effectively, and, in the case of ClientConnect, even bring in separate revenue streams. Certainly, in terms of innovation, the legal services themselves aren't always what are most important.

Law Firm Accountability: A Review of State-of-Art Budgeting and Case Management Oversight

I t is no longer helpful to divide the inside/outside dynamic into, first, how law firms get legal business and then, how they then keep it. Rather, for sophisticated buyers, the two phases should dovetail. These days, when outside counsel pitch client prospects, they must now address, at one point or another, the issue of accountability.

Branding, marketing, reputation, and credentials all decisively affect how companies find law firms. These are the calling cards that get lawyers to the table. They generate opportunity.

Once firms are at the table, however, they must do more than reiterate their bona fides or somehow convince the prospective client that their qualifications are more stellar than those of competing firms. At this point, the corporate buyer assumes that the candidates who have survived the first cut have all the requisite elements to litigate a lawsuit or negotiate a transaction. Now the issue is: *What are you going to do for me?*

Accountability thus becomes the crucial factor. It's the answer, in one word, to that definitive "What's in it for me?" question. As much as the technology systems discussed in Chapter 5, a law firm that can make an iron-clad commitment to undergoing periodic reviews of its work, to staying within a budget, and to clearly defining all the client's business and legal alternatives is making the crucial promise of value-added service. More than any sales technique, or some magic bullet to fire during the beauty contest interviews, this solemn promise determines who, among those found, will now be chosen. The ones who make the best promises, and seem the likeliest to keep them, emerge triumphant.

Accountability seems to be a fairly obvious buyer/seller dynamic, but it took corporate America decades to achieve accountability in the legal services purchasing process. Until the mid-1980s law firms held many of their clients in a state of mystical thrall. The lawyers were ostensibly doing work no-one else could do. The client could not bother them. The client was never to question how the lawyers did their work or how much they charged in the process. Gradually, aggressive buyers such as Robert Banks, former general counsel at Xerox Corporation, got fed up. Banks in particular was pilloried by law firms (and even some law departments) for urging his in-house colleagues to question fees, deny disbursements, and insist on strict case management procedures.

In time, aggressive lawyers were hired in-house, usually alumni of law firms who knew how the game was played and weren't much impressed when outside counsel tried to insist on their own entitlements rather than the client's. A few good law firms got the hint, and then a few more. They became client-friendly. Soon the tide turned, and the budgeting and accountability techniques that we will discuss in this chapter became, blessedly, more norm than anomaly. The revolutionary "convergence" pioneered at DuPont in the mid-1990s represented a new epoch in inside/outside relations. As we will discuss in Chapter 7, it was significant for many reasons. At this point, let us note that if nothing else, convergence was the culmination of the trend toward accountability that had begun a decade earlier.

However, there remains a good deal of posturing among in-house counsel. "They talk the talk, but they don't always walk the walk," says Peter Zeughauser, formerly GC of The Irvine Company, and now a consultant to law firms. Some of today's accountability is a charade. There are formalized documents, including retention letters, that spell out the obligations of outside counsel in terms of performance review, fees, and staffing. Often, though, these standards are not followed even though both parties often have every intention of enforcing compliance. Once the game starts, however, the rules get rewritten.

"Some law firms simply don't read engagement letters," observes Zeughauser. *"Ever."*

Zeughauser's career pointedly highlights the trends affecting the inside/outside dynamic. As Irvine's GC, he became prominent as one of the main commentators, post-Robert Banks, on corporate legal needs and how law firms can best serve them. This second generation of corporate counsel was delivering the clients' message with equal precision, if less confrontationally than Banks. Enough time had also elapsed since Banks first broadcast the message to the profession. These corporate coursel were no longer shocked to hear that, for example, in-house lawyers were insisting on conformance to budgetary projections.

Considering Zeughauser's prominence as an in-house messenger—a spokesman for what in-house counsel want, and what they don't want—it seems appropriate to review a simple but powerful document that Zeughauser developed while at Irvine, and subsequently redesigned as a teaching tool. The document shows how corporate counsel formalized their accountability demands. Its language is both broad enough to allow leeway in the buyer/seller arrangement and focused on specific questions that clients must have answered if they are to maintain control of their own costs.

The document pertains to litigation, but it can also be used to develop similar standards for other types of legal work.

GUIDELINES FOR PRELIMINARY DISPUTE RESOLUTION ANALYSIS: STRATEGIES AND BUDGETS FOR SUBSTANTIAL DISPUTES*

"1. The analysis and budget is to be based on preliminary interviews with all available percipient witnesses. An estimate for

---

* Reprinted with permission of Peter Zeughauser.

the cost of preparing the analysis and budget shall be obtained before it is undertaken. The analysis and budget shall be completed before a complaint or an answer to a complaint is filed by the Company.

"2. Executive Summary not to exceed two pages to include:

"(a) Key issues and problems with the case

"(b) Likely outcome of key issues in percentages

"(c) Cost estimate

"(d) Staffing Plan

"(e) Timetable for resolution

"(f) Settlement recommendation

"(g) Alternative dispute resolution recommendation

"3. Full Analysis to include:

"(a) Recital of relevant facts known to date

"(b) Identification of all outcome determinative issues, and discussion of application of relevant law to those facts

"(c) Likely outcome, in percentages for each issue

"(d) Identification and discussion of possible issues and facts not yet known with enough certainty to ascertain their impact on outcome.

"4. Budget and Strategy to include:

"(a) Dispute Resolution Strategy that includes:

"(i) schedule for all contemplated pre-trial motions and justification on cost benefit basis

"(ii) schedule for all contemplated discovery and justification on cost benefit basis

"(iii) identification of necessary experts

"(iv) estimated length of trial and pre-trial preparation

"(v) staffing plan

"(b) Short-term (twenty-four months) and full-term costs (high/low range is acceptable) for each item in strategy, including number of hours for each attorney and hourly rates

"(c) Anticipated blended rate for entire matter

"(d) Optional alternative fee arrangements

"(i) hourly fees

"(ii) contingent fees

"(iii) flat fees

"(iv) segmented fee arrangements for different segments of the matter

"(v) hybrids of any of the above

"(e) Discussion of settlement alternatives, recommendations, and strategies

"(f) Discussion of choice of forum, including alternative dispute resolution options

"5. With each monthly billing statement the billing partner shall submit a one-paragraph statement indicating how the services rendered during the preceding month furthered the dispute resolution strategy."

The document, unusual for its time, requires further explication because it typifies the formal standards that so many other corporations have since articulated. Significantly, Zeughauser created the document for use as part of a request-for-proposal (RFP) process. In considering potential law firm candidates, he wanted to obtain a sense of the degree of commitment they were willing to make to these written standards. Within a few months, however, he realized he could append the document to all retention letters as terms of engagement.

His doing so reiterates the point with which we began this discussion. Business-getting and client-responsiveness comprise a fluid dynamic. The same document that Zeughauser used to hire a law firm was also used to manage the firm after it was hired.

When, in the late 1980s, this document was incorporated into law firms' engagement letters, only about half of them actually read it, according to Zeughauser. The majority of lawyers who did read it were junior partners or senior associates. "They thought it was important," says Zeughauser. They "hadn't been around long enough" to affect more cynicism about their clients.

Indeed, if law firms are today more responsive to guidelines such as Irvine's, it's because of "generational" changes, believes Zeughauser. Of course, competition has spurred responsiveness among a greater number of lawyers in general. "There's just so much business up for grabs," observes Zeughauser. Yet it is equally true that, in many cases, those same lawyers who were willing to read and conform to client demands a decade ago are now in charge of their law firms in the twenty-first century. There has been some progress.

Acknowledging the existence of these standards, and committing to adhere to them, comprise the first step. The second step is to actually know what they mean, and what the client expects at each stage. Again, Irvine's document is instructive. Guideline 1 is self-explanatory. It involves talking through the parameters of the case. At this stage, outside counsel should be able to make some estimates as to how many documents the case will require, how many witnesses will be needed, and what the relevant legal issues are.

Two of the points to be included in outside counsel's executive summary are especially important. One is the likely outcome for the client on each legal issue that will arise during the litigation. The other is staffing.

The projected outcome of each legal issue involved in the matter must be expressed as a percentage because, with that kind of concrete estimate, the firm and the client can begin to evolve a determinative case strategy. If the case could hinge on a particular legal issue, a 50% chance of prevailing on that issue is unacceptable. In such a case, the strategy would then immediately turn toward settlement, and how to best pursue the most advantageous terms.

Notwithstanding such less-than-optimal odds on the critical legal issue(s), counsel might elect to explore certain less central legal issues that would help win the case but might not be crucial to the final result. In those instances, the lawyers might decide to go forward in any event. The estimates themselves can be obtained through formal probability analysis, although Zeughauser suggests that good lawyers ought to be able to "eyeball" the likely percentage risks.

The Executive Summary is based on preliminary interviews and estimates. To whatever extent possible, it anticipates the fuller strategic discussions outlined in Sections 3 and 4 of the Irvine document. But Zeughauser stipulates that the summary is not to exceed two pages. Obviously, then, the document submitted by outside counsel must be extremely precise. The staffing plan must simply disclose the number of attorneys, identify who they are, and—a point particularly emphasized by Zeughauser—guarantee that these attorneys will be assigned to the case until its final resolution.

Follow-up discussions with the client address whether the attorneys assigned to the case are the best ones at the firm for that case. To ascertain this, Zeughauser asks:

♦ What firm partners have supervised the associates or junior partners? The client can then identify the firm's heavy-hitter partners. If an attorney has consistently been on one or more of those partners' teams, it is likely the firm considers him or her to be top-notch.

♦ What other matters have the associates and/or junior partners worked on? Being assigned to important cases doesn't always mean the firm places great confidence in an attorney, especially if those cases were mega-matters that required large staffs of lawyers doing mainly research or playing other unexceptional roles. Therefore, if an attorney has not been assigned to important or complex matters, he or she might not be the best attorney who is available.

♦ Does a partner you know think highly of the proposed team member? Here's another example of a topic we touched on in Chapter 2: The value of a relationship partner. Especially with a large client like Irvine, partners who enjoy close relationships with the GC understand they cannot hem and haw or overestimate the ability of their own associates.

♦ Is the proposed staff member likely to make partner? It is easy for the law firm to lie about this possibility since, in the Byzantine world of law firms, even a "good shot" at partnership never guarantees an actual promotion. Again, though, the GC should be able to rely on the relationship partner for a good-faith answer.

The full analysis requested in Guideline 3 should be attached to the Executive Summary. This analysis involves a fuller elaboration of all the issues that have emerged to date, including more detail on the percentage chances of victory on the specific legal issues that appear in the Executive Summary. In this part of the document, there should be no doubt whatsoever as to the legal issues that "we've just got to win on, or begin [to think] settlement," says Zeughauser.

THE NUMBERS GAME

Guideline 4 is the most interesting as well as the most detailed part of the Irvine document. The budget and strategy discussions outlined in Guideline 4 are crucial because these are the specific areas where in-house counsel can really exert their leverage and determine, at this early planning stage, who the boss will be. For example, the first item on the discussion agenda, a cost-benefit analysis of proposed pretrial motions, clearly demonstrates how power in the inside/outside relationship gets fixed at the beginning.

As Zeughauser points out, many litigators instinctively file motions for *demurrer* or summary judgment. "They do it because it's the thing to do in litigation," says Zeughauser. "But *demurrer* motions aren't often won. So why are we bothering?" Sometimes a summary judgment motion is effective because it sets a tone for the case. Even if it's not granted, it has some value in placing on the record the client's position that the opposing party's argument does not merit further adjudication.

But mostly, quips Zeughauser, "they do it because they do it . . . and I've heard some weird rationales." For example, law firms used to tell him that a motion for summary judgment was worth filing because "it doesn't cost much." As Zeughauser points out, it doesn't cost *them* anything. It's not their money.

At this point, the client may challenge any of the normal procedures of law firms that simply don't redound to the client's advantage. After all, a cost-benefit analysis of, say, a proposed motion sends outside counsel the immediate message that every component of the case strategy must be weighed for its economic impact, and that no further action is to be taken for granted if it involves the client's money. This is a valuable message once the case reaches discovery, and the Irvine guidelines call for the same scheduling and cost-benefit analysis for discovery as they do for motions. Discovery abuses may be notorious for their deleterious effect on the justice system. They are also assaults on the client's checkbook.

The decisive moment in the planning process is set forth in Irvine's Guideline 4(b). It's where the actual budgeting occurs. Here, outside counsel provides the cost projections that it will either meet or, as is still too common, exceed. Once outside counsel render these projections, a poker game of sorts ensues between client and law firm in which both may sometimes conceal their positions as carefully as they do in the high-stakes "game" with opposing counsel. From the law firm's perspective, overruns require justification. From the client's perspective, those overruns must be controlled or, at least outside counsel must feel maximum pressure to justify excess costs and fees.

Those younger lawyers who actually bothered to read Zeughauser's document would typically ask him the salient question: *"How do I actually develop the numbers you want to see in the projected budget?"* Even assuming utter honesty by outside counsel, the best budgeting practices are still elusive. They're simply not taught in law school. Nor is there any reason to believe that this question of how to budget a case puzzles outside counsel, especially the younger partners, any less today than it did ten years ago when clients like Zeughauser began demanding useful numbers.

In-house counsel are well-advised to help law firms provide the most accurate possible projections. In fact, on these budgeting tasks, they may be the best instructors for younger associates at the law firms they are using. As Zeughauser has advised them, first list all the overall steps in the litigation. Then break down these steps into their actual logistics. What are the smaller steps? What will you actually have to do to complete the task? Will you need to modify a brief? How many lawyers will be involved? How many support staffers? Will there be research? Will you need to travel? By this approach outside counsel wisely avoids simply estimating, say, $250,000 for discovery. Rather, counsel estimate the actual hours that each discoverable component may take to complete. They estimate the number of attorneys involved and calculate costs by using actual hourly rates.

The real value to the client is thus a budget based on a calculation of a maximum number of possible contingencies. If $500,000 is the number that results from measuring all foreseeable increments, then that's the number the client ought to be given as a controlling estimate. Higher numbers are more useful, it would seem, since they advise the buyers of potential escalating costs as the case progresses.

The Irvine document calls for twenty-four-month estimates in addition to the full-term cost estimates. Zeughauser breaks that down further, advising preparation of ninety-day projections as well. With those shorter-term estimates he expects "more clarity." There are fewer imponderables in the short term and fewer unanticipated hurdles requiring unanticipated expenditures. With the full-term estimates, he'd naturally expect and tolerate more significant actual cost fluctuations against projected costs.

Once the short-term and longer-term steps are broken down as much as possible, there should ideally be three cost estimates for each stage, three estimates for each step in each stage, and three estimates for the case as a whole. Although the Irvine document advises that high/low estimates are "acceptable," Zeughauser advises that a third "ballpark figure," presumably somewhere between the high and low estimates, should also be provided.

On the one hand, Zeughauser may really be allowing outside counsel to play a game of self-deception in that, as the in-house client, he would typically look at the law firm's high-end estimate on any of the tasks involved in the litigation—and calculate that the "real cost would wind up double that amount!"

On the other hand, the budgets generated by law firms do represent "tremendous value-added," affirms Zeughauser. That perception of value should be imparted to the lawyers who are responsible for the numbers. Rather than regard preparation of the budgets as an extraneous, onerous chore, outside counsel must understand that budgeting is in their own interest because it makes them more attractive to the client. Budgeting gives outside counsel a competitive advantage, of course. But it's also part and parcel of the "partnering" of inside and outside counsel. This process illustrates how institutional relationships gradually develop between law firms and their corporate clients.

The Irvine guidelines include an anticipated "blended rate" which is unexpected as a standard best practice since, as Zeughauser points out, such rates are "out of favor now." Blended rates are hourly rates for entire teams. They more or less average out the different hourly fees of all the team members. The client is billed at one rate for everybody. Today, there's resistance among many buyers because too much work might be getting assigned to relatively inexperienced associates who bill out more hours at higher rates than is economical for the client.

Blended rates were popular in the late 1980s and early 1990s, so it's possible their inclusion in the Irvine guidelines is a reversion to those earlier market trends. However, Zeughauser also figures there are advantages for the client when more work is delegated downward, even if it means paying a higher fee for junior practitioners. For example, a blended rate could discourage law firms from wasting mid-level or senior attorneys on mundane matters. The overall effect is often a more productive legal work environment. With blended rates, the firm has no incentive to be inefficient. And morale is often better when timekeepers are too challenged by the work to spin their wheels.

There are a variety of situations in which blended rates have benefited both buyer and seller. Zeughauser recalls instances when firms wanted to install newly recruited lateral partners on their Irvine teams. A new partner would no doubt bring value to a team, but Zeughauser might have demurred if his or her rate were relatively high. With a blended rate that additional partner's hourly fee has less impact. At the same time, the law firm is spared having to ask a new partner to decrease his rate in order to join the Irvine team.

Finally, the blended rate works for both buyers and sellers because it creates an exemption from the "most favored rate" schemata. Typically, law firms draw a line in the sand when a major buyer requests a rate reduction. "No," they may say, "we never cut partner rates more than 10%."

"Okay," says the client, "but we want your most favored rate, which means, if you do go to a 12% or a 15% write-down with any other client, we are immediately entitled to the same consideration."

But blended rates don't count in this fee bargain. The law firm can stick to its maximum "write-down" policy even though a partner, working on a particular deal, is actually billing lower, sometimes much lower, than, say, the 10% cut that might constitute a most favored rate. The firm is not compelled to offer the attorney to other clients at that blended rate. Meanwhile, the benefit for the buyer is obvious. The buyer is paying much less for a partner without compromising the seller's integrity.

The Irvine guidelines also call for discussion of alternative billing arrangements, and we'll discuss these more along with convergence in Chapter 7. It has been a constant struggle in the legal profession to find alternatives to hourly rates. What makes it so difficult, observes Zeughauser, is that you often really have to start from scratch with each new matter. No particular kind of alternative, or "value" billing, is appropriate for all cases, or even whole classes of cases.

Some work might lend itself to contingency fees. Even major law firms have been known to experiment with contingency awards, which are often thought to be mainly the province of the smaller plaintiffs' firms. It's hard to feed hundreds of mouths waiting for a big pay-off that may or may not materialize. However, in particular situations, megafirms like Houston's Vinson & Elkins have taken a calculated risk on contingency fee arrangements, and very successfully.

We must stress that the decision to do so must be made on a case-by-case basis. Flat fees are similarly appropriate in some instances and not in others. "Segmented" fees, in which the firm is paid differently for different segments of a case or matter, are possibly useful, provided, of course, that the work can actually be coherently segmented.

As Zeughauser observes, most clients believe that law firms have delayed aggressive creation and institution of alternative fee arrangements, whereas most law firms believe that clients are much less receptive to change than they say they are. Both sides probably have motive enough to stick to the good old billable hour. Firms guarantee themselves revenue, whereas clients can rate-shop.

THE END OF LINE-ITEM REVIEW

It's important to note what these Irvine guidelines do *not* include in terms of cost-control. They do not include line-item review. As in-house counsel began to search for ways to control the costs of legal services, a fairly simple but more effective approach to case and management review began to emerge in the 1980s and 1990s. Instead of reviewing every expenditure, the Irvine document budgeting looks at *total* costs, with the understanding that outside counsel will bill as close as they can to those projected numbers.

In contrast, with line-item review, every hour or part of an hour and every disbursement is itemized. When in-house counsel first revolted en masse against the excesses of outside counsel, line-item review was often the favored expression of their new-found tough-mindedness. It was essentially the approach that was passionately advocated by the early pioneers like Bob Banks.

It's understandable why they took such an approach. Law firms were charging literally hundreds of thousands of dollars annually just to photocopy documents. At 25¢ per page, it's no wonder that the executive director of a mid-sized firm in Los Angeles once quipped to this writer that, "we make more money photocopying than litigating." He was only half joking. And photocopying was just one of their disbursements.

One upshot was a cottage industry of outside auditors who parsed law firm bills and generated millions for corporate buyers in recommended write-offs. Were there four associates on a conference call all billing their hourly rates for the time? Why were there four? Why wouldn't one or two have been sufficient? These auditors were hired by clients to examine the billing records of some of the most prestigious law firms in the country. Most of those top firms are spared this indignity today. However, some auditors are still hired by insurance companies to scrutinize bills of insurance defense law firms, many of which have continued their notorious habits of overstaffing and running a fast clock. (The high volume of insurance defense work, coupled with the low rates that are typical in this sector, have always encouraged overbilling.)

Both the auditors and the entire practice of line-item review generated ill will between clients and law firms. Indeed, a mood of distrust darkened the industry well into the 1990s. Further, line-item review had limited usefulness for the client. First, an isolated expenditure doesn't necessarily have any meaning. A quick trip to Sacramento may or may not have been useful. To assess each item therefore requires follow-up conversations. Auditing can therefore be very unwieldy as well as costly. Also, heavily itemized bills are hard to dispute. Even if the client has the time to review all the entries, the mere appearance of an excruciatingly detailed document tends to deter additional inquiry. Firms can just overwhelm the client and still flagrantly overcharge.

Second, line-item review disserves the client because it can make outside counsel less effective. It forces good lawyers to track their own movements so painstakingly that it detracts from their ability to practice law on the client's behalf.

Today, the concept of control is defined not by itemization, but by knowing in advance what to expect in terms of cost. Some companies have gone further than the Irvine guidelines. As Zeughauser acknowledged, he would naturally double what outside counsel projected in good faith, and assume that the higher number was the real working budget projection.

Throughout the last two decades, in-house counsel have developed systems with real teeth. An early pioneer model, which is still valid today and still widely applied under various iterations by corporate clients, is a matrix system that ties payment to compliance with cost projections. One example, developed at the Emerson Electric Company in St. Louis in the mid-1980s, is still a valid system.

The diagram below offers a simulacrum of the Emerson matrix that corporate buyers can utilize. Although it was drawn up for litigation, it can be redesigned for corporate and other legal work as well. The case name, the responsible attorney, and the date appear on top. The matrix then includes:

CASE STAGE	(1) First Evaluation	(2) Formal Discovery	(3) Ready for Trial	(4) Trial/ Post-Trial	Total
Budget					
Fees to date					
Percentage of stage completed					

Let's say outside counsel projects $25,000 for the first evaluation, which is 100% completed. But fees charged thus far equal $30,000. The client pays only the $25,000 and the $5,000 overage is put into an escrow-type account. It is then applied to the next stage. If, in that stage, the law firm is $5,000 under projection, there is a wash, and the client pays the full bill to that point. It should be emphasized that, as this model was originally applied by Emerson, and continues in force at many companies today, the company could still wind up paying any or all overages. But that payment is delayed, pending an assessment by the company.

The attraction of this model is that it makes the budget real, not just some numbers that outside counsel may diligently provide but wind up exceeding anyway. It allows the client to be as tough as nails. At the same time, it allows the client to relent, depending on the performance of the firm and the company's relationship with it. The agreement to pay a final overage could be painless in some instances. In-house counsel can be similarly amenable (and usually is) to communication with outside counsel about any new case exigencies that may require changing the budget at any given stage. But the existence of a matrix ensures that that communication will happen, sooner rather than later.

The model lifts the opprobrium of a line-item review which, however well meant on both sides, creates inevitable tugs of war over minutiae. It can even drive quality beyond expectations. If, for example, outside counsel comes in $5,000 *below* estimate, that money can be invested in the next stage, with a mock trial that wasn't originally planned, perhaps, or hiring a jury consultant who might not have been part of the overall trial strategy.

When Emerson first adopted the model, there was a subsequent 15% reduction (about $1 million) in legal fees for product liability, as then-GC Charles Hansen reported to this writer. It should be noted that the budget numbers themselves can be estimated or, more commonly, determined by financial data from past cases (adjusted for inflation, if any).

The substantive difference between the Emerson model approach and what was once typical cannot be overstated. Theoretically, if a firm can successfully complete a case within budget while its members eat a thousand superfluous four-star dinners or fly first-class whenever the spirit moves, fine!—so long as the crucial numbers are preserved. In other words, the outside litigators can still practice law any way they see fit.

In a sense, these sorts of budget arrangements return us to an older way of doing business, when trust still drove the inside/outside relationship. This model, however, promotes a reinvigorated trust based on verifiable results.

"Convergence": The Decade's Dominant Inside/Outside Event

It was, according to some in-house lawyers, an utterly fundamental adjustment of the inside/outside relationship. To others, it is in practice nothing more than the natural result of good management. Still others continue to see it as a glib response to the intrinsic problems of purchasing legal services, a response that can—and has—backfired against some of the companies that moved in this direction.

The process is called "convergence," an ungainly bit of jargon referring to how in-house counsel have reduced the number of law firms on their approved list. The idea is to establish strong "preferred provider" relationships with a drastically smaller number of select firms. The goal is to establish closer inside/outside relationships, to "partner" with the outside providers.

"Partnering" is another popular buzzword, of uncertain and varying application. However, as we've discussed in earlier chapters, the salutary essence of partnering involves a generally closer identification by lawyers with corporate goals, corporate interests, corporate culture.

Specifically, the partnering achieved through the convergence process allows for a more streamlined approach to high-volume, multi-jurisdictional matters and cases. The client is better able to keep abreast of casework because in-house legal managers no longer have to maintain oversight of what many hundreds of firms are doing on its behalf all over the world. Some companies have indeed excised hundreds of law firms, big and small.

Along with keeping closer tabs on outside counsel, convergence helps clients extract any number of commitments from their newly designated preferred providers. These commitments involve a range of best practices, from what kind of technology the law firm will use to what sorts of progress reports it will submit as a case progresses.

The benefit for the surviving firms is a guarantee of a certain volume of business from the client. This provides a predictable revenue stream that allows the firm to better plan its own hiring and work assignment schedules. In return, there's a final, very direct benefit for the client: money. At the same time, it's ostensibly economical for law firms that survive the convergence process to offer rate discounts or fixed fees or other cost-saving reductions in return for the dramatically greater volume of business they will get.

It is, in simplest terms, buying volume cheaper—and critics of the convergence strategy hasten to point out that such arrangements assume that legal services can be bought and sold like department stores buy TV sets from wholesale distributors. Defenders of the convergence strategy warn that the arrangement is never just a wholesale deal. To the contrary, convergence is a quality-based approach in which efficiency and good work count as much toward a firm surviving the cut as any discounted price arrangement.

The logistics of convergence are difficult and time-consuming, and naturally vary. Usually the corporation sends requests for proposals to all their current law firms, informing them in the process that the company is consolidating the purchase of legal services, and that each of the firms currently representing the company must win the right to continue doing so. A round robin of beauty contests ensues. Often, new firms that have never done business with the company are invited to participate. Sometimes the process is *pro forma* since some firms, based on poor prior performances, are already on the hit list. Others, because of excellent past performances, are shoo-ins.

Convergence strategies are one more example of how corporation-wide cost-savings initiatives that began during the recession of the 1980s were expanded to include the law department. Some law departments reduced in-house staff in response to those initiatives. Some centralized their operations. Some increased in-house productivity by bringing more work inside without increasing staff. And some looked to the convergence model as a way to achieve the greater efficiencies their corporate fathers were demanding.

The truth about convergence is probably an amalgam of the differing perspectives in the debate. No doubt, convergence was an effective management tool in some instances and ill-advised in others. No doubt, it is an inherently meritorious idea for some companies in certain situations, and less so for others. The devil is in the proverbial details, as a look at germane examples, past and present, may suggest.

A TURBULENT HISTORY

Historically, the opposite of convergence was actually more fashionable, at least in the 1980s. Companies then tended to bid out virtually every piece of business. The thought was, more suppliers means more competitive pricing. But for many companies, the result was an ungainly, inefficient mess. Just getting law firms up to speed on how the client operates can be a lengthy and costly process. Repeating that process umpteen times in umpteen jurisdictions is inevitably an exhausting, wasteful ordeal. So the pendulum had to swing back. One day in Wilmington, Delaware, it swung back with a vengeance.

The most famous example of convergence occurred during the 1990s at DuPont. Howard Rudge, who'd been the GC of DuPont subsidiary Conoco, was appointed to oversee the pruning of hundreds of law firms in what had become an unmanageable mélange of attorneys handling DuPont work worldwide. Even detractors of the convergence model acknowledge that DuPont had to do something. As one in-house manager puts it, "Things there had gotten to the point where a slow, natural selection wouldn't be enough. [The company] needed something radical."

Rudge turned to Daniel Mahoney, a member of his department, to do the job. Mahoney, now an independent consultant, is still the first name in almost everyone's mind when the subject of convergence arises. He continues to personify the strategy. A tough, articulate man, Mahoney was a good choice, considering the mood of the time. By 2000, most law firms, even some of the world's most arrogant, were resigned to the convergence ordeal. They knew they had no choice.

In 1992, however, when DuPont first embarked on its dramatic initiative, many of the law firms that were affected were surprised and outraged. Mahoney tells of managing partners who went directly to the CEO to undermine the effort. They got rough justice. DuPont was utterly committed, top to bottom, to the program. Mahoney had a remarkably free hand.

DuPont had some illustrious models to learn from. It may have been the most dramatic convergence ever, but it was by no means the first. By late 1993, as the company was still putting into place a strategy that reached fruition two years later, Olin Corporation had already reduced the number of firms on its approved list from 366 to seven. In Detroit, General Motors and Chrysler had also moved along similar lines by that time.

Olin's four-month-long convergence in the spring of 1993 was part of a drastic company-wide reduction program that also saw in-house staff slashed by half, from thirty-two to fifteen. It was clearly a recession-driven initiative, a response to an informal cost-savings directive suggested by the Vice Chairman of the Board. DuPont's initiative was somewhat more formal, and more directly inspired by the company's reliance on an excessive number of law firms.

The effort by Olin is nonetheless relevant to any discussion of convergence because—just as clearly as DuPont's or any other corporation's experience—this early example crystallizes the objectives of consolidation and the standards by which law firms can survive the process.[1]

Consider the following:

♦ Meetings with law firms often lasted from early morning to late evening. Then-associate GC Johnnie Jackson, Jr. told *Of Counsel* magazine that candidates' willingness to "eat that time" was a first important criterion in the selection process.

♦ Olin's in-house lawyers emphasized candidates' listening skills as paramount: not "Here's what we do," but "What is it you need?" In a convergence process, such sensitivity looms even larger as a selection criterion, because most of the firms have already been working for the client, some for many years. Too many of them assume they already know what the company is all about and what it needs. Firms in convergence beauty contests are thus best advised to assume a *tabula rasa:* that they are, in effect, talking to the company for the first time.

♦ Knowledge of the company's business was essential. Firms new to the company can particularly impress with such knowledge. Husch & Eppenberger, a firm in St. Louis with a strong litigation practice, wowed Olin five years before the convergence by taking the time to learn how the guns manufactured by Olin's Winchester Group subsidiary actually worked. Not surprisingly, perhaps, Husch was one of the firms that would later survive the consolidation process.

♦ The successful candidates agreed to both periodic planning sessions and periodic reviews with non-

---

[1] For a full report on Olin's consolidation, see "Olin Outsources and Consolidates in Bold Plan for the 1990s," 12:17 Of Counsel (Sept. 6, 1993).

lawyer business managers. Again, remember the historic context. The recession was going on and, to that extent, it was a buyer's market. But such enforceable layers of accountability, especially accountability to non-lawyers, were still not something with which many law firms were then comfortable.

♦ Efficient staffing and task performance, more than billing rates, were on Olin's mind. Husch, for one, impressed Olin with a refurbished database that cut the time needed to produce interrogatories by two-thirds.

♦ Candidates had to agree to monitor local counsel hired for cases only on an as-needed basis by the lead firms. Olin was able to eliminate a permanent support staff position by persuading outside counsel to commit to this increased oversight.

♦ In one particularly good example of how partnering during the convergence process is really a two-way street, Wiggin & Dana in New Haven, Connecticut, won Olin's intellectual property without at that time actually having an intellectual property practice. Yet Wiggin told Olin that it had been looking hard for a way to develop in that area. So Olin "outsourced" three of its own IP attorneys to Wiggin. Everyone made out as a result: The client reduced in-house costs, hired outside counsel it needed to hire anyway, and the law firm suddenly found itself with IP practitioners and a guarantee of work to support them.

♦ Lawyer training is enhanced. Outside inefficiencies are the inside lawyer's main bugaboo. As such, the unbilled time that law firms spend on lawyer training goes far to reassure the client. Olin itself featured an in-house culture highly oriented toward training, so the in-depth program developed by McKenna & Cuneo of Washington, D.C. fit in nicely. It helped McKenna & Cuneo survive the convergence.

In Olin's case, all the firms interviewed had worked for the company already. Competent legal skills were thus assumed. The linchpin was responsiveness. DuPont did not, therefore, need to invent the convergence wheel. It simply spun that wheel a lot harder or at least more conspicuously than anyone else had up until that point.

As Mahoney describes it, DuPont wanted to unabashedly adopt the same sort of customer/supplier partnering that drives the rest of corporate America. Mahoney, for one, seems impatient with the attitude that legal services are too special, too personal, too esoteric to fit the basic business rules that govern supply and demand everywhere else.

Soon after the DuPont convergence reached fruition, Mahoney published an article describing a three-fold sequential process: (1) reducing the number of outside law firms from over 300 to thirty-four; (2) developing value-based rather than hourly-based billing systems; and (3) fostering a more aggressive use of technology.[2]

Mahoney emphasized that none of the three steps were sufficient unto themselves. The strategic partnering DuPont sought required a seamless integration. Like most companies that have converged, DuPont was focusing on litigation—that's the area where most companies are forced to rely heavily on outside counsel—but Mahoney argued that any legal services could be bought and sold in the same way. That had already been evident in the Olin convergence. A few years after the DuPont event, Genentech, Inc. was another example of a company consolidating non-litigation services when it concentrated its outside patent applications and prosecutions in fewer firms.[3]

In litigation, DuPont still wanted to emphasize winning cases (with ADR as an acceptable route), but not, as law firm

---

[2] Mahoney, "When Pruning Is in Order: DuPont Takes a New Look at the Corporate-Outside Counsel Relationship," Business Law Today 48 (July/Aug. 1996).

[3] See the Genentech discussion below.

applicants were made to understand, at any price. To discourage fishing expeditions and other inefficiencies fostered by hourly billing, DuPont explored fixed fees for single cases and groups of cases. There were contingency arrangements struck for some matters that would decrease overall costs while providing outside counsel richer rewards for success. DuPont understood that simply cutting law firm profit margins was a short-term solution at best.

The survivors of the DuPont convergence were going to be, above all else, *trustworthy* firms inasmuch as their interests and the client's would coincide as never before. Hourly rates separate buyer and seller. Value-based fees create a mutuality of interest based on shared risk and shared reward. Real partnering provides outside counsel the incentives of additional business volume, referrals, cross-selling opportunities, and handsome premiums. At DuPont, other enhancements such as ten-day turnarounds on legal bills via electronic funds transfers sweetened the kitty for the law firms.

By 1996 Mahoney was able to claim concrete successes. Four years earlier, when the convergence began, all but two DuPont cases were billed on an hourly basis. By the end of 1996, there were approximately 330 cases based on non-hourly or blended rates, including some of the company's biggest lawsuits. In the first half of 1996, two law firms had already received success bonuses totaling $500,000.

Even more impressive, outside litigation fees decreased by 23% from 1994 to 1995 even as the caseload increased by 18%. Savings on hours that were never billed because matters were staffed more efficiently, technology brought to bear for better document management, and expensive crises avoided, are all harder to measure, but certainly added to the total benefit.

On the technology front, the DuPont convergence carried the client/law firm interface to a new level. As we saw in Chapter 5, sophisticated law firms began sharing automated systems in the 1980s with institutional clients: King & Spalding with Coca-Cola Company, Davis Polk & Wardwell with Goldman, Sachs, etc. In some instances, the firms may have instigated the interface; in other instances, the clients. No doubt the firms were happy about the new efficiencies such connectivity made possible. But from a marketing standpoint, the shared hardware and software was a windfall indeed. After all, shared systems only reaffirmed the institutional nature of the buyer/seller relationship. It was a reassurance of permanence.

DuPont had something more in mind: a Wide Area Network (WAN) linking the company and all its firms in a dedicated loop. The system maximized efficiency without any dependency on a participating firm. The WAN even attracted media attention in *Forbes*.[4] Meanwhile, a new automated system was introduced to facilitate case management reporting. Enthusiasm for such technology, and the aptitude to implement, were prime tests for the law firm candidates during the DuPont beauty contests.

For corporations, the DuPont experience underscores a number of best practices to ensure that a strenuous convergence effort achieves its objectives. As Mahoney enumerates them, the first step is to quantify specific goals and formalize specific performance standards. In the same vein, there has to be a project team and, ideally, someone like Mahoney who is identified with the cause and whose main job it is to advocate for and spearhead the process year in and year out. It's no accident that Mahoney's title at DuPont was "Corporate Counsel and Manager, Law Firm Partnering." Thus, he wasn't just an Associate GC or Deputy GC who headed up the partnering and convergence effort. Instead, Mahoney was, formally, the lawyer in charge of partnering.

Yet the most important lesson of the DuPont experience is that there has to be more to convergence than simply buying a lot for less. Convergence is not, ostensibly, simple cost-cutting. Companies like DuPont are quick to remind us that they can and

---

[4] Forbes ASAP (June 1994).

have fired law firms after those firms were successful during the convergence process, often because lower rates led to inefficient staffing or simply because the quality of their work was disappointing.

Conversely, firms that succeed during the convergence and maintain their status afterward stand to reap a marketing windfall (and one is often surprised that more firms don't play this card more aggressively). The spring of 1999, for example, saw the merger of two firms, Hartford's Murtha, Cullina, Richter and Pinney and Boston's Roche, Carens & DeGiacomo. The fact that both firms are DuPont survivors in good standing would seem a most effective selling point for the merged entity.

In any event, such a merger seems to culminate in a goal articulated by Mahoney: That, as a result of the convergence/ partnering strategy, DuPont's approved firms would be parts of veritable joint ventures, interconnected technologically and working together on solutions to the company's problems. As early as 1995, Mahoney noted approvingly, DuPont's firms were also practicing together on non-DuPont matters. Actually, in this current merger-intensive market, one might wonder why more of the company's primary firms haven't gone down the bridal path like Murtha and Roche.

BEHEMOTHS FOLLOW SUIT

When we take a look at the current climate of opinion, we do indeed find a mixed bag, with a great deal of skepticism as to whether the course DuPont followed is universally applicable. It may not even be universally relevant if, as some GCs say, the situation Howard Rudge inherited was unique to DuPont or a handful of other big companies like it. Yet it's germane that convergence was still as much an option for corporate counsel in the recent unprecedented boom market as it was in the bearish days of the early 1990s.

The reason may be that, whatever other specific relevance the convergence strategy has for legal managers, it culminates the shift of power that, in its early stage, was so palpable at that 1986 ACCA conference discussed in Chapter 1. It's a shift that has a lot to do with basic sound economics, and less to do with what sort of market may exist at any given time. Clearly, the empowerment of the client that the mere notion of convergence implies is now permanent and formidable, in good times or bad.

Since the mid-1990s, more companies have converged but, in some cases, they have emphasized different benefits than those at DuPont. In other cases, converged company goals seem somewhat more modest, or the companies are pursuing consolidation less furiously and over a longer period of time. Among the post-DuPont examples, Motorola's seems to typify how and why the convergence strategy has survived. It merits particular attention for that reason.

Motorola's law department has long been open to a variety of managerial initiatives, often because directives from top corporate management left no choice. Thus, under former GC Richard Weise, Motorola's law department was among those to adopt Total Quality Management ("TQM") initiatives along with other sectors of the company. These days, TQM elicits predictable derision from most legal managers as a benchmarking agenda utterly unsuited to legal practice. Yet in the mid-1990s the TQM canon still seemed somewhat relevant, and in-house managers like Dan Mahoney were even describing convergence as a TQM-based strategy.

There were a couple of reasons why the connection was made. First, TQM focused on the value being delivered to the customer. Convergence also focused on the buyer, especially as DuPont and Mahoney conceptualized it far beyond rates and volume discounts. Second, TQM stressed looking beyond one's narrow frame of expertise, and seizing on innovations being developed in other disciplines or industries. That aspect of the TQM sensibility was similarly eminently agreeable to someone like

Mahoney, who was decrying the legal industry's insistence on its own uniqueness, a professional mystique ostensibly immunizing it from commonsense free market principles.[5]

Given the "quality" context, it's not surprising that Motorola VP and Director of Litigation Management Kathleen Bryan, a company veteran with over ten years at Motorola, tends to emphasize increasingly efficient case management more than measurable savings in hard dollars as the salient benefit of Motorola's convergence initiative. The savings are not insignificant—Bryan estimates 5% to 10% lower outside costs as a result of consolidation—but the really operative word here is "control."

Convergence is a broader initiative than TQM, says Bryan, because the former is more of a "front-end" model. In addition to the General Counsel, there is a discrete group of in-house lawyers at Motorola who deal with all departmental management issues. Another five attorneys are responsible for each of five Motorola main business units, such as automotive and semiconductors. But there's also a separate entity called "Communication Enterprise," which embraces a number of subsidiary businesses, whereas other attorneys are assigned to the businesses acquired when Motorola merged with General Instruments. Finally, there are Motorola lawyers who work at and hire for Motorola's overseas divisions. *In toto*, over 200 attorneys practice inside.

Like DuPont, Motorola found itself with far too many law firms on its list; Bryan says the number was about 300. She spoke to DuPont and other companies that had converged, and she read all the articles. The model was clearly applicable, with one important difference. There was no easy way to categorize the types of Motorola litigation as, say, toxic tort or ATV mishaps, or whatever. Instead, Bryan devised a tier system into which nearly all the work could fit.

---

[5] See Mahoney, "Where It's Leading," 1:1 *Revolutionizing Litigation Management* (March 1995).

The consolidation occurred at three such tiers throughout 1998 and well into 1999:

In Tier One four firms were selected for major matters. This tier does not comprise an absolutely exclusive list of firms, but it is the one the company tends to pick from rather constantly.

In Tier Two Motorola picked five to ten firms on a regional basis for commodity matters and small cases.

In Tier Three there were another twenty firms selected for a range of specialty practices: antitrust, government contracts, and product safety are among the main such areas. This part of the convergence began as in-house lawyers identified the firms with which they were already working. Those specialty firms did not have to reapply for the work—a contrast with how some companies in "beauty contests" (either as part of a convergence or in discrete RFPs) do force current outside counsel to re-interview and re-negotiate.

The lion's share of the convergence would thus happen at the Tier Two level.

Motorola had thought about a "transfer" of work from all its current regional counsel to one centralized "hub counsel" per geographic region, but this turned out to be an unwieldy process and was replaced by a full-blown convergence. A majority of the 300 original firms were allowed to continue their ongoing caseloads which, in turn, has led to a more gradual consolidation than had occurred at DuPont. Many of the 300 firms are still in transition, although the actual business of the convergence is now over and the preferred providers signed up at all three tiers. The four Tier One firms were also grandfathered in and did not participate in the RFP and beauty contest process. Those firms were already doing high-stakes work; their *bona fides* were already pretty well established.[6]

---

[6] They were Chicago's Kirkland & Ellis, New York's Fish & Neave, and Steptoe & Johnson and Arnold & Porter, both Washington, D.C.-based.

Not all the 300 were invited to compete. Based on input from its in-house managing attorneys, Motorola created a short list of firms from which to solicit bids. For the regional firms, geographic areas were drawn up so that one firm would be responsible for everything in, say, Texas-Mississippi-Arkansas not included with the work designated as either Tier One or Tier Three. This commodity work included litigation and transactional counseling, among other matters.

Like most companies, Motorola emphasized litigation in the convergence bidding; DuPont was really an exception to Dan Mahoney's insistence that all varieties of legal work can and should be converged (if they are not being handled in-house). However, Motorola's in-house lawyers make their own determinations as to whether to farm out non-litigation business. A transaction that involves fifty countries exceeds the in-house capacity and therefore goes to law firms, to be handled by one of the preferred providers.

Since the Motorola process is ongoing, there is still an opportunity for law firms to get a piece of the company's work even though a final selection of preferred providers has already been made. Client dissatisfaction or law firm realignments could certainly force changes. As of this writing, Motorola hasn't yet fired a preferred provider, but because the current preferred providers weren't hired until the 1998-1999 period, this may change. As Bryan also points out, Motorola may have selected a firm because of specific individuals with specific capabilities. With all the movement of lawyers from firm to firm these days, the relationship with any law firm can change at any time.

The fact that convergence targets law firms as a whole does not therefore mitigate the policy, stated and restated by virtually every corporate buyer, that "We hire lawyers, not law firms." Change the law firm letterhead, and you may undo the results of a convergence like Motorola's.

According to Bryan, the very fact that so many law firms look so alike on paper supports an extensive convergence, or at least supports the wisdom of periodic beauty contests. That's because important "differences became very dramatic when we met with the firms," she says—when Motorola saw and heard, up close and personal, "how they were going to structure their discussions with us, the people who would come and talk to us, as well as the substance of what they had to say."

Motorola didn't really structure the meetings. Instead, the client let the firms take the lead. Some did very formal presentations and brought in associates, which meant day-long beauty contests. Others chose to bring in dynamic individuals, smaller groups, or different attorneys to illustrate different parts of the firm. Motorola had no real preference one way or another. It was the ensuing substance of the discussions that mattered. The interviewees' palpable excitement at the prospect of working with Motorola mattered. So did their willingness to deal with budgets. Their enthusiasm about technology was also important.

What buyers like Bryan look for is not, "I've tried 1,000 cases and won 900." It's really much more, "This is how I approach a case. . . ," or, "I know cost control is important. Here's how we deal with it." Bryan also wants to hear about the larger picture: the trends in product safety, for example, or where mass tort litigation in general is heading. "That's where I know I've either connected with someone or I haven't," she adds.

Motorola identified in-house teams for selecting counsel in each region. That gave the in-house rank and file a vested interest in the process as something that would directly affect their daily lives, in a way that would redound to their own benefit. "They met the firms," says Bryan. "They saw the possibilities."

Such a process will naturally change the way in-house counsel view their own clients as well. As Bryan points out, a benefit of convergence is that the inside people must focus less on specific cases and more on groups of cases—in fact, on the entire litigation picture. In turn, that pushes them to think in broader terms about how the company as a whole is being generally represented.

It can indeed be a radically new role for middle-level inside attorneys to realize that a particular law firm might not be the best for a particular case, but that there's an overriding benefit to putting that case in a package and then assigning the package to that firm. At the same time, the convergence has made Motorola's in-house staff focus more on the value of the individual cases, in terms of both complexity and risk. How important is the case? Should it be packaged with others? Should it migrate upward to Tier One status? As such, the reassignments have had the desirable dual effect of encouraging thinking that is simultaneously broader and more in-depth.

On costs, Motorola saves more as it converges more. In other words, it rewards the firms that save the company money by assigning them increasingly higher caseload volumes. Alternative billing and premiums are very much a part of the discussion as well although, as Bryan points out, the Tier Two and Tier Three cases really haven't lent themselves to discussions of premiums in part because the packages aren't quite big enough. But the potential remains, says Bryan, if, for instance, the employment caseload increases and the outside provider dispatches the work with a high success rate and/or brings it in well below budget.

In any event, the current focus at Motorola remains on volume discounts as well as billing rates: how those rates are perceived to reflect the quality of the work, how they compare to the rates of other firms. The mix of timekeepers assigned is naturally crucial too, especially because law firms will vary in the seniority of the attorneys handling the work. As with most in-house consolidations, all firms must also agree to follow careful guidelines for disbursements.

Because Motorola is still at an early stage of convergence, measurable hard-dollar figures aren't that dramatic yet, especially since Motorola still spends a significant amount on its Tier One cases. But the overall benefits of better management, although they can't be directly computed, have already proven to be tangibly significant. Even client auditing—the process by which law firms formally assess client satisfaction—is encouraged by the convergence process.[7] That's because "there's a lot more conversation after a convergence process," Bryan comments. "There's a certain amount of pride, there's a certain amount of marketing that goes on to win a preferred berth." Having gone through so much to win the berth, the law firms don't want to lose it after the fact. Also, as a result of the convergence, in-house managers are matched up with a "relationship partner" at the firm. So the post-convergence "How are we doing?" dialogue almost inevitably ensues.

Such dialogue provides another natural benefit of convergence: It guarantees that the client will be important to the law firm, especially great law firms that turn away so much work in a boom market, or give some existing clients short shrift. According to Bryan, the biggest problem is in patent practice. "You can shift litigators around, you can shift commercial lawyers around, you can shift around resources associated with any number of practice areas," she says. "But it's very difficult to shift around lawyers with intellectual property expertise."

Motorola's preferred Tier One provider in the patent area, Fish & Neave, "has been, I'm sure, a little selective in their work," adds Bryan. "If you're not a major client of theirs, you can be in trouble. But we are a major client of theirs, so I can't say enough good things about them."

The relationship benefits and management benefits affect every aspect of both inside management and the inside/outside dynamic. Since it need not worry about managing 300 relationships, Motorola can evaluate more closely, complain about budget overruns, and monitor everything that's working or not working. It's a simple fact of life: the client can discuss twenty cases in one telephone call. The savings in in-house time alone are thus obviously very significant.

---

[7] See Chapter 13 for a discussion about this law firm marketing technique.

The biggest savings, as Bryan puts it, is in doing the right work, not in the discounts. Of fifty depositions, forty-eight might not be useful in trial. The closer communications ensure that those forty-eight never get taken. The two depositions that do get taken might then be handled by associates rather than partners (although, for the Tier Three specialty matters, it's usually the partner-level expertise that attracted the client; for this work, partner-level rates are usually preferable to associate-level rates anyway, because the partners simply do it more efficiently).

At the other end of the spectrum, convergence also allows Motorola paralegals to manage cases in both the Tier Two and Tier Three categories. In fact, Bryan says it's these paralegals who now do most of the day-to-day work with outside counsel because in-house lawyers spend the majority of their time on oversight and case strategy. The logistics of discovery, and of identifying and maintaining contact with the key persons in the case, are now delegated further downward than ever before. With preferred providers, there are no wheels to reinvent, so there's no reason why a paralegal can't learn the drill for a whole package of cases. The lower salary structures at the paralegal level clearly mean that substantial savings are passed on to the client.

Selection of the firms combined historical working relationships with new challenges. Thus, Motorola had been using Arnold & Porter for many years, but the firm became a preferred provider only after it demonstrated a wonderful command of the company's Y2K problems. But A&P's prior history with Motorola remains significant in any event, for that is where a crucial understanding of the company culture which A&P developed over the years could be brought to bear right at the outset.

One criticism of the convergence process is that it's onerous for the outside providers.[8] At Motorola, Bryan acknowledges that some law firms have gotten a "significantly lower" volume of work

---

[8] See, for example, Caterpillar GC Rennie Atterbury's comments *infra*.

than they expected. But she reminds us that discounts and volume are directly related. If firms are getting less, they're not forced to relinquish as much. At the same time, it's also an education process for Motorola. "We'll stop and take a look at it and say, 'Wait a minute, are there people here [at Motorola] who maybe should be giving them work that they aren't getting?' So, we'll readjust."

Another potential downside for law firms, and for the company as well, is attracting the best outside counsel to even compete. For Motorola, the problem might seem especially serious, since the Tier One work is really pretty much locked up among four firms. Would a top-flight firm want a Tier Two role handling relatively mundane matters such as, say, regional counsel to the company's Texas-based semiconductor operation?

It's a telling case in point because it was a big top-flight Texas-based firm, Vinson & Elkins, which did, in fact, win that business during the early stages of the Motorola convergence. Motorola sorely lacked a good relationship with a law firm in Texas, even though there was a lot of local activity, so Texas was chosen to be the first stage in consolidation and a test run for the whole convergence strategy. Two lawyers from the semiconductor company, along with a litigator from the central law department, conducted the interviews.

V&E obviously sees this work as a worthwhile foot in the corporate door, and Bryan doesn't disagree. It's a cross-selling opportunity, and a chance to learn the company culture in preparation for the time when opportunities to handle Motorola's Tier One business might expand. Again, the convergence process is relatively fluid. Otherwise, surmises Bryan, V&E would not have been as "enthusiastic" or as effective in its presentation. The downside, as she concedes, is that it's often very difficult to demonstrate skill sets in Tier Two cases that might commend a law firm for a Tier One opportunity. At the same time, Motorola discusses Tier One cases with firms handling Tier Two matters more explicitly than with a firm that hasn't survived the convergence at all.

Among other corporate behemoths, Sears, Roebuck has reduced outside firms from several hundred to seventy-five. Sears is fairly comparable to Motorola in a number of respects. As at Motorola, the verdict isn't yet in on hard-dollar cost savings. Here too, whereas VP and Deputy GC Bobbie McGee Gregg says "we're pretty much there" in terms of the final cut, the process is described as ongoing, with possible modifications and replacements still to come on the list of preferred providers.

Sears' legal needs are very broad in both litigation and corporate areas. There is immense variety in the type of work, its complexity, and its geographical distribution. Much of the convergence process at Sears thus entailed not only selecting the best firms, but rethinking who'd be doing what kind of work. The arrival of GC Anastasia Kelly in February 1999 catalyzed the process. Often, a corporate convergence is directly catalyzed by an individual lawyer/manager.[9]

At Sears, it was the senior law department members who largely conducted the beauty contests. According to Gregg, line attorneys were "not discouraged" from participating, but the huge time demands that are inevitable when large companies consolidate their usage of outside counsel tended to limit staff involvement. Also, by 1999, when the Sears convergence occurred, large law departments already tended to recruit outside counsel through senior members of the firm. As more mainstream companies converge, both in-house lawyers and the law firms vying for the work consider this process to be more acceptable. Five years after DuPont accomplished its sea change, convergence became a fact of life.

To an even greater extent than Bryan, Gregg emphasizes the cross-selling opportunities in a major convergence. Even with law firms that had long-standing relationships with Sears, new

---

[9] The convergence described below in this chapter of outside patent work at Genentech, Inc. is another good example of how one managing attorney—not necessarily the corporation's Chief Legal Officer—drives the initiative.

possibilities were unearthed. Firms that the company had until then only used for tax work were suddenly able to market credible expertise in, say, intellectual property. If the beauty contests didn't generate work in these other areas immediately, the participating firms at least had a chance to get right on the short list. Since the client requests and sets up the meetings, it's an easy context for expanding the conversation and talking about new partners or new offices or growing practice areas. For bashful lawyers, it's an open invitation.

Sears was looking for law firms that would partner with the in-house attorneys and, in this case, that specifically meant respecting the talents and advice of inside practitioners who have a lot of litigation experience. Gregg sought more than mere acceptance of such partnering. She was eyeing law firms that she thought would actually feel comfortable with an inside/outside team approach.

So far, the real cost savings at Sears may be more an indirect result of convergence. As Gregg explains, there were really two things going on at once: interrelated but separate initiatives. On the one hand, after Kelly's arrival, the company revisited what work would stay inside and what work would go out. On the other hand, Sears wanted to establish a more efficient use of outside counsel. But Gregg believes the more tangible economic benefits achieved thus far are due mainly to the fact that the law department has been handling a higher volume of work. The convergence gains remain less palpable at this point, at least in terms of specific percentage savings.

A ONE-FIRM CONVERGENCE

New corporate convergence initiatives come to light on an increasingly regular basis. One example, first reported in *Corporate Legal Times*,[10] resulted in the Los Angeles law firm of

---

[10] Corporate Legal Times (April 2000).

Manatt, Phelps & Phillips winning just about the entire litigation portfolio of Ultramar Diamond Shamrock Corporation, a $14 billion downstream oil company.

This is a particularly interesting example for a number of reasons. First, there's the somewhat unusual outcome of only one firm emerging as a preferred provider for the company's most important cases.

Second, in obvious contrast to the DuPont model, Ultramar and Manatt negotiated specific management, budgeting, and billing agreements after Manatt was selected, not before. Even so, the benefits of the convergence involved improved case management more than hard-dollar savings. In fact, Ultramar projected a 5% total savings for the 2000-2001 period, about half what other companies now say they want at the beginning.[11]

And third, the selection of Manatt resulted in Ultramar's Associate GC and in-house director of litigation, Marylin Jenkins Milner, joining Manatt as a partner. It's an obvious boon for the client since it saves a salary while it gets an outside lawyer intimately familiar with Ultramar's business. For the firm, the benefit is also clear. Milner's arrival consolidates the Ultramar relationship even as Milner is free to develop additional business as well. Manatt's selection earned the firm $5 million to $7 million in litigation business in 2000.

Ultramar's main cost concern, as Milner expresses it, was a little different than DuPont's. A preferred litigation provider would allow for more *predictability* in litigation costs, not just an alternative to hourly rates. Historically, litigators have argued that cost overruns are unpredictable because cases take on lives of their own. Litigators thus see themselves as *"artistes,"* to use Milner's term. But CFOs and accountants have come to take a rather jaundiced view of such "art as opposed to science," especially when costs began rising so precipitously.

---

[11] See also the discussion in this chapter *infra* of the patent practice convergence at Genentech.

In formulating and adhering to budgets, Ultramar does echo one familiar DuPont theme: shared risk. On the one hand, there may always be events that force the client and law firm to reformulate and expand the budget. On the other hand, absent such agreed-on modifications to the governing budget, overages negatively affect the fees paid to the firm.

Specifically, Manatt will reduce its fee by 10% or less to match any overage. If the firm beats the budgeted numbers by 10% or less, it earns that amount as a premium. Bills may still be based on hourly rates, but the incentive to be efficient is nonetheless present.

Overages or savings beyond 10% are shared by the firm and the client. Matters that are resolved without significant work by the firm benefit the client directly since they cost little and therefore reduce the total budget. Presumably, outside counsel would still be motivated in those situations to be efficient—to dispatch or settle cases without much effort, if appropriate—because it's still doing volume business. It's not in Manatt's interest to needlessly protract a single lawsuit on an already very full plate. Besides, the system is flexible and can be adjusted if needed. In fact, one benefit of Ultramar having picked Manatt before negotiating the terms of engagement is that the relationship was born in trust. There's no sense that Manatt agreed to anything onerous to get the job. The firm had it anyway.

The selection of Manatt—in which Ultramar was assisted by Arthur Andersen's General Counsel Solutions Team—culminated a process started in 1998 when the company began to cut back from 200 to a dozen firms. It was a painstaking series of beauty contests; the client's guiding objective was to have a limited number of firms that could manage large case portfolios on a multi-jurisdictional basis.

As Milner recalls, some firms fell quickly by the wayside. It's worth noting that, at any given point in time, there are very specific factors that sway corporate decisions as much as fundamental questions such as, "Have you ever handled this kind of work before?" or "Are you willing to lower your rates?" In 1999, interestingly, e-mail was just such a decisive factor for Ultramar. Some firms simply didn't have systems in place yet and, as a result, they didn't get very far past the Ultramar cuts.

Like DuPont, Ultramar was clearly using too many law firms. Part of the problem for such companies is that they pick up a lot of firms as they make acquisitions. Two or three dozen firms on an acquired company's approved list can often easily slip onto the acquiring company's approved list. Milner recalls that, when Ultramar acquired National Convenience Stores, the joke was that each store came with its own lawyer.

The next serious stage took Ultramar from twenty-five to twelve firms. Here, the key factor was Ultramar's perception of the kind of client service it would likely get from a firm and, particularly, the ability of its lawyers to communicate and to be open to suggestions on how to handle cases. Milner figures there are no concrete rules of thumb by which interviewers can assess who will likely be good partners in this respect. But, says Milner, "I litigated for twenty years, so at some point you can begin to rely on pure instinct."

The final stage leapfrogged Manatt to preferred provider status without another beauty contest or further ado of any sort. Milner had worked with Manatt partner Craig de Ricat at Graham & James, and she considered him one of the nation's best litigators. That, combined with the size of the firm, cast the die. The other eleven firms settled for regional counsel slots. They handle high-volume local insured cases that Ultramar wanted entirely outsourced, with no involvement by in-house staff. (The company owns many gas stations and retail stores, so there are a lot of slip-and-falls.)

It's not all commodity work, however. In addition, there are what Ultramar calls "managed matters." For example, the company may have a major case arise in, say, Michigan. Ultramar will join with its regional firm there, Dykema Gossett, in handling it. As a result, the selection of the final dozen firms was an important one as well. The company wasn't going to assign potentially significant cases to law firms of indifferent stature. Also, the prospect of handling those cases keeps the local firms enthused about working for the client instead of exasperated because they didn't win the final higher-volume, higher-quality prize.

The size issue here is instructive. In a market where mid-sized firms are often depicted as outgunned by behemoths with greater national or global resources, Milner specifically sought to avoid hiring a megafirm as lead outside counsel. She wanted to avoid the bureaucracy. Also, a client such as Ultramar Diamond Shamrock will invariably be very important to a 250-lawyer firm like Manatt. The attraction of a mid-sized firm is that it thus reinforces a fundamental rationale for converging, which is, again, that a client becomes proportionately more important to the firms it retains.

Ultramar sees itself saving more than 5% in the long run as the efficiencies brought about by consolidation are effective. Specifically, earlier case assessments and better budgeting are expected to yield dividends, although those are hard to quantify. Similarly, reduced liability represents significant potential savings once cases are better coordinated in fewer hands.

Indeed, more proactive preventive counseling is among the predictable benefits of effective convergence because outside counsel can better spot potential trouble areas throughout the company. Such counseling is sometimes distrusted as a way that outside counsel can "beef up" billables by, say, reviewing employee manuals or needlessly auditing patent portfolios. However, a firm engaged on a fixed fee or similar project basis may do this work as part of the engagement without the risk of churning.

Even on an hourly basis, Milner believes a preferred provider can do preventive counseling efficiently and honestly. A Manatt partner will know the company better, she says, and, as such, can provide fast answers to questions pertinent to possible exposure. This is a small billable investment that will yield a large return, although, again, not necessarily a measurable one. The cost savings are theoretical because, obviously, they pertain to lawsuits that never happen.

For Milner, the new efficiencies achieved through convergence are apparent. She cites an FTC matter facing Ultramar that had a substantive component similar to a FERC matter. Eventually, the similarity was picked up and both matters were handled more expeditiously as a result. However, had a single firm been handling them, Milner says the similarity "would have been seen at once." In the same way, preferred legal providers save on discovery when there are similar patterns in multiple cases. Especially when outside counsel is billing on a non-hourly basis, it's to everyone's interest to use the same boilerplate documents or procedures in multiple-case discovery.

Yet the very success of the Ultramar experience suggests one reason why convergence as an elaborate process of reformulation could constitute overkill. After all, Ultramar picked Manatt and then negotiated some of the most important aspects of the engagement. It begs the question, "Why not just negotiate directly with the firms you like?"—the assumption being that, if the relationship has any chance of survival, these agreements on oversight and billing will evolve anyway. Even in an over-lawyered situation like Ultramar's, why go through the process?

CONVERGENCE RECONSIDERED

In fact, that's very much the viewpoint of in-house managers such as John Liftin, GC of the Prudential Insurance Company. At the Rheem Manufacturing Company, GC Jan Hoynacki says convergence is just "common sense." It's what happens as a result of simply negotiating and managing wisely with the law firms you already use. Jeffrey Kindler, General Counsel at McDonald's Corporation, echoes the point. Kindler refers to a "natural convergence" as opposed to DuPont's programmatic approach.

However, Liftin candidly offers one of the more jaundiced views of the convergence process. His reservations are especially noteworthy, since the consolidation of outside counsel by Prudential, which occurred under Liftin's predecessor, James Gillen, was the best known and most wide-ranging after DuPont.

In early 2000 Prudential was under exceptional cost-cutting pressures as part of the company's plan to go public in 2001. Total legal costs in the 1999-2003 period were to be reduced by 25%. Outside costs were cut by 10% in 2000. As a result, Liftin and his in-house colleagues have had some serious conversations with the firms they now use.

But those conversations were not part of a second convergence process.

Prudential is a very hierarchical organization even by corporate standards. Of the 300 or so lawyers who work in-house, seventy-five are part of the property/casualty group and handle small matters, mostly representing insureds. The others, encompassing securities, life insurance, asset management and investments, litigation, employment/labor, financing, tax, and regulatory, are significant users of outside counsel. There have been serious cuts in in-house staff as a result of the public offering, including a March 2000 reduction in force of 10% at all law department levels. A great deal of the decision-making with respect to hiring law firms remains in the trenches nonetheless. According to Liftin, retention decisions of approved firms can be made as far down as three reports from the top.

Gillen's convergence stretched through 1997 and into the spring of 1998. Over 600 firms were dropped from the approved list. The current roster is about 200. The fact that, before the consolidation, there were about 100 firms at the very top end of the list gives some idea of the enormity of the process. Responses to RFPs led to a barrage of interviews and beauty contests. Firms were challenged to prove what benefits they could provide the company. The winners signed RFP contracts that covered a two-year period, and so have expired. Their expiration inspired Prudential to rethink convergence.

A problem, both initial and ongoing, was to convince the in-house staff that the convergence strategy represented a significant improvement over current practice. Part of Liftin's criticism of such a round of RFPs and beauty contests is that, at a company with as many in-house managers as Prudential, it's not practicable to get the key rank-and-file lawyers—the ones who actually hire outside counsel—directly involved in the interviews and evaluations. The very notion of "oversight" is a tricky one, especially since the law firm associates who do so much of the work are also not personally included in the beauty contests.

"I don't believe in micro-managing the use of resources by outside counsel," states Liftin. That is, competently selected law firms that stay within budget or commit to fixed fees ought to be able to self-manage how they use their attorneys and paralegals. If they can't, the fault lies in the retention. And, Liftin suggests, law firms know this.

As Prudential faced mounting cost pressures, Liftin saw more efficient ways to reduce the budget than by re-instigating a consolidation process. A major purchaser like Prudential could have wrung discounts from its suppliers in a much simpler way: just eliminate all the firms earning less than $1 million in annual fees and negotiate with the others. Yet Liftin and Mahoney are of one mind on two key points: (1) simple cost cutting is not in itself an efficacious way to manage the inside/outside relationship, and (2) the convergence model cannot be justified simply as a way to obtain discounts. DuPont demanded shared risk value billing arrangements, and Liftin says Prudential is headed toward modified fixed fee agreements as well.

Corporate buyers are always well-advised to ask what is also best for the seller, since a profitable law firm will likelier be more motivated and more client service-oriented. Thus, Liftin points out that fixed fees, or other such alternative payment modes, can dramatically increase partner realization rates. The negative for major law firms is the leverage question: how to employ hordes of lawyers on any basis other than hourly rates. In any event, you don't need a convergence model to pursue alternative billing negotiations, as the discussion of Ultramar Diamond Shamrock suggests.

When Liftin was interviewed, he and his colleagues had just concluded discussions of alternative billing options with three major New York law firms. At the same time, Prudential launched a pilot program in late 1999 in which half a dozen firms were signed up for certain M&A and litigation work on a fixed fee basis.[12]

The Prudential experience is also important because, as part of the convergence process, a set of best practices was evolved and presented to the law firms as conditions of retention. Not only is the consolidation process itself suspect, but many of those best practices are—each and every one of them—also suspect in Liftin's view. In fact, a large number were jettisoned by Prudential after being formally agreed to by the law firms.

These not-so-good best practices included:

♦ Having all firms use the same Prudential e-mail system as a way to buttress confidentiality. Such an imposition simply wasn't needed to safeguard communications.

♦ A new computerized billing system that would result in faster payment. The benefits to outside firms were marginal. There were practically no direct benefits to Prudential.

♦ Use of a time and billing system for more frequent case and matter review instead of reliance on detailed review of bills by inside staff. This was abandoned because it was too time-consuming. Whatever benefits emerged were scant compared to the investment required.

---

[12] These were Debevoise & Plimpton; Clifford Chance Rogers & Wells; Cahill Gordon & Reindel; Wilson, Elser, Moskowitz, Edelman & Dicker; and Sonnenschein Nath & Rosenthal.

- Task-based billing. This refers to the system first developed in the late 1980s by the American Corporate Counsel Association and what was then Price Waterhouse to work out a universal system of identifying specific legal matters by code. Presumably, this system serves as an efficiency tool and a pricing guideline. It "fell by the wayside" at Prudential, reports Liftin. (Task-based billing is still viable for many companies; Ultramar Diamond Shamrock is using it with Manatt, Phelps.)

- Knowledge management systems. This refers to technology that collects all the intellectual capital of an organization or a part of an organization in databases and on intranets. "It's not a bad idea," says Liftin, but it's also frontier technology—at least it was in 1999. Actually, Prudential is now using Domino.doc, but the original system which Prudential rejected had too many bells and whistles.

- Use of outside legal research companies. These providers serve a wide range of corporate clients with briefs and other legal products prepared by professors and experts at a cut rate compared to what a young associate at a major law firm would charge. However, the particular company employed by Prudential has a policy of not identifying its experts or allowing end users to talk directly to opinion writers. Prudential balked at that and soon fired the provider, without seeking a replacement.

There are at least a couple of cautionary lessons to extract from this across-the-board retrenchment. As Liftin comments, lawyers tend to be "undisciplined" when it comes to business and management. One best practice or two may be practicable. A systemic overhaul is much tougher.

Second, a lot of best practices look terrific on paper. And consultants must always be selling something. Many of them don't work, however. Most are better introduced, not programmatically, but as commonsense responses to specific situations. In fact, an emerging attitude on the issue of whether to formally converge is just that: Certain companies facing certain problems *may* be advised to pursue a dedicated consolidation model.

Profession-wide, there remains similar skepticism. The time problem is huge. Even at Ultramar Diamond Shamrock, Marylin Milner refers to the initial 200- to twelve-law firm reduction as "a terrific waste of time"—despite the fundamental gains in efficiency that she says resulted from the process. So, we have two tough alternatives facing companies that worry about too many law firms on their approved lists: (1) They can expend massive managerial hours or (2) they can take Liftin's (somewhat ironic) suggestion and simply eliminate everyone below a certain fee threshold, then bargain with the survivors.

"NATURAL CONVERGENCE"

There are a number of possible ways to navigate a moderate middle course: Again, like Hoynacki or Kindler, not everyone sees convergence as radical surgery. Unlike DuPont, not every firm has faced an untenable proliferation of outside counsel or ever had the budget to amass such a number of providers in the first place. At McDonald's, for example, ten law firms handle an estimated 80% of the company's work, but McDonald's regularly does business with another twenty to thirty firms. As Kindler describes it, use of outside counsel converged naturally because of the recurring nature of much of the work. McDonald's simply came to rely on the same law firms over and over.

McDonald's caseload is well-defined as well as fairly repetitive. According to Kindler, the heaviest caseload in terms of volume of claims and suits is "customer-related litigation." This is anything a customer is aggrieved about, from food-borne illness to security issues to the notorious hot-coffee-in-the-lap cases. For these, McDonald's is self-insured up to a point, but, in many instances, managing them is complicated because 80% of the restaurants are franchises. The company is not directly exposed but its brand is affected. Although there are many law firms that handle these cases for McDonald's, three or four became the primary providers over the years.

Second, there is real estate-related litigation: a fairly steady docket of disputes with landlords and lessees over properties where restaurants are located as well as zoning issues, permitting issues, etc.

Third, there are franchisee disputes. These were particularly voluminous in the mid-1980s. In the 1990s, however, they decreased as the relationships between the company and its franchisees improved, or as the company prevailed in a number of cases. When Kindler arrived at McDonald's in 1997, many franchisees were alleging "impact," i.e., the company reduces the franchisee's sales by opening a second restaurant too close by. McDonald's consistently prevailed by arguing that its franchise agreement only extends the right to operate a store at a particular address, not the right to any sort of territorial exclusivity.

At the same time, from a business point of view, McDonald's has willingly involved franchisees in development decisions, so more often there's neither injury nor perception of injury. When managers talk about outside counsel partnering with the client, it's just this sort of non-legal negotiation they mean, and to which they expect their law firms to contribute.

Fourth, McDonald's defends occasional lawsuits from suppliers or wannabe suppliers. These involve the alleged failure of the company to adhere to purchasing agreements. According to Kindler, although these claims are few in number, they can be significant in terms of potential damages.

Finally, there are the oddball trademark or other intellectual property disputes. In these, McDonald's is usually the plaintiff, asserting its rights against infringers.

A salient fact about all this litigation is that none of it is "bet-the-company" stuff. None of it involves wrongful deaths or million-dollar judgments. This more moderate level of casework has also encouraged "natural convergence" insofar as the company doesn't have to go shopping when its regular law firms aren't up to some particularly crucial task. Kindler can "count on one hand" the cases where the risk justified hiring a Fred Bartlit-level trial attorney.

McDonald's doesn't fire law firms often, although Kindler points out that it has been known to happen. Part of the company's "natural convergence" involves firms with which it has had a long-standing institutional relationship, particularly Chicago's Sonnenschein Nath and Rosenthal. Sonnenschein currently does more work for McDonald's than anyone else and, says Kindler, is "way ahead of whoever number two is."

"By virtue of this long relationship," says Kindler, "the Sonnenschein lawyers understand our business extremely well and, as a result, can deal with many of our legal issues very effectively and efficiently. This kind of relationship provides significant benefits that you can't really achieve with single-matter engagements, even though those have their place as well."

The relationship extends back to a friendship that partner Donald Lubin established with Ray Kroc in the early 1960s when Lubin was in his early thirties. Since then, partner Alan Silberman, for example, has handled 80% or 90% of all the McDonald's franchise litigation. Again, the preferred provider is more efficient if only because the motions have all been written, Sonnenschein has all the boilerplate, and it wouldn't make any sense to bid out this generic litigation.

However, McDonald's will go to another provider if a franchise case is filed in a jurisdiction where Sonnenschein does not have any lawyers. When that happens, related work also gets naturally consolidated in the hands of local counsel, if they do a good job. Even in the context of a convergence strategy, or where there is an extremely well-established relationship, newcomers therefore still have a chance to get on the approved list or even chip away at the advantage enjoyed by a primary vendor regarding the client's national or global caseload. It's one reason, to be sure, why so many law firms have abandoned compunctions about growth, and have adopted aggressive expansion initiatives to maintain or extend their service to favored clients.

Significantly, too, Kindler says, "I just don't think it's a good idea to have one firm do all of your work all the time. I think you get fresh ideas, you get a little competition, you keep people on their toes. We don't want to be taken for granted. We need to bring in a new generation of people so that we know we have new lawyers over time who are knowledgeable about our work."

This is not an argument against convergence. Kindler's point may actually support a consolidation model that results in a handful of preferred providers. The coterie delivers the best of both worlds: maximum efficiency plus some variety.

Echoing this perspective, of convergence as a natural process, or as common sense, or as an *ad hoc* solution, Caterpillar, Inc. GC Robert Rennie Atterbury III describes it as something that happens as a result of "good tight management." Caterpillar keeps a reasonably tight rein on costs—the company paid just over one-half the national median in total legal costs, according to the prestigious PricewaterhouseCoopers survey of the profession—and tends to stay with law firms a long time.

With a full spectrum of legal needs world-wide, including a hefty product liability caseload, Caterpillar would thus seem to be "tightly managed" indeed, obtaining efficient services from a small group of firms without having to re-engineer the entire retention process. There are 100 firms servicing Caterpillar, but Atterbury says the vast majority are local counsel in foreign nations.

Like McDonald's, Caterpillar "naturally" converged. Washington, D.C.'s Howrey Simon Arnold & White is a major supplier of litigation services to Caterpillar, especially antitrust and other bet-the-company matters. Chicago's Mayer, Brown & Platt covers a spectrum of corporate and transactional work. Chicago's Seyfarth Shaw handles employee benefits and other labor/employment matters, except for collective bargaining, which is done by Chicago's Winston & Strawn.

Also, as at Prudential and McDonald's, retention decisions are typically made well below the General Counsel's level or even the Associate General Counsel's. As such, a rigorous convergence model is not, again, necessarily practicable, since there are too many lawyers making retention decisions to participate meaningfully in protracted RFPs and beauty contests. Atterbury similarly agrees that convergence is a more applicable strategy for companies that have much bigger legal budgets. At the same time, costs at many of those bigger corporations were out of control. Caterpillar's never were.

Atterbury is also aware, and wary, of the negative effects of convergence at these bigger companies. We've noted that Manatt, Phelps could, theoretically, have an incentive not to settle Ultramar cases because it would decrease the overall budget. Elsewhere, suggests Atterbury, an opposite but equally undesirable scenario has proven to be more than just theoretically dangerous. Companies paying fixed fees now have a reason to simply veto settlement opportunities, figuring it won't cost them more to litigate.

It's a double whammy for outside counsel when, further down the line, clients try to pressure the outside firm to further lower average costs per case. Those averages have gone up as cases that were once settled now start costing $50,000 or $100,000 instead of $0. Then the client says, "Our average costs are too high. If you want to stay on board, cut your rates even more."

These companies are "stretching outside counsel's resources," warns Atterbury. "Law firms complain to me about it all the time. But they're between a rock and a hard place if they want the work."

SELECTIVE CONVERGENCE

Genentech, Inc. offers a particularly good example of how the programmatic convergence passionately advocated by Mahoney has become a more selective, less ideological phenomenon. By the late 1990s, GCs were more likely to be adopting some aspects of the DuPont agenda and ignoring or rejecting others. Convergence has filtered through and been incorporated as one tool in the inside arsenal, and inside managers wield the tool on an as-needed basis.

Specifically, at Genentech, some outside services were converged, whereas for others, the company responded by doing the reverse, unbundling work handled by one law firm and spreading the wealth around town. The decisive issues are quantity of matters, the nature of the work, and the volume that is handled in-house. Genentech merits a closer look as an example of a major corporation able to go in both directions.

Genentech has two functional departmental sectors: corporate and IP, with patents by far the dominant aspect of the latter. In 1997, with the arrival of Sean Johnston, Vice President, Intellectual Property, and Senior Patent Counsel and Manager, Patent Litigation, various categories of patent applications and prosecutions were consolidated in significantly fewer outside hands. Litigation, which is usually the area for which companies adopt consolidation strategies, had always been handled by a relatively few number of law firms. Echoing Kindler, Johnston says that that area had naturally converged over the years. However, with a huge number of new patents since the mid-1990s, Genentech faced an efficiency challenge that would demand a more programmatic approach to applications and prosecutions.

In contrast, beginning in 1994, Genentech's corporate matters—under the aegis of Cynthia Ladd, Vice President of Corporate Law until her departure for a small biotech start-up in early 2000—were gradually taken away from Cooley Godward, a Silicon Valley-based firm. They were distributed among over a half-dozen other national and local law firms.

To a certain extent, convergence, for Genentech, is a way to efficiently handle commodity work, which, of course, is a sharp contrast to how DuPont consciously assigned some of its most significant lawsuits to the convergence pot. According to Johnston, there are primary, secondary, and tertiary patents. Genentech carefully sizes up each new patent. The ones identified as primary get handled by the in-house staff. The feeling is, no outside lawyer can have as good a *business* perspective on a vital biotech patent as the in-house lawyers who deal with the company's nonlawyer strategists on a daily basis. Nor can outside lawyers relate as well to the scientists and technicians who create the products. There are exceptions. Three or four law firms have had long-term relationships with the client, and from time to time they are trusted with the primary patents.

By and large, though, they stay inside, and are handled by the seventeen patent attorneys plus patent agents on Genentech's payroll. So definite is this prioritization that secondary patents that become unexpectedly more important from a business standpoint are taken back from outside counsel and handled inside. The assessment process isn't perfect, says Johnston, yet this policy of retrieving work that proves more important than first thought is extremely unusual. It is also why Johnston would debate our use of the word "commodity" to describe the patents that have now been consolidated among fewer firms. The very fact that they can become more significant than first anticipated means that these matters always have top-shelf potential, and should be treated accordingly.

All the secondary and tertiary products are farmed out, and that is no inconsiderable volume of work. Johnston says Genentech has gotten better prices by converging this volume. From a quality standpoint, convergence gave Johnston the opportunity to meet law firm managers as well as the lawyers who actually do the work. Volume was the immediate, critical spur, however. The less important prosecutions simply cannot be done with in-house staff, nor would it make economic sense to staff up—especially not with the kind of discounts attainable through convergence.

A half-dozen firms won this work, including a couple of Genentech's longstanding outside counsel (the firms that will occasionally handle a primary patent for the company as well), a couple that had already been doing patents for the company, and a couple that were brand-spanking new to Genentech. These firms (which Johnston declines to identify) are spread out around the country.

Much more so than DuPont, Genentech was looking for very specific discounts when the company converged its patent practice. According to Johnston, these discounts involved specific percentages or hard dollar amounts that would result in those percentages. Firms had to offer discounts of at least 10% to get them to Genentech's table; Johnston says 10% to 25% was the overall range.

Johnston stresses another significant difference between Genentech's convergence and the sort that garnered the DuPonts of the world so much publicity. Genentech did not actually fire law firms in the sense that outside counsel that did not win a share of the secondary or tertiary patent work were necessarily excised from the department's approved list. Those firms are still eligible for additional business as such business may arise. Indeed, Johnston sums up the difference between Genentech's experience and DuPont's by suggesting that, at DuPont, the problem was too many law firms. At Genentech, the problem was too much work, and convergence was just a way to more handily manage it.

Stephen Juelsgaard, Senior VP and GC, explains the explosion in patents. "A race had begun among the biotech companies to identify all the genes in the human body, and make intellectual property of it all," he says. Genentech targeted secreted proteins as a source of therapeutic products (whereas competitors were all over the place, patenting genes from every sort of protein). Despite its sharper market focus, Genentech's Secreted Protein Discovery Initiative begun in 1997 has resulted in hundreds of new patents per year. Before, the normal caseload was ten to twelve new patents per year.

The ten or so lawyers in the corporate practice faced a very different situation. They are able to handle the lion's share of Genentech's work in-house. In fact, as Juelsgaard puts it, for work to go outside, "we first have to be damned sure it can't be done inside." Right off the bat, then, such a view of the in-house function mitigates against any aggressive outsourcing of significant and high-volume work to preferred providers.

At the same time, there are matters Genentech can't handle in-house. The corporate practice does find itself strapped from time to time. Juelsgaard refers to a licensing matter in which Genentech did not have the manpower to handle a related stock purchase transaction and, as a result, farmed out that part of the job. More typically, though, Genentech goes outside for corporate work when it needs solutions in very specific areas such as antitrust or securities or real estate. There are partners at law firms who have that expertise, which is too specific and too recondite to find at most in-house departments.

These specific legal needs don't necessarily lend themselves to a consolidated approach to hiring. As Juelsgaard sees it, convergence in this area makes less sense for two reasons. First, such work usually involves solutions to problems that a single partner with an associate or two can handle. Hourly rates for the work would be relatively high anywhere. There's nothing to discount since the work is not leveraged like major lawsuits or high-volume patent prosecutions might be.

Second, this kind of work is ideally farmed out to individual practitioners identified as the best in their area. The best on Matter X might be found from a partner at Firm Y and on Matter A from a partner at Firm B. Breadth is not the criterion since the client is essentially needing to fill holes. As Juelsgaard describes this de-convergence, "Each time we had a new matter, we asked, 'Who's the best?'"

Not that Cooley, which had represented Genentech since 1985, didn't have the option to compete in each of the specialty areas. However, as Cooley's share of the client's work dwindled in the mid-1990s, it eventually made no sense for Cooley to maintain the relationship at all, since doing so would conflict the firm out of higher-volume lucrative business. Today, Genentech uses Latham

& Watkins for antitrust, Wilson, Sonsini, Goodrich & Rosati for securities, Morrison & Foerster's Los Angeles office for real estate and real estate financing, a boutique in Washington, D.C. called Hyman, Phelps & McNamara for FDA work, Heller Ehrman White & McAuliffe for employment—and so forth.

Yet Juelsgaard acknowledges the benefits of relying on firms that offer one-stop shopping for such diverse legal needs. A young company, he says, will naturally want full service rather than have to expend time and resources searching for different law firms to handle different areas. Other, bigger companies might also prefer to simplify retention practices as much as possible.

Once again, another benefit of one-stop shopping speaks directly to a fundamental reason why convergence is a coherent way to buy legal services: Most Favored Status for the law firm guarantees Most Favored Status for the client as well. It's called partnering. Juelsgaard is well aware that firms naturally give higher priority to clients with which they've converged or partnered or which simply happen to buy a broad range of services from the single source. Juelsgaard says that, on the corporate front, Genentech has thus taken a "calculated risk" by keeping its buying practices narrower. He concedes that not being a primary work source for outside counsel is a potential "downside."

In the mid-1990s, when Genentech began to cast a wider net, it was already a potent corporate name that could command the attention of almost any law firm. Now smaller clients abound which, because they buy all their legal services from single suppliers, can actually compete with Genentech for the attention of major law firms (especially when those firms own big equity shares in the clients). If those law firms are also the preferred providers for larger companies, that competition only gets steeper.

In certain situations, it may thus be true that major buyers of legal services have no choice but to converge, simply because other, competing buyers have done so.

How GE's In-House Revolution Changed an Inside/Outside Dynamic

> *"I spend infinitely more time . . . worrying about hiring, retaining, and promoting good people than I ever have about law firms."*
>
> —Ben Heineman

Convergence is the most conspicuous change affecting the purchasing of legal services by corporations, in part because it is such a direct and purposeful process. Yet the inside/outside axis of the early years of the twenty-first century was equally determined by how, in the 1990s, corporations rethought the structure and focus of their own law departments.

In other words, retention practices over time have changed, and continue to change, as a byproduct of corporate restructuring. The oil companies, for example, habitually draw new organizational charts with each periodic increase or downturn in the cost of a barrel. Law firms are directly affected by the extent to which any corporation moves from, say, a centralized to a decentralized model or vice versa. In and of itself, that naturally changes who at the company buys legal services. In turn, the volume of work staying in or going outside changes as well. So too do client expectations in terms of accountability, budgeting, or pricing. Sometimes the changes are purposeful, such as when the client sees in the process of reformulating the law department an opportunity to improve its retention practices. Other times, the changes just seem to happen.

Generally speaking, the dominant motif is control. Convergence is one way to gain control of an unwieldy process. Rethinking reporting relationships within a corporation is another. If the decision is made to focus legal (or any other kind of) decision-making in a central office, it's often because a strong CEO wants all policy and practices overseen there. That controls operations.

Conversely, a decentralized model ostensibly delivers more control over the specific goals and problems affecting local management. In this kind of thinking, a corporate nerve center in New York cannot exert optimal informed judgment on how a lawsuit in Oregon is being handled. In the decentralized model, local counsel in Oregon, with a "dotted line" report to New York, provide the best input on local business operations and potential legal problems. The proximity of lawyer and client leads to better prophylaxis and surer control. Companies such as IBM, Citicorp, and GE—the subject of this chapter—perennially wrestle with the balance of power implicit in centralized/decentralized models.

A number of factors have made this evolutionary search for balance almost imponderably complex. Control is a dominant motif, but cost-efficiency is a fundamental theme as well. The conflict between these two imperatives of corporate management is nowhere better seen than in the legal arena because, theoretically, all corporate legal functions can be outsourced to law firms. As such, we've watched an almost three-decade peristalsis of work going inside one day and outside the next, of in-house staff being reduced one year and increased the next.

Adding to the complexity, in-house practice began by the late 1980s to attract a higher caliber of practitioner. Again, remember that first ACCA conference discussed in Chapter 1, and the palpable sensation at the conference that corporate counsel were no longer school nurses whose primary function was to call a doctor whenever the schoolboy scraped his knee. By the late 1990s, prominent partners at law firms all over the country were leaving for in-house jobs, attracted by a number of factors. One was the opportunity to run a more hierarchical organization and pursue global business goals without having to vet every decision with committees of argumentative lawyers, each one having his or her own separate clientele, practice area focus, and personal agenda.

At the same time, corporate benefits offered economic security and even great wealth. In-house managers were negotiating better deals than they could get at most law firms. Salaries weren't shabby either. By the end of the decade, chief legal officers were earning over $1 million per year at companies like GE, Philip Morris, and RJR Nabisco, and that doesn't include benefits and options worth ten times as much.

Even managing partners were leaving their firms. John McGoldrick, for example, had been the managing partner of Newark, New Jersey's McCarter & English. He departed for the top legal slot at Bristol-Myers Squibb. Peter Haje was a partner for twenty-one years at New York's Paul, Weiss, Rifkind, Wharton & Garrison before leaving for what is now AOL Time Warner, and a compensation package well into seven figures. But no such move was more conspicuous, or would have more lasting impact, than the arrival of Benjamin Heineman, Jr. as general counsel of GE. He'd been running the Washington, D.C. office of Chicago's Sidley & Austin.

For outside counsel, one effect of these moves, and many others like them to less prominent corporations or to less prominent in-house positions, was that they were now dealing with equals or superiors on the client end. They could no longer gull or bully their in-house counterparts. They couldn't mystify their work with overstaffed conference calls and protracted or superfluous expenditures of billable hours. They were dealing with people who knew all their tricks.

But Heineman had a profounder vision than simply managing outside counsel more aggressively. With so much talent available, GE could create what he came to refer to as the "in-house law firm." It would be the best of both worlds. On the one hand, it was still a corporation and would function with all the top-down efficiencies of a corporation. On the other hand, the legal department would be a flatter organization as well and provide the benefits of a law firm where lawyers have the expertise to deliver and oversee focused services at the practice group level.

The in-house counsel office would be flatter because a layer of management involved in the intake of legal work was drastically reduced. Lawyers who, previously, were primarily charged to assess a matter and assign it to someone else were suddenly the ones *doing* it as well. They became, perforce, specialists. As at many law firms, lawyers can be specialists in more than one area and therefore practice in more than one group.

GE lawyers still assign out matters that land on their desks but do not fall within their substantive expertise areas. Yet their primary function is to practice law—and this at a company where, historically, the only specialists were patent attorneys and some labor lawyers. Now, the only generalists are the general counsel, including Heineman and his counterparts at GE's subsidiary business units who report to him. There remain a few exceptions. At small GE business units, including a number of the foreign offices, lawyers really must be jacks-of-all-trades, although Heineman expects on-going growth overseas to result in the same sort of focus on specialization that has characterized the development of corporate counsel stateside.

What followed at GE was an impressive flurry of top-level hiring. GE was, in fact, "cherry-picking" lawyers who were dominant practitioners in different specialty areas, just as an acquisitive law firm cherry-picks during a period of expansion. New York's Dewey Ballantine was an especially rich source of talent for GE. Alumni of that firm included John Samuels, one of the nation's leading tax lawyers, who was recruited from Dewey's D.C. office.

To keep this sea change in perspective, however, GE is so big that, even with this decisive shift in-house, legal is still only a small part of the corporation compared to, say, human resources. Size factors have probably furthered Heineman's goals because there's been more room to expand and certainly more buying power than at most other companies.

For law departments, GE is a provocative model if only because top lawyers are migrating in-house and corporate managers want these highly compensated star practitioners put to the best possible use. For law firms, GE represents one more sea change in how big-money clients buy legal services. A review of the specifics of the GE experiment, and an update on how that experiment has affected outside counsel, are, therefore, very much in order.

The "In-House Law Firm"

The complexity of GE's business made the move to specialization that much more decisive. When Heineman set about his task, the primary legal needs of the parent corporation were environmental, trade and international business, labor, tax, and patents. But the business units were gigantic purchasers as well. For example, GE had acquired the National Broadcasting Company. There, the legal practice groups included intellectual property, libel/defamation, corporate, transactional, employment/EEO, litigation, contract negotiation, FCC regulatory, and lobbying. Under the Heineman regime, NBC lawyers were themselves handling specific sorts of matters on a repetitive basis until they developed real parity in expertise with most outside counsel.

Similarly, at GE Appliances, lawyers who had once been assigned to specific divisions such as manufacturing or marketing were now compelled to become resident experts on antitrust, trade, and international law. Yet, corporation-wide, Heineman's new schemata presented definitional and organizational conundrums. For example, litigation itself was a practice specialty, but doesn't libel/defamation encompass litigation?

GE's solution was to have it both ways. There were specialists in depositions, briefs, etc., and there were also lawyers specializing in defamation/libel issues apart from litigation. There was a similar definitional problem regarding the vast body of tax law significant to the corporation: How to categorize a lawyer such as John Samuels, who oversees the entire tax practice from the Fairfield, Connecticut home office? Is he a tax specialist or no less a general counsel than the legal managers at the business units? If nothing else, such examples are important because they suggest that the transformation from intake to practice, from generalization to specialization, was never mechanical or necessarily clear-cut. It is an evolving process and susceptible to exceptions and ambiguities.

Constituting practice teams is also a complicated and sometimes variable process. If a litigation matter arises, who takes the lead, the general counsel at the business unit or the litigation specialists from the corporate legal staff? Often, dollar amounts and potentially high exposure mean that the case goes right to the corporate staff, although those litigation specialists would get involved at some point anyway.

Two overriding developments have made the deployment of GE's lawyers, both in-house and outside, even more complex. One was the accelerated growth of General Electric Capital Services, which itself embraces some thirty separate P&L units. It has its own discrete corporate structure with its own GC and corporate legal staff, a mini-Fairfield, as it were. In fact, as of this writing, half or so of GE's lawyers now work for this subsidiary, which means that the total increase in corporate lawyer numbers has not been particularly great. There are about thirty-five lawyers at GE Aircraft Engines, which is not so many relative to that company's revenue. Similarly, NBC has only about thirty-five attorneys. GE Power Systems is a bit more rotund with sixty-five attorneys.

The other factor adding to the complexity of GE's lawyer deployment was the internationalization of corporate counsel, in part the result of GE Capital's multinational breadth. Yet, like most corporations, GE has as a whole become exponentially more global. Some 200 lawyers are now located outside the U.S., according to Suzanne Hawkins, Senior Counsel, Legal Operations, who was working in Germany when she joined the company in the mid-1990s. At that time, there were only thirty GE attorneys in Europe, most of them Americans. Today there are nearly 120, with another sixty in Asia and a handful of others in Latin America. Shifting workloads provide a particularly dramatic index of corporate globalization. In 1998, 10% of GE's legal work was outside the United States. By the end of 1999, that number increased to 30%.

The transformation at GE from general legal management to specialization practice has generated a new breed of general counsel who are both businesspeople and policy-makers. As specialists better manage their own practices, just as they would at a law firm, the GCs are free to pursue more public-oriented objectives. They help make the law, as Samuels did, lobbying Congress during the early 1990s when new tax legislation was percolating.

They focus on public issues that have a direct impact on GE's bottom line, and on problems that they, as lobbyists, can help solve. (Heineman would like to see product liability reform, for example, but he doesn't think that that's going to happen in his lifetime. So GE lawyers don't waste their time fighting for it.) The GCs at the business units similarly negotiate directly with foreign governments, and they take a more responsive approach to the media, in marked contrast to the icy indifference of many in-house lawyers to press inquiries.

Not surprisingly, these pointed alterations in the very fabric of in-house practice have generated skeptical questions from other law departments and legal profession pundits. We've already seen how, for most companies, in-house lawyers are the preferred providers of, say, preventive law. General counsel like GE alumnus Jeffrey Kindler of McDonald's believe that in-house staff are closer to the business of the client than outside counsel. As a result, they're better positioned to take a proactive legal view of the client's long-term business needs and potential exposure. But some observers wonder if specialists can really evolve the business skills, and the business understanding, that is such an integral part of the in-house lawyer role. They suggest that the immersion of lawyers in specific practice areas could result in lawyers suffering the same myopia as outside counsel who see the world too much from the perspective of their individual specialties.

Wouldn't such a pronounced emphasis on specialization especially mitigate against GE attorneys being able to spot legal and business problems *outside* their narrow expertise, vitiating the main reason for staffing in-house lawyers in the first place? Internal memoranda from the early 1990s suggest this was a concern within GE as well, even as the in-house transformation was under way.[1]

Some GE lawyers were a lot more comfortable talking about "expertise" than "specialization," since the former seemed to suggest more flexibility in their professional roles. For all that, no profound impairment of the proactive function has apparently occurred at GE during the last decade, suggesting that the dangers were more theoretical than imminent. This development is also a result of the steady, rather than frenzied, pace at which the transformation has occurred. Again, the changes are not yet a complete transformation since some GE lawyers are still hybrids, specialists in their practice areas but also on general assignment to a business unit.

There is, finally, a level at which the GE model isn't radically dissimilar from what happens at other companies as more talented attorneys migrate in-house from law firms. They bring specialization as part of their total professional skills package. The specialist/generalist hybrid develops as a matter of

---

[1] See Cotton, "GE's Specialization Plan: Will Other Corporate Law Departments Follow?" 9:22 Of Counsel 10 (Nov. 19, 1990), which includes a memorandum written by NBC's GC Richard Cotton to Heineman emphasizing the need for additional focus on spotting potential legal problems within NBC as the focus of Heineman's lawyers' work continued to change.

course, and there's more room for lawyers to both manage and do the expert legal work that traditionally went to outside counsel.

As such, the question becomes ever more piquant: Where does all of this leave law firms?

Intensified "Partnering"

These days Ben Heineman is an in-house innovator who doesn't devote a great deal of attention to the inside/outside dynamic in general, or to what law firms GE is currently hiring and why. Interestingly, in the early days of the Heineman revolution, there were widely divergent views on the subject of outside counsel. Richard Cotton told *Of Counsel* that he foresaw increasingly less use of law firms, and he, for one, looked forward to "no longer having to finance the education of outside counsel."[2] In contrast, Samuels imagined there could even be a greater reliance on outside counsel as increasingly focused in-house specialists uncovered an ever-growing range of unexpected, complex legal issues.

Suzanne Hawkins is currently GE's point person on outside retention. Hawkins joined the department in 1994, a time that offers a particularly good perspective from which to view the inside/outside dynamic at GE. The move toward specialization was, for all intents and purposes, a *fait accompli* by 1994. Lawyers who could not fit into the new scheme had mostly left, and the ones arriving in the mid-1990s knew exactly what sort of departmental philosophy and approach awaited them. Also, as specialists, they were compensated better than at most other companies. The upshot is that the turnover at GE has become relatively low.

Hawkins is described by Heineman as the department's "managing partner," responsible for technology initiatives, integrating new lawyers, and all vendor relationships, including

---

[2] *Id.* at 12.

law firms. (She's the chairman of the law department's management committee.) Five years before her arrival, there were 300 lawyers practicing in-house at GE. By July 2000, there were 700. Significantly, Hawkins is still the only lawyer in the Fairfield corporate office (besides Heineman) who can be characterized as a generalist, further suggesting, perhaps, that the company has not substantially backtracked from the specialization-oriented goals and standards introduced in the late 1980s and early 1990s.

If anything, the number of specialty areas has grown, from about ten to approximately seventeen, according to Hawkins. Among the new ones are more commercial transactions sub-specialty teams, along with a new e-commerce specialty group. Heineman seems particularly focused on the e-commerce practice. An e-commerce specialist hired in 2000 and staffed in Fairfield reports directly to Heineman. The e-commerce group is also an example of how intricate practice area deployment can be at GE, since an independent e-commerce practitioner works side by side with e-commerce specialists who also practice as members of different specialty teams.

For law firms, the GE experiment has predictably meant even closer management of, and partnering with, outside counsel. Hawkins is the generalist in charge of all the vendor relationships and the policies that guide them. However, the day-to-day legal work is still managed by the in-house specialists themselves. At GE, those lawyers will simply have more substantive legal knowledge in their fields than at companies where there isn't the same emphasis on specialization. Many of these GE specialists may be fresh from law firms where a very different style of practice management exists. Hawkins acknowledges that, "We may have some lawyers who are much better at it than others."

Clearly, GE's specialization strategy is supported by an emphasis on selecting law firms as preferred providers. Because these firms are retained by specialty area, GE lawyers are working with outside counsel who have track records practicing with other GE lawyers in their specific areas. These relationships constitute a built-in support structure that, to a greater degree than seems the case with the convergence strategies of the other companies we've examined, adds value by more closely pairing in-house expertise and outside expertise. If nothing else, this historic refinement of the client/law firm relationship means that inside and outside lawyers are more similarly compensated than elsewhere, their academic credentials are comparable, and their knowledge of the legal matters at hand fairly equal. "Partnering" indeed!

The career opportunity such an arrangement presents for the lawyers on both sides is significant. In the early 1990s, Heineman was prescient in understanding that these pairings generate entrepreneurial potential. Just as he was recruiting top specialists from law firms, he openly acknowledged that GE lawyers might certainly travel in the other direction as well. Law firms and laws departments had been seconding attorneys for decades, but Heineman had in mind something closer to a current market phenomenon in which clients and law firms recruit together and exchange staff on a regular basis.

Companies such as Lucent Technologies have gotten on this bandwagon by beginning, in 1999, to make recruitment trips to law schools with a favored law firm, San Francisco's Orrick Herrington & Sutcliffe. The message to recruits is that they needn't cut off options; by going to work for the law firm, they could also spend a few years at Lucent (assuming Lucent survives its current economic woes). The reverse naturally applied; recruits could start at Lucent and practice at Orrick later on.

Heineman implemented a similar covenant at GE: Young lawyers who agree to restrict their practice to a few specialty areas get, in return, a chance to shuttle back and forth between law firm and law department employers. In some cases, they'll have multiple law firms from which to choose.

Specialization thus means closer management of outside counsel, but it also adds depth to the whole idea of partnering. With regard to litigation, though, GE's specialization strategy could, especially as a model other corporate clients might some day try to follow, prove disquieting for law firms. At GE, in contrast to current policy at most corporations, the in-house specialists do trial work as well as depositions and discovery. Other companies may be closely overseeing the cost and progress of litigation, but the work that comes inside is generally corporate or in other non-litigation areas. GE, says Hawkins, has forty to fifty "true litigators," five times as many as in the early 1990s.

NBC has been particularly keen about litigating its own cases, soup to nuts, and refuses to hire law firms at all for most of this work, at least not until cases get to trial. At companies like Caterpillar, in-house lawyers may, as GC Ronnie Atterbury says, "rewrite briefs at the drop of a hat," but at NBC and other GE companies they write them from scratch. Those brief-writing or deposition-taking specialists collaborate with other GE specialists from the business units, so that the expert on motions is working with a product liability expert from GE Plastics or a contracts expert from GE Aircraft Engines. There doesn't seem to be much left for outside counsel to do.

GE has also had considerable success with ADR, or early dispute resolution (EDR) as it's known there. Of course, both in-house staff and law firms can pursue litigation alternatives, although, like many in-house managers, Hawkins believes law firms aren't quite as motivated to choose EDR on a consistent basis. She estimates that, as a result of intensified dispute resolution efforts, litigation fell from about 45% of GE's total legal work load to about 37% during the 1995 to 2000 period. Part of that overall reduction is no doubt due to the predominance of transactional work at GE Capital. At the same time, it's another indication that, whereas GE's in-house attorneys became more specialized, they were still able to perform the sort of general prophylactic oversight by which law departments typically keep their clients out of trouble.

In any event, an 8% reduction in litigation, along with an 80% increase in the number of "true litigators" in-house, sounds daunting for outside counsel. GE generally seems a tough customer in this area. "I think people over fifty can't litigate any more because they don't really have the stomach for it," comments Heineman. "It's just too hard. It's like wrestling or boxing. It just requires this enormous amount of energy."

The "hard thing" in litigation, as Heineman sees it, is to "find the people who are on the way up, not on the way out." For big law firms, it must be particularly troublesome when corporate managers such as Heineman talk like this, since these megafirms are known for not letting their younger associates cut their teeth in litigation to any meaningful extent. They barely go to court until they're partners. To the extent that these large national firms are wasting so much talent, often callously, the shortage of experienced litigators on the way up is a problem the firms may deserve.

At the same time, the fact that the only generalist on the corporate legal staff is charged with the hiring and oversight of law firms suggests that the need for outside counsel obviously still exists even though a slew of specialists now ply their trade in-house at GE. According to Heineman, the inside/outside shift has changed between 1990 and 2000 from 60% outside and 40% inside, to 60% inside and 40% outside. That may be a conspicuous reversal, but 40% of GE is still a tempting prize for outside counsel.

SPECIALISTS RETAINING SPECIALISTS

In fact, with GE's world-wide growth, the company has not, in terms of real dollars, appreciably decreased its spending on outside counsel, despite the 60/40 switch. As Hawkins agrees, John Samuels' early prediction—that more and better lawyers inside would naturally unearth new legal issues which would need to be addressed and which, in turn, would generate new opportunity for outside counsel as well—has proven fairly reliable. By definition, such work will be high-level work as well, since the new issues that specialists discover in the course of their practice are going to be recondite and professionally challenging. Indeed, outside counsel are always telling Hawkins that the work they get from GE is really of very high caliber, and that they *learn* more from working with GE than with many other clients.

If GE is now in a fortuitous position, the key was in the aforesaid pairing of specialist insiders with preferred providers outside. But that partnering wasn't achieved in a DuPont-like triage. GE was too decentralized. It had too many businesses, with very strong general counsel who weren't likely to appreciate Fairfield dictating how to retain outside counsel or which firms to hire. Nor did Fairfield care to erode their responsibility for cost control and success. Nonetheless, with Heineman's support (and Jack Welch behind him), Hawkins still felt the corporation was using an excessive number of law firms, and that the situation needed to be rectified.

When, in 1996, Hawkins set out to converge outside counsel in this corporate maze, the only area that had a preferred provider program in place was the environmental group, which was mainly in Fairfield and was therefore a more centralized practice than the other practices. The complex intertwining of practice areas described earlier illustrates how difficult it is to simplify the retention of outside counsel. When, for example, there's an e-commerce practice in corporate central, and there are e-commerce practice lawyers in the business units as well, who hires outside lawyers?

GE had to choose one path in the labyrinth, and Hawkins was convinced that the way to hire was by specialty. The result would be a collection of law firms diverse enough to simultaneously provide for all the needs of the business units. The key to success would be getting those business units to sign on to the process. It couldn't be driven top-down, as it was at DuPont. Moreover, the specialty groups themselves had to agree that it was as practice groups, rather than as members of their own business units or as part of the corporate staff in Fairfield, that they could optimize their use of outside counsel.

Some groups such as labor/employment had already been thinking about preferred providers, and they got going right away. Others took a year or two to resolutely move forward. By 2000 all GE practice groups had preferred providers, including some, like M&A, that were initially skeptical that their practices lent themselves to this strategy. Some groups hired a handful of firms; other groups, like the e-commerce antitrust practice, only needed one. GE Capital already had what might be thought of as a preferred provider program in place. There were 100 firms (with specialties in corporate, real estate financing, etc.) that they'd been using in the mid-1990s, and are generally still using today.

As of 2000, some 120 law firms served GE as preferred providers. There were 475 firms used *in toto* in 1990, although that number included foreign law firms retained by smaller GE offices around the world. Without the convergence, Hawkins estimates the company would now have upwards of 900 firms on the gravy train. The fact that the biggest percentage of GE's current 500 outside counsel are still based overseas suggests that the company doesn't feel it has to rely on megafirms with global resources. They're just as likely to buy from smaller firms in far-flung jurisdictions. Heineman continues to maintain that the best lawyer in Budapest or São Paulo is still preferable, even in this day and age of law firm mega-expansion, to any law firm behemoth that happens to have offices everywhere. By the same token, the value of size should not be altogether gainsaid, especially for important practice areas such as M&A. For that work, Hawkins confirms, it is useful when firms have one or more offices outside the United States.

While Hawkins wheedled and negotiated for a specialization-based convergence, GE immersed itself in a quality initiative that, for the in-house legal staff, meant actually measuring their use of outside counsel as part of a formal evaluation process. Hawkins designed an online system that all lawyers would use toward that end. In addition, there are formal company guidelines, derived from the quality program, setting forth how some legal matters, especially GE's commodity work, are to be performed. A case in point is patent applications: The company's preferred providers in this area have very well-defined procedures they must follow to ensure both quality and efficiency.

These guidelines, derived from TQM-type initiatives that were undertaken as late as 1998 and 1999, are always worth mentioning now that it's become *de rigueur* to glibly dismiss the programs as inapplicable to the realities of law practice. Apparently, one of the world's largest corporate consumers of legal services takes no such dismissive attitude toward measurable pursuit-of-quality paradigms.

With so many specialty groups making retention decisions, GE relies on a comprehensive Web-based database that was rolled out in 1999. *Inter alia*, that database includes information regarding who at the company is using what firm, the fees involved, and what percentage of every GE practice group's law firms are preferred providers. This system is a refinement of a manual system that was previously in effect and that included data on every matter for which GE spent $25,000 or more on fees paid to any one law firm. Putting the manual system on the Web (on an intranet) directly supports GE's preferred provider strategy because it allows all lawyers in the field to access and input information. It allows more efficiency at the specialty group level as attorneys identify both the preferred providers in any jurisdiction and contact names, as well as input their own data on the firms they're using.

The system also helps complete the convergence by gathering information about which firms currently used by GE are not preferred providers, and why they're still being used. Sometimes there's a conflict situation that requires the exception, or sometimes a prior relationship persists for whatever reason. In one instance, the labor/employment group needed work done in Nevada and there wasn't a preferred provider available there, so the group went outside the preferred list. Senior practice group leaders retrieve such information and decide what, if anything, to do about it. In Nevada, for example, GE simply went out and found a preferred provider that now covers the state.

At the same time, there are always situations that justify departing from the preferred network. Heineman recalls one case in a Hispanic community where the plaintiff's lawyer was a priest. GE was only able to win the case by retaining a former United States Attorney who was also Hispanic to defend the company.

With seventeen or so specialty areas to retrofit with outside counsel, GE was looking at a Herculean, time-consuming task. Most of the practice groups underwent the typical round of interviews and beauty contests with prospective law firms. In some instances, the GCs at the business units sat in and advised. Hawkins was closely involved in each selection process, usually accompanied by the senior practice group leader and one or two lawyers from his or her staff.

A few groups were already set. Antitrust was happy enough with the firm it was using, Arnold & Porter, whereas John Samuels' tax group was a centralized in-house team with fifteen or twenty law firms it was accustomed to rely on. With these practice groups, Hawkins' staff merely had to enter vital particulars into the online database. More often, however, the convergence process demanded time and more time.

Many of the companies discussed in Chapter 7 were clearly driven by cost and billing methods in their convergence strategies. If they weren't rate shopping or demanding specific discounts, they were focused on risk-sharing billing methodologies. As Hawkins describes it, GE was more consciously focused on quality than cost. During the interviews, GE teams were extremely interested in how a law firm would staff the work: who the lawyers were and how good they were. The firms that turned up for the interviews at GE with the attorneys who'd actually be doing the work gained a strong head start on the competition. The client wasn't just interested in managing partners and practice group heads.

One illustration of the extent to which GE focuses preferred providers at the practice group level is the company's three different IP preferred provider programs: IP litigation, patent prosecution, and patent opinions. All three interview and retain separate outside counsel. Most corporations don't formally separate litigation and prosecution, even though the two are obviously distinct. A separate opinions group is unusual indeed.

GE's approach to IP underscores a crucial point made earlier, that law firms tend to compete for, and appreciate doing, very high-level work from GE—notwithstanding that a corporation this size also has a tremendous amount of commodity work to ship outside. In IP, as Hawkins describes it, GE wants both true trial experience and "really cutting-edge theories. We are not looking for the standard, tried and true patent litigator—the guy that comes out of the Patent Office or whatever." In an era when competition for commodity work is often what beauty contests are all about, the fact that this company is shipping out a relatively high volume of top-shelf work punctuates the importance of GE's decisive tilt toward specialization.

The interviews themselves must have been grueling: Highly compensated, top-level in-house specialists grilling outside counsel on very specific substantive matters. Firm résumés were reviewed rigorously as well. For M&A, GE looked at the volume and nature of the deals the firms had done, but they also scrutinized the counterparties to those deals and did due diligence on how the firm's lawyers actually handled negotiations. For litigation, GE looked up the win-loss records of the prospective preferred providers.

For all the emphasis on quality, cost was naturally still a factor as well, especially since GE has such buying power. GE will usually get discounts as a matter of course from all its vendors. What's interesting, as Hawkins describes it, is that this "You-get-volume-if-we-get-a-deal" approach, obviously a key component of most corporate convergence strategies, seems to have been a natural part of GE's purchasing philosophy even before other corporate legal departments began revising retention policies on that basis. It permeates the overall corporate approach, which is also remarkable in light of the kind of high-level work which, as we've seen, law firms have come to expect and appreciate from GE. Here, then, is one of the biggest corporations in the world that, instinctively, does not pay top dollar, yet bids out top-shelf legal services as a matter of course. "We're sort of a pain in the ass," quips Heineman.

But, stresses Hawkins, GE isn't simply shopping discounts but is also open to the whole value-billing gamut. In fact, she says, "you can't come up with an alternative model that we haven't tried." For example, Hawkins says the company's labor/employment practice pursues three possible billing models. First, law firms can talk about straight discounts. Second, they can negotiate discounts based on budgets that provide that the discounts the company gives increase or decrease according to how well the firms adhere to or exceed those budgets.

The third (and most popular) of the three options is a fixed fee for pre-trial handling of certain kinds of cases (e.g., single-party). As Hawkins points out, outside counsel love these fixed fees because they don't have to do task-based budgeting or worry about discounts. They manage the cases themselves and, since these are recurrent matters, the costs are pretty well-established. With good results, there's a moderate premium. If the case goes south, there's a moderate discount.

GE remains a staunch advocate of task-based billing so that corporations will know what they're spending, although Hawkins concedes that it's not easy to get all the lawyers to use it all the time. "One of the best by-products of it, I believe, is not just the financial aspect, but the strategic benefits that come from it," says Hawkins. "Because you sit down—which is what you should do anyway—you sit down with your law firm and say, okay, how many depositions are you going to do in this case? Are we going to do a motion? When might it be? So instead of just doing that stuff on the fly, you plan it out in the beginning if you can."

Of course, that means cost management as well. The buyer knows what's needed, so the buyer plugs in the seller's hourly rate to predict total fees. Unforeseen circumstances may and often do force adjustments along the way, but, as Hawkins puts it, "It's better than just giving the law firm a blank check."

NEXT STEPS

As Heineman describes it, the next stage in the evolution of GE's "in-house law firm" will revolve around allocation of resources to the corporate staff in Fairfield—a possible tilt toward centralization, as it were. Antitrust, for instance, could be centered in Fairfield or, perhaps, a few more litigators added. This would bring more work in-house and further decrease the number of law firms on GE's list of preferred providers. The business units wouldn't have to hire as much outside.

Here, too, they'll need to do some selling. "If anything, our biggest problem is that the business people like their lawyers," says Heineman. "As I try to change the lawyers, I get more resistance from the business people."

The development of GE's new e-commerce practice is particularly important as an example of how this company builds up internally and will continue to build up on the basis of specialization. But it does so incrementally, hiring new lawyers in new areas as the client and the general counsel perceive a strong business need for these new areas. Throughout 1999, the GE businesses were all launching e-commerce initiatives. The company formed an e-commerce and information technology practice group that would bring together fifteen or twenty lawyers from the different units.

This was a GE-styled specialty team that would evolve best practices and serve as a legal information resource for the company. Following that, GE hired a lateral to work as a specialist in the corporate office. There is still some work for outside counsel in e-commerce, according to Hawkins, although the firms involved haven't been getting as much work as they expected.

All of this begs an inevitable question: What kind of marketing works with this company? If brochures and newsletters are irrelevant with companies that continue to rely heavily on outside counsel, they're no doubt utterly useless here. Yet, just as with those other clients, CLE-oriented seminars are much desired by GE. "Most of our 700 lawyers need CLE now," says Heineman. "So I've told all of our top firms, 'Look, if you want to give free CLE, and invite our lawyers, I'll publicize it'" company-wide.

"I'll let any firm do that," adds Hawkins, including law firms that are totally new to GE, if they're quality firms and well-recommended. GE has also been open to formal audits by law firms of how well they're doing, although neither Heineman nor Hawkins can actually say that that process, so commended by marketing pundits, has been especially useful for either side. In one instance, there were a few wrinkles that were discussed and ironed out but, as Hawkins recalls, it was a good firm to begin with, so not much really changed.

That may be a limit to this sort of client relations marketing—that, sometimes, the firms which are conscientious enough to initiate these audits are the ones that are conscientious enough not to need them in the first place. However, it may be a question of which business unit at GE the firm is auditing. Since the specialists and the businesses do the actual hiring, law firms that market themselves to Hawkins, and certainly to Heineman, may be spinning their wheels. GE is in this respect just a more obvious example of what is now happening at McDonald's, Caterpillar, and Prudential. The general counsel at NBC or GE Aircraft will ask Hawkins who the preferred providers are because, "They want to use the firms we want them to use."

Yet marketing seminar after marketing seminar is entitled, "How GCs Buy Legal Services." That is often a dangerous and lingering solecism if, in fact, as will be discussed in the next chapter, GCs don't buy legal services at all.

CHAPTER 9

Beyond Convergence:
How Law Department Culture
Affects Corporate Legal Purchasing

Jeff Kindler, now GC at McDonald's, is a General Electric veteran. He was more or less there at the creation, in fact, and was very much a part of the process by which Ben Heineman designed the revolutionary in-house law firm. As Kindler now reflects, a lot of what GE has done, other companies have done as well, in terms of pursuing flatter organizational structures. Yet the differences between any of these flat departmental cultures can still be gargantuan, particularly with regard to retaining outside counsel. "The one thing I've learned in the last ten years since I've been an in-house lawyer—both from my own experiences in two different companies, and by virtue of all the communications and contacts I have with general counsel—is that every company to some degree is *sui generis.*"

For law firms, Kindler's remarks suggest that, after we analyze how in-house counsel have configured themselves, and what their general attitudes toward retention of outside counsel may be, it's still a crap shoot. From corporation to corporation, best practices vary regarding retention policies. What individual in-house lawyers may be looking for in prospective firms is similarly unpredictable.

As we've seen among the corporations that have pursued decisive convergence strategies, there are typically significant differences between what a law firm has to show and do to make the cut in one instance, and what it has to show and do in another. Some companies want flat discounts. Others want more complex risk-sharing arrangements. It stands to reason that law firms' myriad other marketing efforts—like taking in-house counsel to a ballgame, or formally auditing client satisfaction levels—are even more imponderable. Some buyers will say, "Yea. Sure, take us to a Knicks game." Others will say, "Nah. We can never be influenced in our buying decisions by anything like that."

Two additional factors complicate the picture:

First, both clients and law firms may be posturing when they speak publicly about how they buy and sell legal services, or they may have honestly deluded themselves into minimizing some factors that do indeed exert significant influence. General counsel habitually dote on high-level referral relationships, and on making ineffably subjective decisions. Their decisions, they say, are sublimely uninfluenced by client newsletters, online bidding services, or eighteen holes in Scottsdale. It's as if they want to emphasize to everyone that no bells or whistles ever affect their thinking. In terms of retention, there's an inner circle of candidates from which they, as in-house buyers, are simply too professional to easily depart.

On the other end of the spectrum, marketers of one sort or another will tell you that, in fact, GCs are as susceptible to good marketing as any other group of consumers. The Internet auctions are a case in point. These services, with names like eLawForum and iBidLaw, allow law firms to strut their stuff online, and give in-house users ample ways to cull more information and vet prospective firms, also online. But GCs often suppose themselves to already have the inside track on who's good for whatever they need. Or, they know what sources to call to find out. They'd be embarrassed to admit relying on a glorified chat room. Yet listen to the online providers and they naturally claim that what they're selling has ignited a veritable revolution that will continue to sweep through the corporate legal community.

Somehow, one guesses the truth is somewhere in between. In-house counsel are more reliant on law firm marketing than they might admit, but less so than the sundry ranks of marketing mavens, which include the Internet providers, have claimed.

Second, even sophisticated law firms don't always know who the buyers are. In case after case, the GC does not make retention decisions, but delegates those decisions to AGCs. In some ways, this delegation contributes to the confusion between how chief legal officers say their companies buy legal services, and how they actually do. Many of these Associate or Deputy GCs are younger and less committed to refined buyer/seller networks. They're more open to being influenced by, say, a client seminar. Or, because they're more technology-conscious than their elders, these up-and-coming corporate counsel fully expect to use online facilities to at least support their retention decisions.

For law firms, the downward delegation of retention authority signals a fundamental change that goes well beyond whether younger in-house lawyers like to go online. There's a more serious general question as well. Marketing seminar after marketing seminar features discussions of how GCs buy legal services. Telephone call after telephone call to the chief legal officer angles for sales opportunities. But it may all be a colossal waste of time if the wrong decision-makers are being discussed, or if the wrong in-house lawyers are getting the telephone calls.

In both instances, the best strategy for law firms is to know their buyers: To know why they're buying, what they're buying, and how they've bought in the past—as well as who does the buying. Knowledge of client business is irreducibly important in any selling situation, but not specific routine knowledge such as how to discharge Olin's firearms or whether Caterpillar is selling a lot of tractors in India these days. We must concentrate on a closer knowledge of the specific legal in-house make-up and, in particular, how departmental culture affects retention.

That, in turn, relates to how different companies view the legal function. As Jeff Kindler suggests, no two may be alike. Some companies like to litigate, others hate it. Some are relationship-driven. Some are open to press coverage of their cases. Others wouldn't dream of talking to a reporter about a pending lawsuit or, for that matter, any lawsuit. Some corporations instinctively look internally for the resources to solve their problems and achieve their goals rather than rely on outside providers such as law firms.

In some instances, law departments acquire their cultural identities from their clients. Lawyers working in-house for a litigation-happy CEO like Sumner Redstone at Viacom are going to have a very different practice than in-house counsel serving Japanese executives, who may still expect that apologies sufficiently redress public grievances. In other instances, law departments take on a cultural life of their own if an extremely autonomous or idiosyncratic GC is at the helm.

Kindler's company, for example, has a unique propensity, traceable to Ray Kroc, for having handshake relationships with suppliers. McDonald's doesn't use contracts and 99.9% of the time that works out just fine. Once in a while, there's a disaster, like the famous defeat of McDonald's in the Central Ice Cream case at the hands of trial lawyer Gerry Spence. Clearly, lawyers, inside or outside, must adjust to the company culture if they expect to do work for this company on a long-term basis.

"Culture is defined as what's really important to us," says Kathy Bryan, Director of Litigation Management at Motorola. "We're an engineering company, so the personalities of engineers come through in how we make decisions, or what we think is important when we discuss risk." That's number one. Number two is the multiplicity of businesses owned by Motorola and the fair degree of independence enjoyed by those companies. Both factors permeate how the law department does business on a day-to-day basis, and what it expects from outside counsel.

The underlying theme of this chapter is therefore departmental culture, and the knowledge that law firms with limited or no experience serving specific clients must gain if they are to develop and expand a relationship. We'll take a closer look at a few of the companies we've already visited in earlier chapters, along with other global purchasers. We'll pay some particular attention to McDonald's as one corporate culture that, in a less noisy way than DuPont, but with equally long-range implications, illustrates why law firms must redefine who they are and how they do business.

We'll also look at companies such as Sears that seem more instinctively friendly to law firms *qua* law firms, and we'll look at how this cultural genus affects the inside/outside sales dynamic. Finally, we'll discuss a much smaller company, Rheem Manufacturing, which is still big enough to face some of the same issues in hiring law firms as the multinationals, yet small enough to put the crucial partnering imperative into a very different perspective.

An "Acceptable Risk" Culture

Companies such as McDonald's present a conundrum for outside counsel. On the one hand, they are clearly interested in building up in-house counsel in order to handle as high a volume of non-litigation matters as possible. On the other hand, they are not beset by chronic bet-the-company lawsuits. So law firms must find a way to target what is really a middle-level caseload which, presumably, might be handled equally well by any number of qualified firms.

Differentiation strategies by the outside vendors won't really work because Jeff Kindler doesn't really care about the unique attributes of one law firm versus another. Prospects for new firms to acquire business at companies like McDonald's is further clouded because these clients have long-standing relationships with competitor firms.

One solution is to identify a major case exposing the company and pounce on it. Kindler mentions a lawsuit that McDonald's thought had the potential to be "very serious from a brand point of view." Kirkland & Ellis, a Chicago firm with a bankable reputation for handling critical matters, got the job— and a chance to demonstrate its expertise in such cases. Kindler says McDonald's now uses Kirkland "more and more for advice and counsel with respect to a whole category of cases of that nature. No particular case within that group is going to turn out to be the trial of the century, but one of them could [at least] become very serious." At the same time, Kirkland has positioned itself to handle more generic work, not substantively related to the original litigation, should it want to litigate those cases for McDonald's.

Kirkland's lawyer had won the opportunity in a beauty contest for a trial lawyer on another case that originally appeared to be more serious than it was. When that case seemed headed for trial, Kindler gave his in-house attorneys names of three or four prospective trial lawyers to interview. The fact that Kindler initiated the process by providing the names of these lawyers is worth noting. Kindler is one in-house manager who particularly emphasizes that retention decisions are fairly diffuse at his company, and that, as chief legal officer, he's not really the person to whom outside counsel ought to be marketing. Having said that, in this instance, it didn't hurt the prospective hires that they were well known to the GC.

The lawyers Kindler recommended were simply people he knew. He himself was a trial lawyer for twenty years. Especially for a case that merits the involvement of a major firm like Kirkland, it's still the GC's little black book that matters the most. The above example somewhat belies Kindler's own point, that the key retention responsibilities are downwardly delegated. At the same time, it supports Kindler's view that, at least for higher-level work, no shrewd marketing can replace the confidence that decades of observing lawyers in action can instill in a market-wise buyer.

When we spoke to Kindler, he had just received a call from a colleague at GE seeking advice on an outside lawyer he was using. Clearly, the GC's clout is decisive even as a third-party commentator or an indirect referral source. The Ben Heinemans of the world may claim they spend "infinitely" more time worrying about their own departments than they do about law firms, but even a sliver of any powerful GC's attention can lead to boom or bust for a law firm. And in-house counsel pride themselves on being "straight shooters" when they talk to each other. "If I call one of my fellow inside counsels, I know I'll get a very direct reference," says Kindler.

Here, too, the best marketing is to existing clients, not just as a way to expand existing business, but as a way to get new business via referrals. "That's true, by the way, in all business," comments Kindler (including the hamburger business).

Kindler is one example of a whole generation of in-house counsel that have concluded—to a point where it's practically an article of faith—that repetitive, non-litigation legal work will usually be handled more cost-efficiently in-house. In real estate, for example, the transaction costs steadily diminish as corporate counsel assume control. Not only is the learning curve for outside counsel eliminated, so too are the myriad small costs of doing business, such as visits to the client, talking through the issues, etc., that add up significantly from start to finish.

For non-litigators to sell to Kindler, they have to become so familiar with the work that they become the equivalent of inside lawyers. Such familiarity can only be based on their having done the work for the client as long as in-house counsel. Thus, the institutional relationships that companies like McDonald's have developed with certain law firms become all the more formidable for would-be competitors, since the alternative for the company isn't usually another law firm to handle the mature and repetitive legal tasks, but rather the inside staff. At the same time, Kindler points out that law firm billing rates go up every year and new associates must be brought up to speed. The inside route may thus be cheaper in any event, especially if, as inside salaries go up, staff can be redirected to handle a variety of other client matters as well.

It is in this context that the hourly rate for buyers such as Kindler becomes a real source of friction. "Outside counsel are diligent, they want to be efficient, they'll give you all kinds of reasons why they have an incentive to be efficient, and many of them are," says Kindler. But Kindler will "beat a path to the door" of any firm that can come up with an alternative value-based system that truly puts an incentive on efficiency.

Part of the problem, acknowledges Kindler, is that in-house counsel are risk-averse in terms of venturing new arrangements with outside counsel. The end results of premium billing, contingencies, or fixed fees are uncertain. There's a "Better the evils we know" approach by inside counsel. And outside counsel know it.

As long as McDonald's is less than optimistic about achieving viable alternative billing systems, its preference for in-house practice will remain very strong. "The reality is that inside lawyers have a much, much greater incentive to be fast because they're not being paid by the hour," says Kindler. "They've got a tremendous list of things that they've got to accomplish. They're working extremely hard, and the faster they get a project done, the faster the client is happy, and the faster they can move on to the next project. And they want to go home."

According to Kindler, in-house attorneys will also offer more value because they are better positioned to "compromise based on a prudent look at risk," which in turn means an additional efficiency the outside lawyers can't offer. The outside lawyer will take a deposition because there's a 15% chance it will lead to something the client needs, or will foreclose something that could hurt the client. It's an extra step the in-house buyer also expects the outside lawyer to take. It's not wheel-spinning; it's a professional obligation.

"I don't want [outside counsel] to think about whether or not the deposition is a waste of time," says Kindler. "But I want to be able to have the right to say, 'You know what? As the client, I'm going to make a judgment, I'm going to make a cost-benefit decision, and I'm going to take the risk that you're going to miss that 15% chance because I don't think it's worth your time doing it.' I get to make that decision [only] because I'm the client. The lawyers inside are constantly making tradeoffs on risk that allow them to save time and money that lawyers on the outside shouldn't be making."

The same dynamic is just as applicable to non-litigation work. As Kindler points out, any advice he asks for from outside counsel ought to occasion a thorough evaluation by the outside attorney. The lawyer may want to research it. The lawyer may even write an opinion letter or memorandum. The lawyer will, and should, pursue a 90% certainty that the advice is correct. "But it will cost me to get that 90% certainty," says Kindler. "I can call the inside counsel and say, 'Give me the answer, and I'll take 50% certainty.' I'm running a business and I've got to make decisions quickly, and I have to live with uncertainty. Business people are constantly required to make decisions based on such uncertainties, and on a lack of information. That's how they move forward."

Kindler originally joined GE from Washington, D.C.'s Williams & Connolly, a firm which practically defines litigation. "But I soon learned that the General Electric Company does not exist to practice law," says Kindler. "In fact, the purpose is to not practice law at all, to the extent we can legally avoid it."

After a while on the job, inside lawyers "get it." They recognize that their duty is to give the best possible answer they can, but also that the answer is more valuable at a 50% level of certainty today than a week from today at 90%. As John Liftin at Prudential puts it, "It's a tremendous disservice to any client to argue every point of a contract, regardless of its significance."

"Getting it" from a business rather than a legal standpoint is what the in-house marketing chore is all about. In-house lawyers have the time and opportunity to convince the client that they know their job is to move business forward rather than impose the delaying concerns that outside counsel are obligated to impose. It's much tougher for any law firm to present itself as similarly business-minded, except when the relationship is long-standing.

McDonald's is thus a prime example of how law department culture creates a possibly insurmountable hurdle for law firms in many situations. On the one hand, the culture determines that repetitive work is done more cost effectively in-house, except by firms that have institutionalized ties to the client. On the other hand, the law department is geared toward levels of acceptable risk that, as Kindler describes it, should not be assumed by outside counsel. This dynamic combination significantly narrows the opportunity for law firms to gain a first-time foothold with such corporate buyers. "When you live inside the corporation, you develop a sensitivity to the things that animate your decisions so much better than if you were on the outside," concludes Kindler.

Yet McDonald's has not stopped using outside counsel or entertaining the possibility of hiring unfamiliar firms. The fact that a GC like Kindler emphasizes the appeal of law firms that have specific expertise in a given area that is typically hard to come by inside is a powerful if implicit endorsement of the strategic marketing plans that are driving more and more law firms these days. "If the inside lawyer is looking for help or the answer to a relatively discrete question, involving a narrow set of legal issues that require a high degree of technical expertise, that lawyer [probably] won't find it internally," says Kindler.

We've seen in Chapter 7 how, as a counterbalance to its convergence strategy, Genentech went shopping around for numerous law firms, each of which could deliver just such focused expertise in one specific area. This strategy seems to be the key to getting a foot in the door at McDonald's as well. The fact that these two companies are so different, with such different legal needs and such different product lines, only further validates the wisdom of law firms' niche marketing strategies.

In a sense, niche marketing is an alternative to branding. As John Liftin at Prudential observes, the most effective brands are the ones that have been achieved by the great lockstep firms. The branding message for these firms is: "Every partner here is good." Such consistency defines lockstep cultures. At the opposite end of the spectrum are the firms built on lateral partners and mergers where, as Liftin observes, "the only thing the lawyers may share in common is a lease." For most non-lockstep firms, Liftin agrees that the best strategy must aim in the opposite direction by marketing—not every partner—but strong niche practices.

Interestingly, the cultural dynamic at a company like McDonald's offers somewhat of an exception to the common wisdom that understanding the client's business qualifies outside counsel above all other considerations. Of course, corporate legal buyers want to see outside counsel manifest some understanding. *Appreciation* of the client business is also decisive. Kindler, for one, is offended by lawyers who flippantly assume that neither he nor they are supposed to eat McDonald's hamburgers.

However, the dynamic at McDonald's puts the in-house counsel far ahead in the race on this score. As a qualifying consideration, "understanding the client's business" by definition favors in-house counsel when the work is parcelled out. Again, we need to be very careful to see through, or at least surmise, that there are profound exceptions to all common rhetoric about the inside/outside relationship. "If I need to know, does the ERISA law let me do this, yes or no, all I want is the answer," explains Kindler. The outside lawyer in that case doesn't need to know whether the client sells hamburgers or pajamas.

Yet Kindler also emphasizes that most interesting and difficult legal problems are not susceptible to technical black-and-white solutions. Inside or out, they usually involve judgment. To that extent, both the inside and outside counselors must still understand the business objectives underlying those more challenging legal issues. "To the business person, law is just a means to an end," comments Kindler. Here, too, the firms with institutional relationships with the client are in an advantageous position, since they're presumably immersed in the client's business cultures and in the objectives that evolve from and express that culture. And, allows Kindler, outside lawyers who steep themselves in the corporate culture do "absolutely" narrow the gap between themselves and in-house counsel. But "there's a talent to that, and a skill to it" that Kindler says lawyers are not typically trained to develop. These days, they talk about it all the time. Talking, quips Kindler, is at least the "first step."

Other law firms are moving beyond that first step, with business courses added to their associates' training regimens. Yet one wonders to what extent such training can ever narrow the gap between law firm counselors and the in-house counselors who live and work in the client culture. Much of this training derives mainly from law firms' desperation to please young lawyers and stem their rising, often exorbitant turnover rates. Also, a lot of nonlegal training is simply a review of fundamental business principles that won't necessarily increase anyone's ability to understand the particular business objectives driving a particular client. Associates might simply know a little about accounting before they arrive on Kindler's doorstep. But, for example, the brand name concerns that underscore the company's legal responses to its franchisees might still elude them completely. The outside lawyer is still counseling in a vacuum.

As an even more basic example, lawyers will always advise clients not to talk to the press during a lawsuit because it will jeopardize the case. The in-house attorney is better situated to understand why a Kindler might actually *want* to jeopardize a case if it means buttressing public opinion in the media. The price of silence, even with a courtroom victory, could mean a nosedive in stock value.

It is, perhaps, nearly impossible from a practical standpoint for a firm that has never worked with McDonald's to convince Kindler it can provide legal counseling based on an understanding of the business objectives of McDonald's. "I guess you just have to start with little cases and work your way up to big cases, because we are not going to turn over a matter of tremendous magnitude to somebody we don't know or haven't had some experience with," says Kindler.

WHO BUYS?

We've assumed that institutionalized client relationships better position law firms to compete with in-house counsel for standard, repetitive work. If nothing else, a time-tested understanding of the client's business culture is another major advantage enjoyed by firms that have such established and durable ties. However, the forces roiling and fortifying in-house culture threaten this assumption as well. In fact, the stronger the in-house staff gets, the more imperiled the institutional relationships may become, for a variety of reasons.

Kindler sums up what's probably the best of those reasons: "If I'm going to hold my inside lawyers accountable for the results of their matters, for the effectiveness of the legal services that they're delivering, I can't do that and at the same time dictate to them who they have to use." There may be high-profile, high-stakes cases where Kindler will at least participate in a conversation about who's getting hired. He'll want to be comfortable with that decision, but for the most part it's not his decision. If he gets a letter or a call from somebody who practices intellectual property law, he'll send it to the McDonald's intellectual property lawyers. Ditto securities or any other discipline.

Once again, Kindler is talking about the transfer of decision-making authority. Reporting to Kindler are a U.S. general counsel, an international GC, and a deputy GC with some corporate responsibilities. There's a matrix in which client responsibilities and functional responsibilities are intertwined. For example, the international GC is responsible for the legal work outside the United States, but the head intellectual property lawyer for the entire company also reports to him. The U.S. GC is responsible for the legal work in the U.S., but all the company's securities lawyers report to her. The deputy GC is responsible for certain clients in the Oak Brook corporate office, but he's also responsible for all antitrust, purchasing, and litigation. Within this global matrix, retention decisions can be made as far down as the middle levels in some offices.

The downward delegation of retention authority represents some opportunity for law firms that have never done a lot of work for McDonald's in the past. "A lot of lawyers from law firms—big shots, you know, high-ranking, powerful and prestigious people— have tried to cultivate me on the theory that, as the general counsel, I control the legal work and so, if they make me happy, they'll get the work," says Kindler. "I'm relatively young compared to some of these people. Some of these people are the kind of people that, if I were in their law firms, they probably wouldn't give me the time of day."

Kindler has in any event communicated to them that they're wasting their time. In the past, it was possible to forge an institutional relationship through the relationship the managing partner had with the CEO, never mind the GC. Now, by contrast, Kindler's present advice to law firms is instead to hook up their young go-getters with up-and-coming counterparts on the inside. Such advice would seem to apply exceptionally well to flat organizational cultures like GE, since such an in-house law firm features thirty-five-year-old lawyer/specialists practicing law like partners, and therefore also empowered to make retention decisions.

How would Kindler try to cultivate his own underlings if he were an outside lawyer? Newsletters and brochures don't cut it. And, social favors may be the worst approach. Kindler would love to have you take him to a basketball game and pay for the tickets. "But you ought to know, if you do that, and later on I'm thinking about sending you a case, I'll probably hesitate," he warns. "I'll be afraid that you tried to influence me by buying me basketball tickets."

Caterpillar is another powerful example of how and why the legal hiring function has moved down the chain of command. Like Kindler, Caterpillar's GC Rennie Atterbury holds his in-house staff responsible for law firms' performances. That being the case, the in-house staff ought to be exerting more authority at the front end.

Caterpillar's organizational structure and departmental culture further support this delegation strategy. As Atterbury describes it, Caterpillar is "dispersed but not decentralized." There are just over 100 lawyers, including two groups in Europe along with others in Asia, as well as the sizable staff at headquarters in Peoria. All lawyers make at least a dotted-line report to Atterbury. There's an approved list of outside counsel to which all inside attorneys refer. Atterbury may send recommendations downward, but practice section leaders submit final approval of the law firms retained. More often, Atterbury accepts recommendations that percolate upward rather than having a direct say himself.

If law firms want to represent Caterpillar in Europe, they should target Geneva, or Kiel in Germany. (On other continents, caseloads can be voluminous. Third-world countries, for instance, are often agricultural nations that import a lot of tractors.) In the U.S., firms would do well contacting Associate GCs. Atterbury feels even stronger about basketball games than Kindler; he just won't go to one with somebody from a law firm.

Caterpillar is not impressed by brand names or reputation. As Atterbury puts it, a Dunhill costs more than a ballpoint pen, but there really isn't much difference in what they do. The Dunhill may even be less serviceable for heavy-duty scriveners. At the same time, Cleary, Gottlieb, Steen & Hamilton—a member, to be sure, of the world's global law firm elite—is Caterpillar's primary firm in Europe. But Cleary didn't become that primary firm because of its brand name or even its overall reputation. Instead, Atterbury praises Cleary because it has local practices in the company's local jurisdictions to a much greater extent than do other firms. Those other firms may have a geographic presence there, but they don't bring the same area expertise to the table. The expertise is the lure, not the color of Cleary's shoes.

If there's one differentiating cultural characteristic at Caterpillar that best illustrates how and why the company spreads out the hiring function, it's the company's strong tendency to help law firms litigate, not just manage them. Every firm is expected to participate in a biannual course at Caterpillar on how the company litigates. Every law firm can also expect Caterpillar to "rewrite a brief at the drop of a hat," as Atterbury puts it. The outside lawyers go to court, but the inside litigation attorneys are all trial lawyers. Any firm that wants to do business with the company ought to understand that that means there's going to be close partnering on every important case.

It is therefore instructive that one of the nation's most prominent litigation firms—Washington, D.C.'s Howrey Simon Arnold & White —is Caterpillar's favored law firm in litigation and has been for many years. The lesson is that the best aren't arrogant. The best are open to suggestions from the client even in areas like brief writing where they feel utterly confident and expert.

According to Atterbury, the Howrey people are equally assiduous in treating the lower-level lawyers and staff well. "The first step in hiring a law firm is to start off liking its people," Atterbury observes. Even in the firm's lean days—when the disappearance of antitrust work during the Reagan years threatened its very existence—Howrey enjoyed a steady flow of business from Caterpillar.

Howrey handles discovery efficiently and quickly, and, says Atterbury, "can't wait to get to a courthouse." The firm's branding tagline, "In Court Every Day," is thoroughly justified, according to Atterbury. On the other side of the coin, Caterpillar's tagline could be, "We fire law firms midway through a case," says Atterbury. "Why not?"

In-house staff meets once a month, and Atterbury holds section leaders responsible for all cost overruns. If they're over budget at any point, they'd better be able to explain why. Rates aren't especially important, but total costs are. Caterpillar doesn't pay premiums. "I'm not paying firms to lose," quips Atterbury.

Caterpillar does experiment with contingency fees, however. These fee arrangements are convenient ways to handle the in-between cases. The company doesn't want to lose these cases, or settle them, but neither does it want to invest significant time or money. A 30% or 40% piece of the likely reward exposure for outside counsel is a practicable alternative.

Chicago's Winston & Strawn, and specifically partner Columbus (Chris) Gangemi, have handled Caterpillar's rather serious union problems over the years even though the firm is not the company's primary employment/labor supplier. Caterpillar relies on Seyfarth Shaw in Chicago for Title VII cases, benefits, etc. As Atterbury observes, Seyfarth "knows better" than to try to wrest the collective bargaining work away from Winston, which has a solid relationship with Caterpillar based on Gangemi's past performance. In such situations, it's simply bad marketing for another firm to try and intrude.

Caterpillar avoids New York firms because they're just too expensive. "Who in New York is better than Howrey?" asks Atterbury. The company does most of its major transactions in-house, although it has used some M&A powerhouses, including U.K. giant Slaughter & May, for billion-dollar deals. However, Caterpillar was impressed by one New York firm, Simpson Thacher & Bartlett, which it observed on the other side of the table in one deal. Atterbury comments that Simpson did "a commercial deal in a commercial way."

Once again, a client was impressed because lawyers acted less like lawyers and more like businesspeople.

LAW FIRMS VERSUS LAWYERS

For law firms that take full measure of clients' departmental culture, the best marketing may have little to do with any of the conventional marketing approaches. As Kindler figures it, one effective way he's seen law firms get business from McDonald's is by offering a test run. Outside counsel will say, "Look, give me a case, any case, I don't care how small it is, I don't care how inconsequential you think it is, I'll do it for you at a cut rate." In fact, the more inconsequential the case, the better, since the client will obviously feel more comfortable taking the flier. The slip-and-falls get your toe in the door, if not your foot, and that's better than nothing. Kindler has seen firms handle trivial cases so well "that [our] people wanted to send them work" right away.

In beauty contests, the best approach Kindler has seen law firms take is to actually start talking about the case. Commitments to periodic management reviews, including budget reviews, also help "immensely." But prior research impresses him most, along with some considered free advice at the beginning: "We've read the complaint in this lawsuit and these are the things I think you should do immediately. We need to get our hands around these records, we need to address this issue, we need to have this kind of witness."

McDonald's has certainly hired firms that took this tack. As Kindler advises,

> "When you're trying to sell something to somebody, the question in your mind ought to be, 'What's his problem and how can I help him solve it?' The process should start with the very first meeting, beauty contest or no beauty contest. Some firms worry about giving themselves away for nothing. Others know that samplers sell the loaf."

Kindler dismisses much of the rest of the current marketing wisdom, especially branding. "I believe in brand names for lawyers, not for law firms," he says. "Fred Bartlit is a brand name. Dan Webb is a brand name." A Kirkland & Ellis may have an image—heavyweight litigators, democratic culture, etc.—but not a "brand" in the sense that there's anything attached to the image that would persuade Kindler to buy its services.

"What do I do, call Kirkland and Ellis, and say, 'Hey Mr. Kirkland, send me a lawyer'?"

In contrast, Kindler would hire Dan Webb "wherever he is." The caveat is that Webb would probably never leave his firm (Winston & Strawn) to join an organization that doesn't have the resources needed to support the mega-cases in which he specializes. Kindler therefore doesn't have to think beyond hiring Webb because he can have implicit faith that Webb won't land some place where he won't be able to do the kind of work that Kindler needs doing.

Yet size isn't the real issue either. Bartlit left Kirkland to form his own much smaller firm, Bartlit Beck Herman Palenchar

& Scott in Chicago, and he has been wildly successful handling very much the same kinds of cases he took on at Kirkland. In fact, even with a Dan Webb, Kindler says he'd rather "unbundle" the partner from the "associate and paralegal mouths he's feeding."

"If Dan Webb is worth $1,000 an hour to me, I'd rather pay him $1,000 an hour and then go hire the associates and paralegals, and the other people that I need, at cheaper rates from someplace else," says Kindler. As it is, he's paying Webb $500 per hour plus a range of other, less value-based timekeeper rates. This is how nearly all the big firms operate. In order to get the partners they want, in-house counsel pay inflated costs further down the line, and that does the profession no real good. When you buy an associate as part of a package, says Kindler, you may not be getting value at all.

The whole point of Bartlit's smaller firm strategy is that the customers pay for what they see. "I want to buy what I want to buy," says Kindler, "because all this other stuff that you're selling along with it is stuff I might be able to get for less." The Dan Webbs needn't worry, adds Kindler. They're probably worth $1,000 an hour, and corporations will likely pay it.

Of course, Kindler is inveighing against the entire organizational structure of leveraged professional services—and that seems a quixotic tilt indeed. For corporate buyers, there's another abiding alloy in the big firm propaganda that makes the Fred Bartlits, and the boutiques and niche practices of one sort or another, look attractive by comparison. As Kathy Bryan at Motorola points out, the inescapable and obvious fact with services organizations of great size is that they have to be uneven *somewhere*. Kindler readily agrees: Don't pitch the fact that the firm has a growing office in Los Angeles or Chicago or Miami. Pitch the partners who happen to be there. Pitch the people.

Again, though, every such bit of common wisdom gets qualified if you dig deep enough. On the one hand, even at dissimilar corporate cultures such as Motorola and McDonald's (only one of which has converged), the in-house managers tend to de-emphasize size and resource immensity as effective law firm selling points in favor of more focus on quality practice and people. On the other hand, as discussed in Chapter 7, Motorola did hire regional firms for its high-volume commodity work as well as firms for its "Tier One" business. Listening to Bryan, it certainly does seem as if sheer quantity, with an assumption of adequate quality, were a determinative factor.

For example, Motorola selected the Florida-based behemoth Holland & Knight for both its northeast and southeast work. Holland & Knight is huge in the southeast and growing in the northeast (where, among other moves, it merged with a fairly substantial mid-sized Boston firm). For the Tier Two and Tier Three matters, "where quality isn't as much of an issue," Bryan views the law firm expansions, and the mergers, as a definite benefit simply because more resources can be brought to bear.

"I haven't worried so much about making sure that the quality is at a tremendous level," says Bryan. "I'm more interested in quantity and that the [outside lawyers] are responsive, and that the key people who are working with us develop expertise and understanding of Motorola."

For Sean Johnston at Genentech, quantity is similarly determinative, especially when, as with many convergence strategies, it's the commoditized work that goes outside. The company has farmed out its lesser patent matters in order *not* to spend top-partner rates getting it done. "I don't care if these big firms are uneven, or if there are people there doing sloppy work, as long as it's not *my* work they're doing sloppily," says Johnston.

Johnston goes even further in saying that, for higher-level, non-commodity work, Genentech would not follow strong lead partners to new law firms if they weren't taking all or a substantial part of their teams along. Such indeed was the case in the mid-1990s when patent litigator John Kidd joined what was then New York's Rogers & Wells. Genentech's business was portable because Kidd didn't move alone.

The fact that GCs and other in-house managers tend to emphasize girth in a way that the Jeffrey Kindlers certainly do not suggests that today's mega-growth is, in many instances, a client-friendly phenomenon. As corporate clients globalize, they have multi-jurisdictional needs on both the commodity side and the high end. Whichever kind of work a law firm wants, wholesale growth, and often a merger, may be the only way to get there.

Indeed, we're at a point in the consolidation of the legal market where many law firms no longer ask their clients what they think of their merging with another firm, assuming there are no conflicts precluding the ongoing representation. Whatever further growth Holland & Knight embarks on, for example, Bryan will still be calling the partners in the offices where the Motorola relationship started, and they'll still be putting the client in touch with lawyers at the practice team level. Those teams will continue to be fairly small. In other words, amid unprecedented global and domestic reconfiguration, it's business as usual.

There's an assumption that most firms are "in play" these days, so they just go ahead and do it. Rogers & Wells, for example, didn't tell Steven Juelsgaard or Sean Johnston at client company Genentech about its historic transatlantic merger with U.K. giant Clifford Chance until it was practically a done deal. All Johnston says he really cared about anyway was that the team handling his work would not be fragmented as a result.

Johnston's response was also a most instructive example of how buyers should behave when their vendors restructure. He asked the law firm what the associates were thinking about the merger, and if there was any fear in their ranks that they'd be "redundant" afterward. He visited with the lawyers to get his own sense of how they were feeling, and to suggest to them that the Genentech work ahead was going to be both plentiful and interesting. If nothing else, the client should help make its firms' mergers work for the client's own interests.

Meantime, mergers have expanded inside/outside relationships that are likely to have a tangible impact on the culture not only of the firms themselves, but of the buyers' corporate law departments as well. It's altogether extraordinary, really, to watch a firm like Clifford Chance suddenly expand its part in Prudential's sexiest legal work. John Liftin—a former Rogers & Wells partner who has used that firm since going in-house—confirms that Clifford Chance will play a major role helping Prudential acquire companies throughout the world. It's a happy dovetailing, where one party to a law firm merger has a relationship with the client, and the other one has the resources with which to exploit the relationship.

"If one of our firms is acquired by another, that's of interest," says Caterpillar's Atterbury. But "it's also of interest if one of our firms suddenly has expanded capacity." When a securities lawyer that Caterpillar relied on died, Howrey's acquisition of a securities team in Los Angeles led directly to new work for the firm. Indeed, listening to GCs like Atterbury, it's pretty obvious why so many law firms are just itching to merge with as many other viable firms as they can drag to the altar.

FOREIGN AFFAIRS

We've seen how in-house predilections at McDonald's tend to favor more work going in-house and staying there. Although it's just a little tougher for new law firms to get inside the door at such companies, there is one salient fact about McDonald's that could promise more opportunity: Only Coca-Cola goes into new countries faster or more often than McDonald's. As such, there are far-flung jurisdictions where local counsel and/or big firms with good lawyers in those jurisdictions can start doing business with this client.

It's also relevant that even companies that, unlike McDonald's, go through extensive convergence often revert in the opposite direction overseas. Kathy Bryan, for example, reports that every single one of Motorola's forty or so in-house attorneys overseas wanted to be using more law firms, not fewer. They were excepted from the convergence process and the company did indeed increase its number of law firms abroad even as it consolidated domestically. Corporations' foreign retention practices are a separate and, usually, more advantageous situation for law firms. The problem emphasized by in-house managers with respect to their foreign legal needs is less often controlling outside costs and more often finding local counsel they can trust.

Toward that end, there's an interesting symbiosis between Coca-Cola and McDonald's. They share overseas referrals and monitor each other's experiences, particularly in the less-developed nations. In the more advanced nations, with strong legal infrastructures and an existing bar, McDonald's interviews local attorneys by interviewing and checking references, much like they'd hire a law firm stateside. McDonald's might also call Baker & McKenzie, which has offices in every part of the world, and which has correspondent lawyers just about everyplace else as well. It's a unique advantage of size when corporate clients use you as a legal resource even if they might not be using you as a legal advisor. This method is not Kindler's first choice, however, since he always prefers that McDonald's find and establish its own relationships.

The downward delegation of responsibility for hiring outside counsel is perhaps even more pronounced in these foreign jurisdictions, since Kindler and other GCs have less knowledge of who's good and who's not over there. The autonomy of overseas legal managers for McDonald's—in fact, all its overseas managers—is representative of how the company generally does business internationally. It's a point Kindler figures ought not to be lost on law firms trying to sell legal services to the company outside the U.S.

In France, for example, the company tries to present itself to the French people as a French company. Indeed, 90% of food sold by McDonald's in France is prepared there. The company's local managing director has a general counsel who was interviewed by Kindler, but her direct-line report is to her client. She's dotted line to the GC for Europe.

"We don't even know about 99% of the decisions that she makes with regard to hiring outside counsel," says Kindler. "What value is there for somebody sitting in Oak Brook to tell a lawyer in France what French lawyers to use? That's a waste of everybody's time and energy."

For all the autonomy, it would still seem that McDonald's global expansion does not change the company's cultural predisposition favoring in-house counsel. China, a particularly good example of how carefully McDonald's hires overseas, is a case in point of how difficult it can be for law firms to compete with what in-house staffs provide, even in so foreign a legal environment. There are perhaps 400 McDonald's restaurants in China. Every U.S. company doing business there wants English-speaking attorneys close by, with English common law expertise. They also want U.S. trade lawyers who are Chinese-speaking and understand the Chinese legal system. They are few and far between indeed.

McDonald's has two such in-house practitioners in China, and it's Kindler's sense that this on-the-ground presence is especially crucial simply because China's professional culture is still evolving. It is not one country, as he points out; it's more like thirty. Shanghai is different from Guangzhou, which is different from Beijing. "You can't possibly function in the legal environment there with, say, [just] Freshfields in Hong Kong," says Kindler. As of this writing, foreign law firms are also subject to a one-office rule in China. There's not enough mileage in that for a company like McDonald's which does business everywhere in the country. The in-house component is that much more crucial as a result.

The fact that so global a corporation would still place such an emphasis on in-house capabilities, even in a frontier legal culture like China's, seems especially portentous for law firms. Indeed, the in-house culture at McDonald's, at least since Kindler's arrival from GE, is thus that much more interesting because it suggests how marginal law firms can be, even in a legal boom market. The fact that Kindler is not personally confrontational toward outside counsel—in the way pioneers like Robert Banks at Xerox used to be in the mid-1980s, or many GCs continue to be in their cost-monitoring and guideline-setting practices—adds impact to his views. Kindler has never sought the role of public gadfly. Yet in-house cultures like that at McDonald's quietly suggest the need for law firms to redefine what they think they can offer global corporations.

It may be more than mere posturing when Kindler says that he just doesn't care about law firms one way or another. "I have no stake in law firms, neither in how they're structured, nor in their institutional survival."

Law firms are probably right in believing that the multidisciplinary practices ("MDPs") have impressed corporate law departments as a step forward in client service. This is an especially pertinent issue overseas where the MDPs are allowed to practice law and can compete directly with law firms. Beyond that, the MDPs appeal to in-house counsel because they feature more business-like thinking, and thus appeal to corporate buyers for very much the same reason their own in-house departments do.

The problem is that most law firms still see the MDPs as a threat rather than an opportunity. When Kindler joined a panel discussing the MDPs, he "was almost embarrassed for my profession. . . . The lawyers were so threatened by this, and so worried about that. They threw around all this rhetoric about professionalism and ethics and integrity, and how that's all going to be ruined if the accounting firms get to have lawyers. Well, why should I care if a lawyer's in an accounting firm or not? They kept saying, 'we want to protect you.' I kept saying, 'let me protect me. Don't patronize me.'"

AUDIT INITIATIVES

The conventional law firm is not totally without viable marketing tools when dealing with a tough customer like McDonald's (with, again, the caveat that, in the world of law firms and their clients, some customers like to sound a little tougher than they actually are). Doing slip-and-falls at a cut rate may be the one tactic Kindler can definitely recommend to firms that have never been hired in the past by McDonald's. But for firms that have gotten in the door, marketing techniques like formal client audits are generally commended. In these audits, firms formally solicit feedback, often via neutral outside consultants, on the quality of their own performances, providing an opportunity to improve a faltering relationship or, in some instances, unearth possibilities for new work from the client as well.

Several firms have formalized these "how-are-we-doing?" initiatives with McDonald's. "I think it's a pretty good idea if they really listen, and if they really want candid responses," says Kindler.

Genentech's Sean Johnston and Caterpillar's Rennie Atterbury represent polar opposites of how in-house attorneys view this brand of legal marketing. "Do law firms really do this?" exclaims Johnston. He's only been "audited" once, and that was by a managing partner who'd just learned that Genentech was firing his firm. Other than that, auditing is a foreign concept to Johnston, who says he'd be extremely receptive to such an overture. Johnston's reaction confirms the wisdom of the marketing pundits who urge this kind of client contact on law firms. It also explains their exasperation that counsel at a major company like Genentech not only haven't been approached for these interrogatories, but aren't even aware that auditing has become established practice in some circles.

From another perspective, Atterbury suspects these audits are analgesics for failed management. "Why should law firms hire people to do *my* job?" he asks.

There's a point at which Johnston's incredulity and Atterbury's skepticism intersect. Both their companies have review processes in place that would seem to mitigate the need for client audits. The issue can be refocused in the same way as the convergence question. If sound management procedures are in place, there's no need to separately tell outside counsel "how they're doing," just as there's no need to re-engineer the number and types of law firms on the retention list.

At Genentech, for example, all litigation firms are subject to monthly reviews. Although the company doesn't exactly rate-shop, "We do [at least] remind law firms when their rates are higher than other firms for the same work," says Johnston. Such rate-consciousness is constant for a company like Genentech that ships out so much commodity work (and demands a 10% discount just to start negotiating).

Furthermore, as rates go down, hours might be going up. It's the proverbial bubble in the carpet. That being the case, Genentech minds the store to such an extent that the company doesn't have to fire law firms because of cost overrides. With monthly rather than quarterly reviews, costs do not get out of hand, and the inside/outside collaboration stays in check. The reviews also provide effective, positive reinforcement for outside counsel when they know they're in the same ballpark with the client, adds Johnston.

One might well ask if client audits are redundant, Johnston's enthusiasm notwithstanding. At Caterpillar, Atterbury expresses the strongest negative reaction to formal or informal check-ups that we've heard. The cultural impetus driving his reaction: A pronounced pride in in-house management such that there's no need for additional layers of oversight. The closest that Atterbury gets to a client audit is an occasional friendly reminder to a managing partner, perhaps during a round of golf, that "you can be replaced."

For law firms that do want to pursue formal client audits of one sort or another, the next question is how to do undertake them. Marketers debate over who should conduct audits. Some believe that managing partners or other partners not directly involved with the client can best get the kind of feedback that will be most directly relevant to the firm. They know the firm, how it operates, where its weaknesses are, and how client feedback can be most effectively processed. However, such an approach can lead to internal political problems. Also, many clients are more reluctant to be totally candid with members of the firm they're critiquing. According to this view, third-party auditors are most suitable.

Then there are the many companies that expect law firms to formally designate "relationship partners" to communicate regularly about the ongoing representation and address the problems that arise. Sears is an example. (At Sears, there's also an in-house engagement manager for each law firm the company is using to any appreciable extent.) This relationship partner isn't necessarily directly involved in Sears work. Los Angeles-based Latham & Watkins, for example, does much corporate and transactional work for Sears, but the relationship partner is a litigator.

These relationship partners are key for Sears. The company hasn't often followed partners to different firms when they move laterally. Yet one example cited by Deputy GC Steven Cook was a relationship partner who had the rather attractive habit of providing answers to the client's questions within about fifteen minutes. He moved from one good enough law firm to another good enough law firm, and Sears followed him there simply because the company valued his alacrity.

WHAT ELSE WORKS?

Caterpillar notwithstanding, the formal client audits seem to impress most folks on both ends of the inside/outside feeding chain as a meritorious way to bolster client service and generate new business. Generally, though, there's a fascinating tug of war between marketing consultants, who prod their law firm clients toward more aggressive marketing, and the prospective buyers of legal services, who greet or feign to greet those aggressive efforts with a yawn. The poor law firm is caught in the middle, between vendors with something to sell them and their own clients who won't always admit to what really influences their retention decisions.

In-house counsel are not loath to praise law firm marketing when it does them a real service. The client audits are one example; CLE-type seminars for clients and potential clients are another. In contrast, it's harder to gauge the effect of a branding effort on in-house lawyers; there may indeed be an impact, yet it's a subliminal one. The buyers only pay conscious attention to marketing that is *immediately* useful to them. They're less aware of being affected by an advertisement here or a directory listing (or online auction) there.

Again, too, the client's business culture comes into play. Interestingly, client size is a definite factor. Mid-level businesses are happy to see their law firms advertise in the local newspaper. It increases their sense of connection to the firm, i.e., that even though they're all lawyers, they're still a part of the human race, enough so that they're not ashamed to play the same commercial games that we, their real estate or manufacturing or retail clients, must also play. That does not translate, culturally, to the corridors of corporate power. Jeffrey Kindler would not, presumably, feel comfortable with law firms who sell their services like his boss sells hamburgers.

"I'm trying to think what marketing effort I've paid any attention to at all," admits Kathy Bryan at Motorola. "I don't go to many ABA meetings, for example. The meetings I go to tend to be exclusively for in-house lawyers, so there's not a lot of opportunity for outside lawyers to pitch us there. Brochures—I get them; I file them away if they're in an area or a location that I might be interested in, but other than that I don't pay them any attention." The opinions of other in-house counsel matter a lot, naturally, as do references. Bryan cites one instance when she let a law firm in the door for the first time because of a call from a third party.

Sears offers an instructive contrast to companies like McDonald's as well as like DuPont. The contrast to McDonald's becomes apparent when, talking to Deputy GCs Bobbie McGee Gregg and Steve Cook, we hear a greater receptivity to law firms as collective enterprises, not just as places where star lawyers happen to work. This is not to say that Sears, a sophisticated buyer of legal services, is beguiled by institutional reputations, or less sensitive to the quality of individual practitioners. Firms have certainly been fired by Sears, confirms Gregg. They weren't "listening" to the client, she adds, and were likely taking the relationship for granted.

What is palpable, however, is Sears' tendency to talk about *whole* firms and what they can offer *as* firms. As a matter of departmental culture, one might indeed divide the world into corporate buyers who have a keen interest in the organizational development of major law firms and those who, like Jeff Kindler, aver not to.

The contrast to DuPont is also significant in that Sears has also converged, and rather dramatically, from over 700 firms to under 100. But the motivation was not to begin controlling an out-of-control situation or to hold law firms' feet to the proverbial fire. Gregg, who oversees litigation and departmental management at Sears (as Cook does for corporate), does not put a dollar value on the convergence. She talks, rather, about a general sense at Sears that the company is now getting more value and more efficiency from its legal vendors as a result of the convergence.

As Cook describes it, Sears' department is organized both around business lines and subject matter expertise. Along with a range of practice sections, which report to Gregg and Cook, Sears has GCs for its various businesses. These GCs also manage teams of generalists assigned to those businesses. This is a fairly new evolution at Sears, occurring in early 2000. In contrast to flatter specialist models like GE and other organizations, the Sears business-based configuration is of obvious import to law firms, since the management of outside lawyers is very much a key function of such in-house generalists.

Sears' in-house strategy of assigning more lawyers to the business units was intended to create a tighter partnership between the business managers and their lawyers. It certainly expresses a corporate culture where there are significant differences among the businesses. Someone knowledgeable in the credit business won't necessarily know much about retail. Similar diversity exists at GE, and the two are alike in that each GE company has its own GC. However, the emphasis on specialization that defines GE's culture is very different than the way in which Sears' seventy-five or so inside attorneys (excluding collections) are expected to operate.

Work from the Sears business units flows directly to the lawyers assigned to those businesses as well as directly to practice sections not assigned to a business. The system requires well-structured communications between the generalists and the subject matter practitioners. Some matters require special expertise. All litigation, for example, is centralized and assigned to Gregg; like most in-house departments discussed above, Sears' in-house department does not litigate.

Both Gregg and Cook report to Sears' GC, Anastasia Kelly. Within Gregg's litigation section there are three practice groups: general (mainly tort) litigation, complex litigation, and employment. All commercial and consumer litigation is subsumed under "complex" litigation. The employment matters under Gregg's wing are handled by the employment practice group which, in turn, also handles non-litigation employment matters. In the last few years, Sears has created a new matter report that is distributed daily to all in-house lawyers to facilitate intake and proper assignment. If, for instance, an employment matter arises at a business unit, the employment litigators see it immediately, without having to wait for the generalist at the business unit to call them about it. The opposite is true as well: A matter that comes to the intellectual property team, for instance, is immediately visible to the affected business unit.

Retention decisions at Sears are also diffuse, although the top managers seem to play a more direct role than the GC does at McDonald's. The GCs and deputy GCs help vet each firm that makes it to the approved list. Beyond that, the decision to send a particular matter to a particular law firm may be made by a practice group head alone or in consultation with either Gregg or

Cook, or with additional consultation with Kelly, depending on the nature of the matter. At the business units, vice-presidential level managers, including non-lawyers, sign off on the retention unless it's a routine matter. In general, retention decisions are thus made at levels both below Gregg and Cook and above them.

There are about fifty to seventy-five law firms on Sears' approved list; the number is fluid, and in some cases firms are used only for very specific matters. But the fluidity of the list is itself significant. At DuPont, the approved list may change if convergence survivors don't perform up to expectations but, until that happens, the firms are very much identifiable as DuPont's preferred providers. At Sears, things aren't quite written in stone.

Sears' more open posture toward law firms as institutions, versus a partner here or a practice group there, is evident in the very encouraging attitude Gregg and Cook have about cross-selling. Talk to the marketing consultants, and cross-selling—whereby outside counsel who is handling, say, IP for a company sets up a business development opportunity with that client for one of his or her litigation or M&A partners—is usually treated like a sacred cow. Cross-selling is a be-all and end-all both because it generates new business for the firm and because it's such a healthy index of the cooperation and support that exist among partners as they market their law firm.

Yet there are dissenting voices. Prestigious consultant David Maister has made the point that cross-selling is really useful mainly to the seller. It may even disserve the buyer if a referral to another firm would result in a better match. As such, for thinkers like Maister, cross-selling often fails the litmus test of all good marketing. That test is: Does it give the client something the client needs, like the client audits discussed above or the hints about case management that Kindler loves to hear? Some in-house managers seem to agree with Maister. At Prudential, John Liftin is acutely aware that cross-selling is a self-serving process. "Sure, I'll listen to a partner cross-sell his firm, if he doesn't mind the risk of burning a little credibility with me," quips Liftin. "It's just hard to say no when they ask to have the conversation."

In contrast, Gregg and Cook welcome the conversation. Again, this may bespeak a more generous attitude toward law firms as total institutions, i.e., "When we hire you, we're open to all that you, as a law firm, may have to offer." This approach differs significantly from that of Kindler, who only wants to pay hourly rates for a single practitioner, not for his or her associates or paralegals or the intermittent contributions of other partners from other practice areas.

Gregg mentions O'Melveny & Myers as a major law firm that never had a particularly solid relationship with Sears. But O'Melveny lawyers who'd been doing a few things for the company found opportunity to cross-sell sophisticated employment work, a complex IP matter, and even a role for the firm in Sears' strategic partnership with AOL. At the very least, cross-selling by lawyers who've done good work for the company gets their partners a quick trip to the short list in almost any area where the seller has depth. From Sears' perspective, cross-selling is an informational asset, if nothing else.

As Gregg sees it, a further justification of large-scale convergence is that it allows law firms to cross-sell. Even firms that were already working for Sears were able, in some instances, to expand their relationship by marketing, say, their tax practices even as they were interviewing to continue to do the company's real estate or IP work. Neither Gregg nor Cook encountered any of the resistance or hostility from outside counsel that Daniel Mahoney reported during the DuPont convergence. One reason is that more than five years elapsed since DuPont's convergence, and expectations and attitudes were now different on both sides of the fence. It no longer comes as a shock for lawyers to hear that they have to interview to survive with established clients.

Gregg believes more firms are seeing the opportunities inherent in a convergence process, and that cross-selling is one of the biggest. Convergence takes the discomfort out of cross-selling.

Law firms no longer have to grope for an excuse or "burn credibility" in the search for a cross-selling opportunity. Quite the contrary, it's the client who's created the pretext by insisting on the beauty contest. The legal profession may indeed be truly "beyond convergence" in the sense that the convergence process itself is no longer a trauma for marketers, but rather an ongoing dialogue which allows law firm business developers to adjust their services to corporate needs and corporate cultures.

Sears is also a company that seems more open to conventional marketing tools, including newsletters and substantive client advisories, if not brochures. Again, free legal information provided by law firms is naturally valued more than most other marketing. It's especially noteworthy how enthusiastically client seminars are commended even by in-house buyers who hold the most jaundiced views of law firm marketing in general.

It is also noteworthy how seminars or other informational resources affect major decisions by in-house buyers. For example, in the early 1990s Genentech hired Covington & Burling to represent the company in Europe, in part because Covington had an office in London, in part because Covington is one of the only U.S. firms in Europe that has a strong food and drug practice. But, as GC Stephen Juelsgaard recalls, Covington's seminars also had a decisive effect on the company's decision to retain the firm for all its work in Europe.

These seminars weren't simply icing on the cake. They were an integral part of the sale. Genentech has since retrenched and no longer requires legal services in Europe. Yet a decade later, Juelsgaard is still impressed by how well Covington developed his business. (In contrast to its U.S. strategy, Genentech was seeking a full-service preferred provider in Europe. As we suggested above, Juelsgaard figures that's the "only way" to efficiently handle matters overseas.)

Cook and Gregg cite a number of seminar programs that, at the very least, have allowed for substantive contacts between

Sears and law firms smart enough to base their marketing on informational client service. This marketing approach cuts across departmental cultures. Everybody loves free advice.

At one program in Chicago conducted by New York's Wachtell, Lipton, Rosen & Katz, senior partner and M&A legend Martin Lipton participated, along with a few of his top lawyers, talking about the transactional environment of the early twenty-first century. This program was attractive not only because of the prestige of the attorneys involved, but because the seminar was also interactive, a major plus as far as Cook is concerned. It was a two- to-three-hour program, which was also a plus, according to Cook, because it didn't include the "fluff" that comes with some of the all-day events that other firms conduct. Wachtell may only do the seminar once a year, or irregularly, which, adds Gregg, means it can really focus on something timely. She much prefers this approach to monthly breakfasts where lawyers are "trying to come up with a topic and there may not be a topic."

Cook says Sears "may use Wachtell for something, or it may not," but it is still extremely difficult for a firm with which Gregg or Cook is unfamiliar to get on the company's legal radar screen. In this respect, Sears is no different from the other companies interviewed. There must be some kind of prior relationship somewhere. Not one GC has a potent recipe for successful cold calling—except, again, that one trump card all firms have is their niche marketing specific expertise a prospective client needs but can't get from its current firms. Here, says Cook, his attention may be drawn not just to demonstrable past successes in the narrow area, but also to the notoriety a firm receives from commenting in a pertinent newspaper or magazine article.

The overall contrast in attitude toward law firms as a whole reflects a cultural difference between Sears and McDonald's, which, in turn, has a lot to do with work volume and diversity. "Given our volume of work, it isn't just one or two partners that we're going to be working with," says Gregg. "It's going to be a host of people in the law firm, [including] paralegals, associates, and partners on different matters. It's great that Dan Webb is at Winston & Strawn, but if Dan Webb's not going to be my guy, I need to know who else will be working for me."

For Gregg, "depth" is therefore important, and "depth" means broad subject matter and expertise. Does the firm have employment lawyers? Does it have risk expertise? Is there OSHA expertise? Discrimination and Title VII expertise? If so, how much? Gregg doesn't want the one great lawyer. She looks for a range of people.

On the transactional side, the firm itself is important because, as Cook explains, the institutional culture is crucial. The company will consider recognized experts, different levels of training from firm to firm, and different client service ethics that are either inculcated firm-wide or not. "There are great people at all these firms," says Cook. But what else have they got?

During beauty contests, Sears will thus want prospective firms to talk about the individual team members who will be working on their matters. As Gregg acknowledges, there's no real way for firms to demonstrate a propensity for partnering or for real client service, although committing to stipulated periodic management reviews is, again, helpful. Beyond that, Sears wants to know who those associates or even paralegals are and why they're good enough to be on the team.

Not surprisingly, Gregg and Cook are more keenly interested in how law firms are faring in their organizational development than a buyer like Kindler. Today's mergers are very significant for them as a measure of the kind of client service they're likely to get. A case in point was the 1999 merger of Chicago's Rudnick & Wolfe and Baltimore's Piper & Marbury to form Piper Marbury Rudnick Wolfe. Rudnick was an important supplier to Sears. Now Gregg says how impressed the company has been with the Piper lawyers brought on to help handle its work.

The law firm claim that mergers are client-driven may be empty rhetoric in some cases, but not this time. If the Clifford Chance/Rogers & Wells merger captured an altogether new corporate client base via merger, the Piper/Rudnick merger—only relatively more modest—enhanced an existing client relationship. According to Cook, the combination has "cemented" Sears' relationship with Rudnick and generated new business for the reconstituted firm. Piper did more than send Sears the customary marketing materials. The firm was anxious to go out to Illinois, introduce its people, and talk about its new capabilities.

It's worth noting—in fact, it's a further cautionary point for law firms—that the culture we've described at Sears may differ from a McDonald's, in terms of overall attitudes toward law firms, but that doesn't mean that Sears doesn't also have an enthusiasm for bringing work inside. As Gregg and Cook describe it, the re-examination of what work could and should come in-house was really a parallel process to the convergence of 1999. There would have been a re-examination of the inside/outside workflow regardless of whether or not there was a convergence.

Furthermore, the in-house buildup began before Kelly joined Sears in February 1999. There were new hires in securities and tax. Ditto real estate, where Sears was significantly increasing internal staff throughout the 1997-2000 period. The achieved goal was to handle real estate transactions from soup to nuts throughout the country, although local zoning matters are still handled more efficiently by outside counsel. Some inside/outside cost comparisons were done formally. Others, says Gregg, could be done anecdotally. It's easy to get an immediate sense of what some matters, like advertising reviews, will cost in-house versus outside.

In fact, Sears is doing a lot of hiring because it intends to keep work flowing inside. According to Cook, the company has enjoyed particular success adding to its employment practice. The gargantuan increases in first-year associate pay around the country in 2000 (with Silicon Valley law firms driving starting compensation over $150,000) created a kind of double bind for many corporations. Because those salaries are driving hourly rates up, corporations have more incentive, and are feeling more pressure, to hire in-house lawyers. At the same time, in order to recruit those lawyers, they have to compete with the very firms that started the problem.

For all that, Cook says that Sears has not been overly taxed. One or two candidates were lost to law firm Midases, but those were exceptions. Quality of life is still apparently a factor luring lawyers in-house, as are the benefits packages that make in-house careers economically viable in the long run.

Sears is concerned about rates but doesn't rate-shop that closely. Nor has it sought or made value billing a big topic in its interviews with law firms. Litigation is still mainly an hourly game, except in some cases where Sears is the plaintiff, and a few other instances where there are incentives for early resolution. Cook knows of no case where the company paid a premium for a successful transaction.

Rates, then, did not drive the Sears convergence, which both Gregg and Cook now describe as more or less complete. Just as Sears wants to know about beauty contestants' associates and staff depth, so too were line attorneys at the company allowed to sit in on some interviews. All senior legal managers, from both relevant practice areas and the business units, participated.

ON THE CUSP

Small companies buy differently than big companies. Their needs are obviously different and, staying with our theme, their cultures are different. In the next couple of chapters, we'll focus on "New Economy" companies, how they buy, how their expectations and cultures differ from the corporate behemoths we've been talking about thus far. Of course, "New Economy" encompasses both small clients and clients that have grown to be Goliaths in their own right. We'll cover both, along with a preliminary look at Eastman Kodak, an Old Economy company on the cusp of New Economy transformation, with additional consideration of Genentech as a corporation that similarly melds Old and New Economy buying issues.

In the present context, Rheem Manufacturing is a decidedly Old Economy company on a cusp of its own. It is small enough, and culturally different enough from the Fortune 100, to march to a different drummer in its relationships with outside counsel. At the same time, the trends affecting the multi-nationals filter down, crystallizing for such smaller companies the same best-practices choices. In some instances, those best practices are directly relevant to the small in-house culture. In other instances, the DuPonts and Rheems talk in wholly different tongues.

Take the issue of following lateral partners to new firms. Rheem will be loyal to one lawyer handling one area, for instance, an attorney who for some time now has been handling a Superfund matter on Rheem's behalf. But with multiple cases involving a number of practitioners, Rheem GC Jan Hoynacki says the company is unlikely to jump ship if one or two partners switch firms. That may seem obvious, but it does bespeak a middle ground of sorts between the "We hire individuals" approach at McDonald's and the "We look for breadth and depth" thinking at Sears. The smaller company has less *a priori* disposition one way or another. It goes or stays wherever it must in order to get the legal work done.

At the same time, the client is vulnerable. If partners leave firms with which Rheem has had longstanding relationships handling multiple cases, it would be cause for real concern. There could be serious work interruptions were the company to either stay with its firm or follow the departing lawyers. More, perhaps, than at the larger companies, in such situations Hoynacki wants to hear something tantamount to "a real hard commitment about the relationship. . . . Who would come, who would be with the firm, who wouldn't, what's the support for the ongoing relationship with me as the client?"

Rheem is a privately owned company with an annual revenue of about $35 million. Primary product lines include boilers and heating units, along with both commercial and residential air conditioning facilities. It was a public company in the 1970s and the target of a hostile takeover. A white knight took charge for a few years until Rheem was sold to KKR in the mid-1980s, which in turn sold the company to a Japanese family that presently holds it. Operations have improved significantly. It's now number one in the water heater business and number three in air conditioning.

Most of the Rheem caseload derives from the water heaters, primarily small cases in which people burn themselves and sue the manufacturer. According to Hoynacki, a "surprising" number of the cases turn out to be intentional, often children being scalded by parents or guardians. Rheem does not settle any of these cases. It litigates, and it wins. Other major cases that particularly require Hoynacki's involvement relate to flammable vapor ignition. Consumers bring gasoline into the house, it spills, the flammable vapor floats over to the open pilot light of a gas water heater, and people get horribly burned.

In 1997, Hoynacki's predecessor conducted a beauty contest to consolidate the cases related to flammable vapor ignition. A fifty-lawyer New Orleans firm, Frilot, Partridge, Kohnke, & Clements, came out on top and has since done what Hoynacki describes as an "excellent job." The first stage was to give Frilot direct oversight of all the lawsuits of this type that other firms were still handling or finishing up. New cases went to the preferred provider, whereas additional local counsel are still retained as needed to go to court in local jurisdictions.

Rheem is possibly Frilot's biggest client, which is an advantage for Rheem in using a smaller firm that Fortune 100 companies don't necessarily worry about. The very fact that, unlike Rheem, Frilot is Fortune 100 is leverage enough, since there's always the promise of additional high-volume and/or high-level work that would presumably be attractive even to a very large law firm.

For the smaller company, the smaller firm often assigns its top people, especially if the company is an anchor client. Such is the case here, since name partner Scott Partridge is primarily responsible for the Rheem business. Partridge is a class action defense specialist who, with Hoynacki's assistance, now represents the entire gas boiler industry in its class imbroglios. Even were Hoynacki to have a similarly close relationship with one or two partners at a bigger firm, he doubts that, for all their friendly intent, they could be available for Rheem "no matter what." The exigencies of their practice would inevitably interfere. Even in-house counsel at the Fortune 100 complain they can't always get the attention of their point people at larger law firms.

At the same time, this is not a "We buy lawyers, not law firms" situation, since Rheem is equally dependent on other Frilot attorneys who do as much or more of the litigating as Partridge himself. Partridge is more like the "relationship partner" that Bobbie Gregg at Sears describes.

Another lawyer Hoynacki has worked with in the past (not at Rheem) is Fred Bartlit, whose firm, Bartlit Beck, also broke off from a larger entity, Kirkland & Ellis. A firm in Denver that handles a variety of Rheem's other smaller cases also spun off from a larger firm. There does seem to be something about these break-off firms—and there are many such entrepreneurial refugees from larger bureaucratic law firm cultures throughout the country—that is especially harmonious with a smaller company that, like Rheem, has high-volume caseloads with potentially high exposure.

"They're hungry, and they want to do new things," observes Hoynacki. In return, the Partridges and Bartlits bring to the table the same sense of boundless resource that is comforting about a bigger firm, but they do so with more efficiency and none of the expensive baggage big firms carry. Indeed, as Hoynacki suggests, partners at these spin-offs know "what's wrong" about how legal services are being bought, sold, commoditized, and bureaucratized in the profession today. "They know different; they know how and why it should be different," says Hoynacki.

The break-off firms pose an especially elegant solution to the problem that Kindler talks about, of having to pay specious rates to a great attorney that obfuscate the cost of associates and staff. McDonald's may need the larger firms one way or another. If it didn't, it could rely solely on lawyers like Bartlit and Partridge who, when they send in their bills, are truly billing for what they personally deliver. The fact that corporations like McDonald's cannot apparently get by solely with law firms of the size of Frilot, Partridge, or Bartlit Beck may suggest that they have no choice but to rely on heavily leveraged vendors. Perhaps they ought to simply accept that they have to subsidize some inefficiency in the delivery of legal services.

However, the experiences of smaller companies for which cost efficiency is non-negotiable may be instructive to larger corporations that have resigned themselves to inefficiency. As Hoynacki points out, Frilot has a database that stores every deposition that's ever been taken in the flammable gas vapor cases, along with every article and every expert testimony transcript. Rheem and the firm hired outside experts to help design the system. The benefits in terms of discovery cost are obvious, as is the company's ability to dispatch myriad smaller cases by relying on the material in the database rather than reinventing the wheel with each new complaint.

The key is cost efficiency, not rates. "I look for fairness, not cheapness," says Hoynacki. Nor did the selection of Rheem's preferred providers hinge in any way on promised discounts or rate shopping. Like most buyers, Hoynacki says he doesn't especially care what a lawyer like Bartlit charges for his personal services, not when there's great exposure. In fact, Hoynacki recently acceded to a request from Frilot to raise its rates. The request was granted with an assurance from the firm that Rheem would continue to be a primary client.

Hoynacki even suggested to one small firm that it charge him higher rates. It was Hoynack's perception that the firm needed the extra revenue to "become viable." And he wanted to be sure that this particular firm would be fairly dependent on Rheem.

When we talk about the emergence of Frilot, Partridge, and a few other law firms as Rheem's preferred providers, we're talking about something well beyond the formal convergence that happened at DuPont and other large corporations. As we saw in Chapter 7, many in-house buyers converge their work "naturally." The consolidation of lawsuits happens as a direct result of good management, as one or two firms simply offer better ways to embrace far-flung caseloads. For the smaller company, legal cost efficiency can be a life-or-death proposition, so the search for lower costs ends up, perforce, in such reliance on fewer vendors.

But Rheem never consciously said to itself, "It's time for a convergence." It was a decidedly more unselfconscious evolution, similar to what happened at United Technologies, where Hoynacki was an in-house counsel for twenty-five years. UT's "underlying relationships" with certain firms became so strong that the firms simply emerged as preferred providers.

To some extent, there's a cultural connection between Rheem and United Technologies that transcends size. Hoynacki observes the plethora of corporate initiatives that engulfs many larger companies as they adopt new procurement initiatives. Purchasing advisory agencies and sub-departments are created. Matrices and decision trees are applied. Yet many of these initiatives are just plain common sense dressed up like management science. In contrast, at UT, Hoynacki says a convergence in legal procurement occurred because in-house buyers recognized sellers whom they could trust. The same thing happened at Rheem, and in more or less the same way.

Another, no doubt rather serious issue for a company the size of Rheem, is how to deal with a big law firm when it absolutely has to. Again, because it's on the cusp in terms of size, an antitrust issue might be complicated enough to require a lawyer who's likely to be practicing at a large firm. The problem is getting someone at such a firm to value a client like Rheem, especially in a boom legal market when high-ticket matters are pouring in from high-end buyers.

The solution lies in relational marketing—finding the lawyer at the big firm who has a reason for wanting to keep the company's business. Presumably, the lawyer will also have enough clout at his or her firm to preserve the relationship when the managing partner or executive committee starts drawing up lists of fireable clients.

As Hoynacki sees it, "personal attention" is the crux of all good marketing, and it's noteworthy that he says he has gotten it from partners at large firms as well as small ones. One can only surmise how much more of that attention was from big firms representing United Technologies compared to his current employer.

One law firm Hoynacki has relied on at Rheem is Pittsburgh's Kirkpatrick & Lockhart, which does insurance coverage work for the company. "I feel a strong personal relationship, with access, and I think the [lawyers] are responsive," says Hoynacki. As Hoynacki acknowledges, however, Kirkpatrick is going through a tremendous growth spurt, with ambitious mergers in the eastern part of the country. Time will therefore tell the extent to which it can continue to be responsive to a client this size.

Rheem's situation with Kirkpatrick & Lockhart may also be problematic because insurance coverage is Kirkpatrick's leading practice area. It would probably be more reassuring for Rheem if it were relying on Kirkpatrick in some relatively marginal area, where the specialist lawyers need to maximize their practice group's revenue in order to strengthen its position at the firm. At Kirkpatrick, Rheem is likely just one drop in the coverage bucket, with little leverage. Only a one-to-one relationship can compensate for the deficit. Were Hoynacki to leave Rheem, the company might not get the same level of service it's getting now.

A final problem that companies like Rheem face is recruitment. Even smaller public companies can use stock options to lure talent away from law firms. But Rheem is privately held. Hoynacki points out that there are opportunities for large cash bonuses based on company performance. Hoynacki himself concluded when he left United Technologies that increases in annual earnings would allow him to do as well at Rheem as at a public corporation. At private companies, everything depends on the compensation structures in place.

Another advantage is that companies like Rheem represent a very stable work situation. At the same time, Hoynacki doesn't pitch "lifestyle" or the notion that in-house lawyers don't have to work as hard as at a law firm. Ten years ago, that might have been a valid message to send to potential recruits. Today, the in-house job is frequently as demanding as any other even if lawyers aren't logging billables and fretting over business development. In-house cultures continue to change as an explosive economy leads to accelerated workloads.

PLAYING IN PEORIA

As a footnote, Caterpillar's recruitment successes speak directly to the effect of departmental culture on how cases are staffed and handled. Caterpillar now has a business-oriented in-house practice. Lawyers with a bent in that direction can be persuaded to relocate to Peoria. The only defections from the department have been lawyers who joined Caterpillar business units. "They are always welcome to return," says Atterbury.

The other lure is the hands-on litigation practice, which Atterbury compares to a Texas Rangers approach: "One riot, one ranger. One law suit, one lawyer." But that doesn't mean a lack of support for the litigator assigned. To the contrary, an attraction of in-house practice in general is that, "Asking for help isn't seen as a sign of weakness as it is at a law firm," according to Atterbury.

Tough as it is to sell Peoria, Caterpillar has recruited lawyers from a host of top-notch firms, including Proskauer Rose, McDermott Will & Emery, and Sidley & Austin (now Sidley Austin Brown & Wood). Atterbury does all the hiring himself. Since 1990, when Atterbury became GC, the department has quadrupled in size despite the loss of twenty-seven lawyers to Caterpillar business units. The projected growth of the company from $20 billion to

$30 billion during the first decade of the twenty-first century will no doubt occasion further departmental expansion.

Atterbury is even contemplating on-campus recruitment. The downside is the lack of time to train first-year lawyers. However, a summer internship program is a possibility. The company's past experience hiring two lawyers on-campus was a happy one. One of those attorneys is now an executive in a business unit.

"Next Economy" Legal Buyers: What Fortune 500 High-Tech Corporations Expect from Outside Counsel

Thus far in this book we've been discussing the great Old Economy giants and the fundamental changes that have affected how they buy legal services and what they expect from law firms afterward. Of course, this discussion is only one part of the picture. The New Economy is the other part. Despite the recent high-tech crash, how law firms approached dot.coms and other venture-oriented clients still provides an important piece of the inside/outside picture.

In the mid-1990s the turn toward the New Economy particularly required the purveyors of legal services to change mindsets in a variety of ways. Because the growth potential of the New Economy companies was so significant, law firms targeted this sector with the same—and often greater—intensity with which they've gone after the DuPonts and Caterpillars in the past. In fact, it has entailed a whole new inside/outside dynamic.

After all, big powerful law firms were now trying to relate to small companies. The convergence issue is irrelevant, since we're not talking here about global buyers with hundreds of law firms on their retention lists, and wondering what to do with all of them. The leverage is different. Some smaller high-tech or other start-ups still offer prospective law firms spectacular promise, but they don't have the clout of major corporations. How outside counsel treat these clients is therefore a persistent issue.

Formerly, equity stakes defined the inside/outside relationship. In California, leading law firms such as Cooley Godward and Wilson, Sonsini, Goodrich & Rosati have been taking ownership positions in start-up clients since the early 1980s. That trend accelerated until it became standard practice among firms doing business in Silicon Valley, Northern Virginia, and other growth corridors.

In Chapter 11, where we will look at the specific experiences of New Economy companies, we'll see obvious differences in what successful public technology companies, as well as start-ups in pre-IPO funding stages, are expecting and getting from outside counsel. The buyers themselves are usually very different. The smaller companies do not have the developed in-house legal capacity that typifies mainstream corporate America. Many of these fledglings are continually wrestling with the question of whether or not to hire chief legal officers. In the meantime, it's usually CFO-types who do the legal purchasing.

At the same time, we'll note some profound similarities between these companies and even the Fortune 100. For example, the responsiveness issue still haunts both quarters. Fortune 100 companies and two-year-old start-ups often sound eerily similar in their complaints about overbilling by outside counsel, or telephone calls that never get returned. And there is often the same strategic concern about how many different firms to retain for diverse legal needs. Do we look around for, say, separate employment counsel, or do we rely on a single vendor for one-stop shopping? It's a particularly crucial strategic point for the smaller companies, since the decision to refer virtually all their legal business to one law firm naturally creates real dependency on that one firm. In such instances, outside counsel become total "partners" with the client, rendering legal advice that will have a decisive impact on every aspect of client operations. The lawyers raise money for the company, they help run the company, and, especially of late, they'll even take it through bankruptcy.

ESTABLISHED WISDOM

One instructive bridge from Old to New Economy lawyer/client
relationships begins with the Fortune 500 companies that are
themselves key participants in the high-tech revolution. They may
be global high-volume purchasers, but their experience on the
cutting edge of high-tech products and services is directly relevant
to the start-ups. They're selling a lot of the same stuff, after all. In
areas such as intellectual property, both sectors need law firms that
are willing and able to rethink the services they provide to clients
on a daily basis.

A convenient way to describe these larger companies is as
"Next Economy" clients. Already established as national or multinational powers, these are the corporations that will carry forward
the innovations in technology developed by the thousands of
Internet or other tech start-ups that fell by the wayside or got eaten
by bigger fish. In a sense, the larger companies represent both the
past and the future. They represent the past, because that's where
they come from. But they represent the future as well because,
after all the shakeouts, they'll likely still be standing as the New
Economy "matures."

A case in point is Genentech, which we've already looked
at as a pertinent variation on the convergence theme. As a
harbinger of high-tech things to come, Genentech merits
additional attention in this context. Senior Patent Counsel Sean
Johnston's description of his company's experiences in the early
days of biotechnology offers a relevant link between the
generations, in terms of the problems that all innovative
companies face at some point in their histories when they must
retain outside counsel.

As Johnston recalls, even as late as the mid-1980s, there
were very few law firms that could do any of the work that
Genentech required. So the client had to educate its lawyers.
Rounds of seminars were developed. Genentech scientists were
providing in-depth tutorials to outside counsel. Significant time

investments, often a solid two weeks at a stretch, were needed to bring lawyers to a point where they knew the professional vocabulary of biotechnology, and could manage its litigation. Additional weeks were required for follow-up.

Astonishingly, in those years from 1985 to 1987 Genentech *paid* outside counsel for this training. "That absolutely could not happen today," avers Johnston. Recently, for instance, Genetech's outside lawyers needed training in interference practice, an esoteric IP sub-specialty. According to Johnston, Genentech made it abundantly clear that it was not amenable to compensating outside lawyers for their time getting up to speed.

The difference between then and now is that no one was doing biotech in those years; Wilson, Sonsini, for example, got in relatively late in the game (which legendary partner Larry Sonsini acknowledges as his firm's one serious competitive mistake during the 1980s). In other words, it was a seller's market. Today, by contrast, the legal market is mature to the extent that no law firm can afford to demand payment for its own training, no matter how small the buyer or abstruse the specialization. For today's start-ups, the lesson is that, if a law firm doesn't get itself up to speed on its own dime, there are other good firms that will.

Sean Johnston's approach to buying and managing outside legal services reflects, in a number of rather attractive ways, Genentech's roots as an early New Economy company. For example, Johnston will go off on his own when he visits a law firm. He'll wander about, and chat with secretaries, clerks, and paralegals to get a feel for the firm's culture. Is it an amiable place to work? How much respect do the partners show other human beings in the course of a workday? You don't have to be a New Economy client to take this tack. Old Economy industrial buyers could visit a law firm and do the same. But they seldom do.

There's a lot of purpose to this method. Johnston simply has to ask the folks he chats with how long they've been at the firm. If everybody says two months, he will have unearthed something questionable about the organization that the most

practiced displays of superficial amicability can't disguise. He'll
also know that, if there's so much turnover going on, legal services
to Genentech could be affected as a result. And that will naturally
be something he'll want to discuss with a partner or two.

Conversely, as associate salaries skyrocketed, attrition
became a problem for the in-house department as well. All
corporations were affected as lawyers chose to practice at law firms
instead of taking in-house slots, or left large companies for
entrepreneurial opportunities. But the pressures are greater on
companies that, like Genentech, depend on lawyers who already
have a predilection for high-tech practice.

"We [had] to raise salaries to compete with what the law
firms [were] offering," says Johnston. "We can't just rely on
options and benefits." In 1999 and 2000 those pay raises
included substantial upward adjustments in addition to scheduled
annual reviews.

The problem is exacerbated because the back-and-forth
movement of lawyers, between law firms and law departments, is
such an accepted fact of life. It more easily allows young lawyers
to capture the best of both worlds. They can work for an extra
$50,000 a year at a law firm until they're in their early thirties,
then move in-house for the long-term benefits. In the 1999-2000
period, Genentech, for one, lost two lawyers to biotech start-ups
and one to a dot.com, according to GC Stephen Juelsgaard. No one
departed for a law firm, which probably meant that the Genentech
pay hikes were effective, not that law firms weren't potentially stiff
competitors for that talent.

In-house managers in the Old Economy sector often bitterly
resent the pay hikes at law firms that both lure away their own
attorneys and result in higher legal fees. But many of the corporate
counsel who operate in the high-tech markets know better than to
cavil at the high rollers outside. Even a high-volume purchaser like
Genentech was told by law firms that it didn't have the time or staff
to take on the company's work. As a result, "we understand that
they have to pay a lot to get enough people," says Juelsgaard.

At Genentech, Juelsgaard seems to see less of a hiring threat from law firms than does Johnston. Juelsgaard points out, for example, that all three of the lawyers leaving Genentech made conscious decisions not to join law firms. In any event, it's by no means an insoluble problem for either side. Law firms and high-tech law departments are partnering to provide benefits all around. As was mentioned in Chapter 8, a major Bay Area firm, Orrick Herrington & Sutcliffe, has gone on joint on-campus recruiting tours with Lucent Technologies. Young lawyers can accept offers that will put them at Orrick for a few years and Lucent later on. In the meantime, because they're working on Lucent matters while at Orrick, they ostensibly provide the company both immediate and longer-term benefits. Immediate, since they're doing Lucent work. Longer-term, since they'll know enough about the company to really hit the ground running if they do finally opt for an in-house position.

Similarly, Johnston has been invited to special summer intern programs at law firms. One advantage is that the firm gets to show off a major client to apprentice lawyers, the message being that this is the kind of sexy work they'll get to do if they accept an offer there. Another is that the interns are also exposed to Genentech as a possible future employment possibility.

A GLOBAL MIRROR

To a great extent, Genentech began life as a New Economy company, dealing in what was then a most esoteric product. Today's New Economy companies can therefore directly translate Genentech's experience in the 1980s relative to hiring and managing outside counsel to their own current situations. Eastman Kodak Company offers a different scenario. It is a much older company that has always dealt in technology. In some ways, this conservative giant also has, during the last decade, confronted many of the same issues with which younger companies are now grappling. In other ways, however, it remains free of such issues as it continues to happily rely on a stable coterie of loyal law firms. In any event, Kodak provides an instructive mirror on how technology companies may now buy legal services in the global economy.

Interestingly, when we interviewed GC Gary Van Graafeiland and Assistant GC James Quinn of Kodak, both men pointed out that we had made too glib a distinction between "Old Economy" companies like Kodak and the New Economy creatures that have sprung up in Silicon Valley and elsewhere. Kodak certainly has the superficial appearance of an old-line corporate buyer. The in-house contingent is 100 lawyers strong. Kodak's in-house group is a centralized department, although fifteen or so Kodak legal teams in about as many countries report directly to the operations managers in those countries or in regionally defined markets around the world. In Rochester, there are five groups: (1) corporate/regulatory, (2) patent, (3) employment, (4) marketing/antitrust/trademark/litigation, and (5) commercial affairs (technology).

Kodak operates through a number of business units. Consumer is the largest, representing a revenue base of $8 billion from film, photographic paper, photo finishing, cameras, and other products. Among the other discrete businesses, there are motion picture film, digital, document imaging, and health imaging. Quinn's marketing/antitrust/trademark/litigation group functions as lead counsel for these business units and advises on marketing and distribution. Individual lawyers within the group act as lead attorneys for different business groups. According to Van Graafeiland, Kodak's global strategy is moving away from nation states toward regionalization. Five years ago, for example, the company had a legal department in England and a legal department in Germany. Now, lawyers in both countries report to a regional general counsel in Switzerland. The move toward regions very much reflects the way business has evolved as trade centers consolidate internationally.

Even more than at the other big companies we've looked at, retention decisions at Kodak are, as Van Graafeiland puts it, directly affected by "thirty-year lawyers or by one-week lawyers." The in-house lawyers manage cases. If they're diligent, and follow Kodak's established best practices, their careers are not adversely affected by a bad choice in law firms. They make the necessary correction and move on. All in-house lawyers with case management responsibility are therefore empowered to the greatest extent possible.

As we'll see, Kodak is somewhat unusual because of the extent to which it can rely on time-tested relationships with a few outside counsel. Yet, with relatively new in-house lawyers empowered to help select law firms, there is also opportunity for firms that have never worked for Kodak to market themselves to these fresh hires at the company. At the very least, some of the newcomers worked at law firms before joining Kodak. Quinn says he can think of two such recent instances when in-house attorneys successfully referred their former employers.

There's no actual list of approved law firms at Kodak, so there are no hot tips on how to get on such a list. As Quinn puts it, "We have experience with firms, we rely on that experience, [and] we have some firms [with whom] we've negotiated special arrangements. Everyone in the department knows what those [arrangements] are, and, because those arrangements are favorable to us, we will tend to gravitate toward those firms." There are about a dozen law firms that have negotiated special fee arrangements with Kodak.

Like many corporations, Kodak has standardized guidelines in place for outside counsel. "We give these guidelines to outside lawyers to gain their attention," says Quinn. "Here's how we do business." (The guidelines are reprinted, in slightly modified form, at the end of this chapter.) The format is a typical example of a generic document that continues to be used by in-house legal managers throughout corporate America. At the same time, like Kodak's, such documents are necessarily tailored to each buyer's particular culture and will encompass each company's individual concerns with respect to outside counsel.

According to Van Graafeiland, Kodak tries to do most of its own work, except for litigation. "We have chosen not to litigate in-house for a variety of reasons," he adds. "We don't have hundreds of thousands of claims [on file], all of which have the same fact patterns. It's very hard to staff for [high-volume] work, or develop a little in-house expertise in a lot of different areas."

Kodak still sends out a fair amount of transactional work as well. The reason is simple: The flow of transactions is very heavy, including a large number of good-sized deals requiring significant support. Half a dozen Kodak lawyers do nothing but transactional work, but that group isn't big enough for the constant volume. As a forecast of Next Economy needs, it's significant that Kodak, despite its size, also cannot develop a large enough patent group inside. As Van Graafeiland observes, in addition to the enormous volume of patent work at Kodak, the growth of IP at law firms has caused an ongoing labor shortage. Law departments at big and small companies alike are continuing to feel the pinch.

A STABLE CREW

The fact that Kodak does not have a formal approved list is in part attributable to the unusually stable relationships it has maintained with a relatively small number of firms. According to Van Graafeiland, 65% of total legal fees are paid to about ten law firms. This stability, involving a pretty small number of firms, means that Kodak has never needed to formally converge.

It's an interesting comment on a company that identifies itself as "New Economy" or "Next Economy" that these relationships are old ones indeed. The challenges of new technology have not forced Kodak to re-engineer its retention practices, mainly because the company maintains close enough relationships with outside counsel. Its law firms can envision where the new substantive challenges are coming from, in terms of legal work, and train or hire lawyers to handle it on Kodak's behalf.

By the same token, there are at Kodak, as at many of the other large companies we've looked at, "crevices" through which law firms can land first-time business, despite this reliance by Kodak on established relationships. Geographical happenstance naturally plays a part since companies like Kodak will invariably need lawyers in places where their usual firms can't help them. Similarly, referrals from other corporations lead to work for new law firms, and Quinn identifies manufacturers and other trade associations, along with bar associations, as important points of contact with prospective firms. Echoing a frequent theme, Van Graafeiland and Quinn dismiss most written marketing materials while being more open to seminars because of their substantive nature.

Despite its stable relationships with outside counsel, Kodak will put on beauty contests, usually for a very specific purpose. Quinn talks about one IP case "where we wanted to see what some of our good firms would put together. We primarily [invited] firms that we already deal with, and we said, 'What would you do for us in this particular case? How would you staff this? What would your approach be and what would your rate structure be like?'"

This procedure is a significant variation on the beauty contest phenomenon, since the sort of interviews that get the most attention, and arouse the most anxiety, are the ones where corporate buyers are intentionally looking outside their established networks. Usually their objective is to change the network in one way or another as a result of the competition. Here, Kodak is interviewing within its existing network for a particular matter, and the network itself won't necessarily be changed when the process is concluded.

The durable relationships that Kodak has enjoyed suggest that it can get the sort of coveted business-oriented counseling from its firms that goes well beyond winning cases, negotiating contracts, and writing coherent briefs. In the context of this discussion, such "business consulting" from outside counsel is that much more valuable for a client like Kodak that, as a technology company, has to ride constant seismic waves of technology-driven change in its own marketplace. In turn, such companies can maintain these long-term relationships with law firms in a volatile marketplace such as technology because it gets something from them besides narrow legal expertise. Kodak may hire a new firm for a very specific matter, but it expects heightened service, and broader service, from the handful of its trusted *consiglieres*.

There are really two different efficiency models. Some companies shake up established relationships if their outside firms begin taking them too much for granted, or to foster creative competition and generate favorable fee and service arrangements. Other companies, and Kodak would seem to be a case in point, tend to leverage established relationships. For example, Quinn reports that Kodak will borrow lawyers from local firms for extended periods of time. This practice is not just another instance of a client seconding associates to help itself handle high-volume workloads. It goes much further up the food chain. Kodak even hired a senior partner from one law firm for four months in 2000, replacing a senior Kodak attorney as the counselor to a key business unit.

LEVERAGING STABILITY

"We've exchanged lawyers at many levels," says Quinn. Kodak negotiated (but didn't ultimately implement) the transfer of one in-house lawyer to a law firm in order to train him for a year in a practice area where the company needed more expertise. Another firm that impressed Kodak loaned one of its key administrative people to Kodak on a regular basis in order to manage and share a variety of technology and research functions. From there it was just a short jump to the firm also sharing relevant case-oriented material with Kodak's in-house attorneys. Since the material was being circulated throughout the law firm anyway, why not take the one extra step of including the client's people on the routing list?

In turn, Kodak customarily includes such firms in a variety of in-house training initiatives. In Chapter 7 we mentioned how some smart law firms have built extranets connecting them to their institutional clients. Here, too, we see the benefits for both buyer and seller in utilizing well-established relationships rather than making outside counsel constantly worry about whether the client's been shopping around.

For such companies, the changes in the legal marketplace over the past few years might be a little more disconcerting. After all, a company accustomed to relying so closely on stable legal service providers might not agree that the reconstitution of global legal behemoths is altogether to its benefit. The most loyal attorneys in Rochester may be less reliable if a larger firm absorbs their firm, replacing its name on the letterhead.

In fact, a primary Kodak provider, Nixon, Hargrave, Devans & Doyle in Rochester, merged in 1999 with Boston's Peabody & Brown to form Nixon Peabody. Nixon was, in fact, the bigger of the two firms in the deal, so there was no reason to assume that the loyalty of outside counsel to Kodak would be at all compromised. Yet the Kodak/Nixon relationship was such a steady one that any major merger involving the law firm inevitably begs the question of how the client relationship might be affected.

That being the case, it's interesting that even under these circumstances—where so much value seems to derive from the longevity of the client's relationships with a specific law firm—Van Graafeiland echoes most of his in-house colleagues at other corporations. "We tend to use individual lawyers, not law firms," he says. The law firm, he adds, is important because it's the entity with which the company has struck an economic arrangement. Beyond that, the focus of Kodak's concern is not usually organizational. ("Firms come, firms go," says Van Graafeiland.)

When Van Graafeiland heard about Nixon, Hargrave's merger with Peabody & Brown, "it was not a huge surprise, considering what's happening with law firms these days." Of course, Kodak, or any other client, will want to hear all about how its own work may be affected in such a situation. But the size of the merger and the publicity attending it are not necessarily the decisive factors.

In fact, Quinn points out that, after Nixon's merger with Peabody, the reconstituted firm went on to acquire a small intellectual property practice that, considering the nature of Kodak's business, was actually just as interesting to Kodak as the much bigger deal that had garnered all the attention. "We wanted to get to know [the newly acquired lawyers], to see if there were some folks over there [at the boutique] that we could use," says Quinn. "It was this small acquisition that, he figured, "could be a real boon for us."

Among mature technology-oriented companies, Kodak does offer a pointed contrast to Genentech in its view of other signal developments affecting the legal market. It may be because Kodak is so large, or else because it is not an integral part of New Economy communities like Silicon Valley, that Van Graafeiland expresses more concern over spiraling associate costs. "When twenty-five-year-olds directly out of law school get $125,000, or whatever these firms are paying, they have got to be productive in a way that justifies their salaries," he says. "There are zillions of lawyers out there, many good ones, who are not employed exclusively by the big New York City law firms or the big San Francisco law firms or the Silicon Valley law firms."

In other words, lawyers who for whatever reason are practicing in Rochester have never been paid these wild salaries and they don't bill out as if they were—yet they deliver equally competent if not superior services. If you represent a technology-based company, it is therefore important to remember that the entire legal marketplace is not being driven to run in this particular rat race. Mature companies such as Kodak still assign cutting-edge work to potentially "zillions" of lawyers around the country who aren't as famous as Wilson, Sonsini. But they can prosper by providing considerable work for comparatively little payment. In fact, not being Wilson, Sonsini is potentially a marvelous way for a technology practice to brand itself.

At the very least, law firms in cities like Rochester can make a very good living by taking pieces of litigation that East Coast or West Coast firms are handling, and doing parts of the work for much less. Quinn cites one case in San Francisco that was taking thousands of hours at West Coast rates. Kodak was able to give the document work to Nixon Peabody, which handled it in Rochester at Rochester rates. In the same way, on another big case in the east, Rochester's Harter, Secrest & Emery handled both document work and witness preparation. Kodak saved money, and the Harter firm enhanced its credibility with Kodak through its superior performance.

The bottom line, according to Quinn, is that top partners in Rochester charge about the same hourly rates as associates in New York City. Again, the additional significance of this, when we consider the nature of Kodak's business, is that it *demystifies* technology practice. New Economy companies make sky's-the-limit allocations on all sorts of legal work because they don't know any better. In Chapter 11, when we take a closer look at the experience of new companies with law firms such as Brobeck, Phleger & Harrison, we'll get an even better notion of how and why the in-house managers at Kodak have apparently found a better way.

DO GOOD, DO WELL

Like many other large legal service purchasers, Kodak is intensely interested in retaining minority- and women-owned law firms. Given the company's overall buying strategy, this corporate aspiration comes as something more than a postscript to the foregoing. Kodak, after all, is a global company that dotes on law firms in its own upstate New York region because those firms are cheaper than the profession-leaders on the East Coast and West Coast, and yet provide comparable or superior work.

Minority- and women-owned law firms provide the same advantage, which means that Kodak is not merely responding to

what it sees as a social and professional obligation, but can further
its own buying strategy in the process. "It's a priority for us," says
Quinn, although he acknowledges only "mixed success. . . . We
haven't been as good at doing this as we would like. The firms that
we have identified have been great, but we're still struggling to
make sure that we have good networks, so we can be confident
about finding [member firms] that deserve our attention."

Quinn says it's also "a real plus" to be introduced to
minority lawyers working at majority-owned firms. But the
inescapable appeal of minority firms is their rates, which are a
"fraction" of what lawyers at mainstream law firms charge.

"They've got blue-chip client rosters," adds Quinn. "We're
also talking about litigation when we talk about hiring outside
counsel. If you look at the composition of jury pools, having a
minority lawyer representing you is just good sense. There are
plenty of good reasons for these diversity initiatives."

APPENDIX *

MEMORANDUM TO OUTSIDE COUNSEL

May 18, 2000

From: Kodak Legal Department

Re: Terms of Retention

This memorandum describes Eastman Kodak Company's practices and expectations regarding the retention of outside counsel.

1. *Identity of the Client Contact*

The Kodak lawyer designated as the responsible lawyer for a new matter will guide outside counsel in the performance of its tasks and will participate fully in planning and implementing all action to be taken.

2. *Early Assessment ADR*

Kodak's practice is to defend or prosecute its lawsuits vigorously. However, the early assessment of actual or threatened litigation is one of the best methods of ensuring that Kodak's legal resources are used efficiently. This process begins with a

---

* Reprinted with permission of Eastman Kodak Company.

preliminary litigation evaluation . . . conducted by the Kodak lawyer and outside counsel.

Kodak has signed the Alternative Dispute Resolution Pledge developed by the Center for Public Resources, thereby agreeing to consider whether the use of ADR techniques would be appropriate in disputes with fellow signatories. Kodak expects its outside counsel to be experienced in, and willing to suggest and use, ADR techniques in appropriate cases.

3. Personnel

At the outset, the Kodak lawyer and outside counsel will agree on staffing—viz., the identity of the outside lawyers, paralegals, and any other law firm billable professionals who will be assigned to the matter, and the extent to which the Kodak lawyer or other Kodak personnel will perform tasks related to the matter. Staffing should not be changed without the Kodak lawyer's prior approval.

The Kodak lawyer must be consulted before experts or consultants are retained.

Throughout the representation, the Kodak lawyer and outside counsel will identify necessary tasks that can be performed more efficiently by Kodak personnel, by other outside counsel (e.g., local counsel), and by third-party contractors (e.g., contract paralegals).

4. Responsiveness

Outside counsel are expected to be accessible and cooperative. They are expected, on their own initiative, to report to the Kodak lawyer on a regular basis, to forward copies of all substantive correspondence and substantive internal memos, and to keep the Kodak lawyer informed of all significant developments. Outside counsel should not deal directly with Kodak businesspeople without the permission of the Kodak lawyer.

5. *Attendance at Meetings and Travel*

The Kodak lawyer should approve in advance any travel by outside counsel or other billable professionals, and the number and identity of firm personnel who will attend meetings, conferences, and similar activities.

Outside counsel are expected to make every effort to keep out-of-pocket disbursements for travel and other expenses at reasonable levels. (For example, Kodak policy requires that domestic airline flights taken by Kodak employees on company business be coach class, and that international flights generally be coach class or, for longer trips, business class. Similarly, Kodak policy requires that expenses incurred for meals and accommodations be reasonable. Where outside counsel wishes to incur additional expense—for example, by flying first class or staying at a luxury hotel—outside counsel should bear the additional expense. The same rules apply to outside counsel, experts, and consultants.) Any significant expenditures should be approved in advance by the Kodak lawyer.

Kodak and Rosenbluth Travel, Inc. have entered into a special discount arrangement for travel undertaken by Kodak employees, including members of the Legal Department. These special rates are very competitive and are available to outside counsel and others traveling on the business of Kodak and its subsidiaries. When making travel arrangements identify yourself as working on behalf of Kodak. (Your firm need not use Rosenbluth if it can obtain a better rate elsewhere.)

6. *Fees*

Prior to a retention, the Kodak lawyer and outside counsel will agree on outside counsel's fee arrangement. Since cost control is a priority at Eastman Kodak Company, including the Legal Department, outside counsel may be asked to discount hourly rates, bid on Kodak legal work, work on a contingency or fixed-fee basis, provide volume discounts, etc.

Kodak normally does not pay retainers. Exceptions will be made only with the approval of the General Counsel.

The Legal Department encourages outside counsel to suggest creative alternative billing arrangements.

7. *Billing*

Outside counsel should submit statements monthly unless the matter is generating monthly fees of less than $2,500, in which case bills should be submitted quarterly. Kodak lawyers may modify this requirement in appropriate cases. In no event, however, should bills be submitted less frequently than quarterly. Outside counsel should send bills to the Kodak lawyer, unless otherwise directed.

Effective January 1, 2000, Eastman Kodak Company pays legal bills forty-five days from the date of invoice. To ensure prompt payment, outside counsel should include on the first page of each invoice the following information:

♦ an *invoice number*, which outside counsel assigns; [and]

♦ a *case number*, which outside counsel can obtain from the Kodak lawyer or his/her secretary

When a bill covers multiple matters, each matter should be separately identified along with its case number, fees, and related disbursements and expenses. Bills should identify the lawyers and other billable professionals performing services, the services performed by each, and the number of hours spent on each aspect of the matter. Unless other arrangements have been made in advance, litigation bills should be in the Uniform Task-Based Management System format. The Kodak lawyer can provide more information about this format, including specimen bills. The bill, as to each matter, should include a recapitulation showing the hours billed, hourly billing rates, the total amount billed by each timekeeper, an itemized listing of the disbursements incurred (including cost per page for faxes and copies), and a statement of the total cumulative fees and disbursements to date. Where a disbursement exceeds $500, backup documentation should be provided in detail sufficient to permit the Kodak lawyer to understand how the disbursement was calculated.

Kodak engages outside counsel to provide it with professional services, which are expected to include incidental office expenses. Additional charges for word processing or routine office work, or for copying or faxing at a rate higher than actual cost, are not consistent with this expectation and should not be made without prior written approval of the Kodak lawyer.

8. *Nationwide Court Reporting Services*

Kodak has entered into a nationwide court reporting services contract with Alliance Shorthand Reporters, Inc. of Rochester, New York.

When scheduling a deposition, please give Alliance as much advance notice as possible and send Alliance a copy of the deposition notice via facsimile. Alliance will choose reporting firms near the deposition sites. Alliance has assured Kodak that it has contracted with top-quality firms nationwide and that it can obtain very competitive rates in most jurisdictions. In addition, Alliance will provide a Word Index and Condensit.

A firm need not use the service identified by Alliance if: 1. it is required by contract to obtain services elsewhere; 2. it can obtain a better rate locally, and Alliance declines to match that rate; 3. the court reporter service identified by Alliance has not performed acceptably in the past; or 4. it would be impractical to change reporting services (e.g., another court reporter service has already performed significant services in the matter).

Since Alliance will bill Kodak directly on a monthly basis, firms should not pay invoices that are submitted directly to them. Monthly reports will be provided to Kodak and outside counsel listing all depositions taken, including dates, times, and pages. Transcript delivery will be handled by the local reporter.

Firms should make sure that all lawyers, paralegals, and secretaries who handle Kodak matters are aware of this court reporting program.

9. Conflicts of Interest

Firms that represent Eastman Kodak Company or *any* other member of the Kodak consolidated group of corporations (including Kodak's foreign subsidiaries) *anywhere in the world* may not represent clients in matters (primarily litigation) where Eastman Kodak Company or any member of the Kodak consolidated group is an adverse party. They also may not represent parties taking legal positions contrary to positions that they are taking on behalf of Kodak or *any* other member of the Kodak consolidated group in the same jurisdiction. Finally, in limited situations, firms that provide substantial legal services to Kodak may not represent Kodak's major competitors. (E.g., Kodak may object if a firm that provides Kodak with ongoing antitrust counseling proposes to provide antitrust counseling to a major Kodak competitor.)

Since there are many situations where dual representation (e.g., simultaneous representation of Kodak in an environmental matter and another client in the negotiation of a lease with Kodak) does not rise to the level of "adverse party" representation, Kodak is prepared to grant dual representation waivers, provided the firm does not represent Kodak in the same matter, and provided that Kodak's confidences and secrets would not be at risk. Waiver requests should be directed to the Kodak lawyer for approval by the General Counsel.

10. Identification of Kodak as Client

Firms should not identify Eastman Kodak Company as a client, in firm advertising brochures, *Martindale-Hubbell*, and the like, without Kodak's prior written consent, which will typically be given where the firm is an ongoing supplier of substantial legal services. Inquiries should be directed to the Kodak lawyer for approval by the General Counsel.

11. *Communicating with the Media*

Kodak's corporate policy entitled "Communications with the Public Media" states in part that, "the company cooperates with the media in order to insure that the information appearing in print or broadcast outlets accurately depicts the company and its interests." Outside counsel who is asked by a representative of the media to comment on a Kodak matter should direct the media representative to the Kodak lawyer, who will refer the inquirer to the appropriate Kodak media relations personnel.

12. *Kodak Policy on Receiving Gifts*

Kodak's policy on Conflicts of Interest states in part that "gifts and entertainment, including trips and invitations to sporting and similar events, of more than nominal value by any organization doing business with Kodak may be accepted only with the documented approval of a company officer." Entertainment of Kodak lawyers by outside counsel should be consistent with this policy. Questions about the appropriateness of proposed gifts or entertainment should be directed to the General Counsel.

13. *MBE/WBE*

As a government contractor, Kodak is required to place a certain percentage of its third-party-vendor business with small businesses, including minority-owned business enterprises ("MBE's") and women-owned business enterprises ("WBE's"). Attached hereto is a form titled "Eastman Kodak Company's Small Business Development Program for Historically Underutilized Businesses." If a firm qualifies as a "small business," as defined in the form, the firm should complete the form and return it to Kevin B. McMillen, Director, Legal Administrative Services, Eastman Kodak Company, 343 State Street, Rochester, NY 14650-0206. Questions should be directed to Mr. McMillen at (716) 724-2897.

14. *Diversity in the Workplace*

The general counsels of many of the country's largest companies have endorsed the following:

"Diversity in the Workplace: A Statement of Principle

"As the Chief Legal Officers of the companies listed below, we wish to express to the law firms which represent us our strong commitment to the goal of diversity in the workplace. Our companies conduct business throughout the United States and around the world, and we value highly the perspectives and varied experiences which are found only in a diverse workplace. Our companies recognize that diversity makes for a broader, richer environment which produces more creative thinking and solutions. Thus, we believe that promoting diversity is essential to the success of our respective businesses. It is also the right thing to do.

"We expect the law firms which represent our companies to work actively to promote diversity within their workplace. In making our respective decisions concerning selection of outside counsel, we will give significant weight to a firm's commitment and progress in this area."

Kodak's General Counsel is a signatory to this Statement of Principle.

Sharks and Little Fish: How New Economy Companies Hire Outside Counsel

Never mind the stock market "correction" in the spring of the year 2000, or the dark clouds hovering over the Dow and the NASDAQ ever since, including the year-end free-fall. Never mind the growing mortality rate among dot.coms big and small. Never mind the fact that her own company's stock has certainly not bounced back to pre-April 2000 levels or that, in November 2000, analysts on CNN were advising that companies "like DoubleClick" will probably not be bouncing back in the foreseeable future.

Elizabeth Wang, Vice President and GC at DoubleClick, Inc., continues to speak with the same confidence and sense of purpose that characterized the Internet world when she first joined the company in June 1998. After all, DoubleClick is still the leading provider of online advertising/marketing solutions for corporate and commercial clients worldwide.

Its market position still affords DoubleClick some of the same purchasing power that the Fortune 500 enjoy when they shop for law firms. Wang's approach to outside counsel is commensurately tough-minded, though without the contentious pugnacity that, as we've seen, was often so prevalent among larger corporate buyers in the mid-1990s. Wang is also more a lodestone for media interest than most of her rather distrustful and inaccessible Old Economy compeers. She's young and female and a risen star in the Internet business, which is still a nice combination for attracting attention from the legal press.

Personally, Wang projects a certain chipper insouciance until, when you get down to business, she'll switch gears and assume a vaguely challenging no-nonsense persona. Like the diverse other GCs we've talked to, Wang is less involved with the direct hiring of law firms than her in-house subordinates. She's nonetheless acutely aware of the power a company like hers can wield in the inside/outside interface. That power is not really so much a function of size or annual billings. To the contrary: hundreds of millions in revenue is, of course, small compared to that of companies that, like DuPont, were really putting the screws to law firms a few years ago.

Instead, DoubleClick's clout among law firms is directly related to the marketing and strategic directions that these firms, wisely or not, have mapped out for themselves in the last five years. Many law firms still want a piece of the New Economy, even when there's not much in their particular institutional histories or current core competencies that suggests they can go this route with any kind of credibility. They realize that the great Silicon Valley firms or their counterparts on the East Coast (like Testa, Hurwitz & Thibeault in Boston or Shaw, Pittman, Potts & Trowbridge in Washington, D.C. and northern Virginia) can no longer be solely dominant in e-commerce and other Internet work. The high-tech downturn has affected the work volume and revenues that high-tech firms were generating. But there are still openings for newcomers. There's also the perception that, one way or another, the whole world is going this route, albeit by fits and starts. Even the most conservative old-line clients may soon be living or dying online, not only dot.coms. If the old-line clients' usual law firms can't help them, the companies will find others that will.

Some of the work these law firms are targeting is with start-ups, or with maturing companies like DoubleClick. Some of it is with the Fortune 100 as those companies install their own Internet businesses or buy up the smaller fry. In Chapter 8, for instance, we noted that GE's most recent in-house hire in 2000 was an e-commerce specialist.

Smokestack and old-line law firms are making the transition. Jones, Day, Reavis & Pogue is building a big information technology practice group. Chicago's Sonnenschein Nath & Rosenthal was the first law firm to ally with First Tuesday, the London-based organization that brings together New Economy representatives at periodic networking soirées. Sonnenschein decided to sponsor a Chicago-based version, and it turned out to be a good idea. With enough fungible legal talent in its ranks, the firm has in the last three years marketed one of the leading e-commerce practices in the United States.

Law firms are counting on being able to hire enough lateral talent to convince New Economy clients that they can actually do this work. Alternatively, they're arguing that an Internet practice does not so much require a new breed of lawyers as it does lawyers smart enough to transfer the skills they have in their corporate practices to what is simply a new array of products and services. The gist of this argument is that the legendary Silicon Valley law firms like Wilson, Sonsini, Goodrich & Rosati or Fenwick & West may be brand names, but at this time they're not featuring anything really unique. This situation is a variation on the debate that first sounded loudly in the mid-1990s when patent litigators argued that the bet-the-company intellectual property cases springing up around the world required the dedicated expertise of patent specialists. Other lawyers argued that any good litigator could handle the substance of these lawsuits. After all, isn't the distinguishing characteristic of all great litigators the ability to quickly master new and frequently esoteric material with each new job?

There's something else that law firms targeting the New Economy must constantly worry about, and that's the likelihood that their clients may not survive. The start-ups are not the only businesses in trouble. Companies like Priceline that once seemed to set the direction for the future of the American economy are now names from the past. As a result, there are law firms out there trying to utterly transform themselves even as the sands are shifting and re-shifting under their feet.

Consider Cummings & Lockwood in Stanford, Connecticut. This is the last law firm one might expect to zero in on New Economy markets. Long known as having one of the best trusts and estates practices anywhere, Cummings historically wrestled with the problem of marketing a talented corporate practice when people thought that the firm simply handled T&E. When, rather suddenly, a high-tech corridor opened up in Connecticut, the firm took careful note, especially since Priceline was then in the vanguard of that local high-tech charge, and Priceline was at one point a client.

High-tech continues to be a shiny lure, Priceline's woes notwithstanding. If nothing else, Cummings & Lockwood can always sell T&E to New Economy clients who are still getting rich, and who need to be setting up trust funds just like the old-time industrialists used to do. But that's the least of it. There aren't a lot of top-name law firms in Connecticut. This new high-tech explosion spelled unprecedented opportunity for the prestigious Cummings to make good on its old strategy and dynamically expand its corporate practice. It is tough, however, to convince the emerging local companies to hire what is arguably the best law firm in Connecticut rather than a middling but dependable firm in New York City.

Imagine, then, what a desirable client DoubleClick would be for any good law firm in Cummings & Lockwood's situation. DoubleClick is East Coast-based, it's surviving, it may even grow. Any strong identification with this company could certainly provide immediate entrée for firms that don't have the benefit of a Sonsini or a Fenwick on their letterhead. For Elizabeth Wang, that spells leverage, both in terms of the quality of services she can demand and the prices she'll agree to pay. By the time Wang landed at DoubleClick, the company was already a real catch for most law firms.

BEGGARS IN THE MARKET

But there's a dark side for New Economy buyers in all this. With so much concern over the viability of dot.coms, major law firms are now being a lot more careful about which companies they're willing to represent. In the 1980s, law firms took on young clients in exchange for equity in the companies. The companies would presumably grow and the firm's representation of them would expand as they grew. Now there are conspicuous questions as to the value of such equity arrangements. The DoubleClicks can still manage the inside/outside relationship as any other company might, Old or New Economy. (DoubleClick did not trade shares for lawyer hours when it came into existence during the mid-1990s.) By contrast, today's start-ups are, as Wang puts it, forced to "bid" for law firms as they might bid for venture capital. They are now in the unenviable position of having to prove their worth to the firms with which they want to work.

Let's look at two examples.

The situation of a company like OrderFusion with respect to outside counsel is precisely the opposite of DoubleClick's. Law firms need the imprimatur of DoubleClick in order to grow their New Economy business. Conversely, OrderFusion, a business-to-business start-up in San Diego offering innovative e-commerce sell-side software, derives great advantage from having a Wilson, Sonsini or a Fenwick & West when it ventures into the capital markets. In that respect, it is just like thousands of other start-ups looking for money. The leverage equation is thus reversed and, in today's market, the new buyers of legal services are facing contentious and rather dangerous circumstances as a result.

First they have to worry about finding a good law firm. Then they have to worry about holding its attention. The Cummings & Lockwoods that would presumably make concessions to get and keep DoubleClick's business don't necessarily fill the bill for companies like OrderFusion that need to be working with established brand name law firms if they want to make progress in the high-tech capital markets. Yet those branded law firms, the ones that can get their clients up close and personal with the VC decision-makers, often don't need OrderFusion at all.

Founded in 1995, OrderFusion was in its second round of funding by mid-2000, reports Jeff Gilford, Vice President of Finance and Administration. As at many similar companies, there is no in-house counsel. The job of hiring law firms falls to the CFO in most such instances. OrderFusion's CEO explicitly delegated this task to Gilford, although he already was meeting with anyone hired to represent the company in a significant matter. OrderFusion is now studying the advisability of hiring an in-house lawyer, and hoping for some helpful "metrics" to guide its decision, according to Gilford.

As late as autumn 2000, OrderFusion's primary outside counsel was a securities attorney named Brad Schwartz, an alumnus of Gibson, Dunn & Crutcher who had been hired in 1996 through a consortium of lawyers called Strategic Law Partners. Schwartz' personality matched the company's needs in that Schwartz is "deal-oriented and accessible," as Gilford puts it. Other outside counsel are hired as needed for due diligence on tax matters, whereas Chicago-based Sidley Austin Brown & Wood handles OrderFusion's IP matters, having begun its relationship with the company by doing its contracts work.

The problem, as Gilford acknowledges, was that, by the late 1990s, it could only be "a matter of time" before OrderFusion would have to accommodate its own growth by migrating to a full-service law firm, Schwartz' good offices notwithstanding. Employment needs "pushed" OrderFusion to look in 1999, and a growing volume of IP issues "pushed" it again the next year. Anticipating an IPO down the line as well, OrderFusion retained Brobeck Phleger & Harrison in 1999. Brobeck, of course, is one of the name brand firms that clients in search of capital typically feel obliged to hire.

OrderFusion soon encountered a problem that law firms serving the New Economy usually fret over more than their clients (at least publicly): lawyer attrition. In the 1980s, law firms lamented the departure of partners for the investment banks; then they smarted as attorneys, both partners and promising associates, left to take jobs with dot.coms. Indeed, the best law firms in the world were losing talent to the New Economy. Elizabeth Wang, for one, practiced at New York's Cleary, Gottlieb, Hamilton & Steen before she joined DoubleClick.

Clearly, though, clients can be hurt as well when partners move laterally from firm to firm or from profession to profession—and none more so than newer companies that have no real clout with outside counsel, and are forced to rely on the partner who originally developed their business. That individual partner usually has some sort of personal commitment to the company or a special faith in its future. In OrderFusion's case, the main contact partner at Brobeck, John Denniston, left for Salomon Smith Barney where, presumably, he's now bringing that investment giant's power to bear in a New Economy context. Gilford remembers that, with his previous employer, Alpine Capital, law firms themselves counted for more. At that bigger company, "full service" meant less dependence on a single partner. With a pre-IPO client, however, the departure of the responsible partner can leave the young company perilously underrepresented.

"Why is no one watching me?" asks Gilford.

When the time came to revise the company's "inadequate" employee manual, for example, Gilford had to go shopping again, this time to a local employment boutique. To replace Brobeck, Gilford "took a run at" Cooley Godward in Palo Alto, looking for the "prestige" that is so essential in a law firm for clients that want to bring impressive names to the negotiating table. But at Cooley, Gilford would have to confront a daunting fact of life in Silicon Valley.

Equity participation in start-ups looks pretty attractive on paper, since it presupposes incentives on the part of the law firm to help its young clients grow. But there are problems. For the lawyers, as we've noted, the risks are sometimes too great to trade billable time for stock in a new company. For the companies, the equity demands often represent too great a compromise; plus, the lawyers are still demanding their hourly "retail rates" as well. Not that OrderFusion, although small, is overly sensitive to costs. Gilford doesn't rate-shop, for example. He assumes that the rates he sees are market rates, and he's willing to live with that.

Yet it was additionally frustrating and puzzling for Gilford because he had already seen CPAs at public accounting firms take "a three-year bath," gambling for handsome returns from OrderFusion further down the line. In contrast, the law firms Gilford talked to were not really taking any risk at all because their work would have been coming in right around IPO time. Were the company to fail at that point, the law firm would not have to write off anything like a five-year investment.

In such situations, buyers like Gilford are really thinking like businesspeople and wondering why their law firms won't do the same. Business entails risks. If a law firm wants to invest in a company, fine—but that means gambling on the payoff. Gilford realized that, in the Silicon Valley legal culture, the better law firms wanted it both ways. They were willing to take a big flier on equity, but they assumed they could hedge their bets with guaranteed rates. This approach is not a business mentality at all, argues Gilford. It's the same old guild sensibility, except that it is also enriched with potential returns on equity bequests.

Another thing Gilford seems to have learned is that, in the professional services, a brand does not equal reputation. They're different concepts altogether. Depending on the situation, both can be bankable, but the brand of a VC-wise, high-tech-savvy law firm by no means guarantees a commitment to quality service and client responsiveness. At the same time, a reputation for blue-chip work does not ensure clout of any sort in the capital markets.

It may be, as Gilford suggests, that OrderFusion was "spoiled" by Brad Schwartz. The level of attention and concern the company is accustomed to getting from Schwartz was not palpably available at a large firm, although it was clear that a large firm was still needed to guide the client as it grew. According to Gilford, that search continues. It is, in essence, a search for "intangibles," for something in a law firm that might persuade the company that the prospective relationship offers reliable chemistry.

Significantly, Gilford echoes the GCs of America's largest corporations in describing the kind of direct marketing by law firms that would most likely work for OrderFusion. Again, it's the seminar that works best and is valued most—direct communication of substantive legal information that is useful to the company—and might persuade it to come back for more on a paying basis.

But none of that solves the definitive problem for a start-up like OrderFusion. The question persists: How can the company be confident that, once inside the door, it won't be shunted into some dark corner? It only underscores the problem that, as this book was going to press, the executive team at OrderFusion conceded immediate concerns about the company's short-term survival prospects.

Sigma Designs, Inc. in Milpitas, California is on the opposite end of the capital spectrum from OrderFusion. Whereas OrderFusion is a new company trying to make its way through the capital markets, Sigma, a semiconductor and digital technology company, was founded eighteen years ago and went public three years later. As of January 2000, it was a $50 million operation.

OrderFusion is bedeviled because it can't find "chemistry" with a brand name law firm that it can take to the negotiating table, and the company has been appalled by the equity deals that Silicon Valley law firms propose. In contrast, Sigma has had its ups and downs through the years, and cannot now excite interest among outside counsel because it has no start-up equity to offer. In their respective stages of development, both companies are guilty of the sin of not being Microsoft or IBM. Their experience points out the penalties of being small in the ravenous world of new technology, and that a culture which in many ways supports entrepreneurial endeavor can, when it comes to the legal component, punish those who for whatever reason are still walking on wobbly legs.

Sigma's history with the venerable Wilson, Sonsini is a piquant case in point. It was Wilson that took Sigma public and it is still the company's primary outside counsel. But the partner who developed this client departed for a dot.com. As with OrderFusion, when its primary contact at Brobeck took another job, this departure would prove to be a dangerous and disheartening event for Sigma.

In the summer of 2000, as John J. Beck III, Sigma's CFO, tells it, Wilson, Sonsini sent Sigma a letter informing the company that, in thirty days, it would no longer be its outside counsel. Beck was shocked. This was a longstanding relationship based originally on a friendship between the company's CEO and a Wilson, Sonsini partner. Some time later, a pallet of company documents arrived from the law firm, the first step in the disengagement process. Only a call from the CEO to the originating partner salvaged the situation. Sigma was allowed to return the documents to Wilson.

Sigma's annual legal fees to Wilson, Sonsini total about $200,000, which may have been a decisive factor once the client's partner contact at the firm had left. That amount is, as can be imagined, a trifle for this particular law firm. Indeed, a powerful sub-theme of law firm economics in the early days of the new millennium was the firing of clients. With business booming, and rising overhead causing unprecedented profitability demands, law firms were finding they couldn't really afford clients who fall below certain fee revenue thresholds. Their consultants were certainly urging them to be tougher. Wilson, Sonsini's actions ought to be understood in that context. In fact, its final agreement to keep Sigma might actually be more fairly deemed an act of some generosity, considering the low fees and how other law firms might have acted were they, like Wilson, Sonsini, operating so near to capacity.

Beck does take comfort from his company's "long history" with the firm, and he says its lawyers are now being responsive to Sigma's needs, although he still finds himself "prodding to get results." Wilson, Sonsini handles the spectrum of Sigma's corporate and SEC work as well as shareholder litigation, and the firm has also made recent changes to the company ESOP and is reviewing Sigma's quarterly press release. Sigma uses San Francisco's Jackson & Hertogs for immigration matters. (Immigration was a fast-growing specialty in the New Economy because these clients are often in a hurry to shift personnel across borders.) However, there is no in-house attorney at Sigma. When Beck was interviewed for his current position, one important question was how he would handle legal needs.

Sigma's misadventure with its law firm is not, however, the only significant part of the story. Beck's attempt to at least explore the possibility of finding new counsel is equally portentous. The SEC-related work that Sigma farms out is too important for the company to risk not being represented. So the CFO had to go shopping even as the CEO went begging.

There simply weren't any firms with Wilson, Sonsini's standing willing to take on a client like Sigma without pre-IPO equity, and it was already fifteen years too late for that. As Beck describes the problem, although the first-tier firms weren't interested, he didn't know enough about the second tier to be sure who was good, or who in that tier had the requisite experience with public companies like his own. He called Sigma's accounting firms for referrals, and asked the Venture Law Group in Silicon Valley for recommendations. Clearly, the networking that most GCs say is the one main way they find and hire law firms was not adequate in this case. Some kind of law firm marketing could have been helpful here.

Beck says he would even have been receptive to cold calls from law firms. His honesty in admitting this is, if nothing else, most unusual. It should also be noted that, when Beck went searching for a possible replacement for Wilson, Sonsini, he was totally unfamiliar with the names Skadden, Arps, Slate, Meagher & Flom; Shearman & Sterling; and Simpson Thacher & Bartlett. These New York law firm institutions all have relatively new branch offices in Silicon Valley. In some cases, they are still having trouble integrating into the local market. They are sometimes seen as creatures from a different culture, bringing New York attitudes and New York styles of lawyering that don't fit, personally or professionally, with local norms.

The fact that Beck never heard of these East Coast firms may suggest an uninformed buyer. But it may also suggest a window of opportunity for the interlopers. A $200,000 client might not mean a lot to Skadden or Shearman, but Beck's problems with the local bar, as well as Gilford's at OrderFusion, bespeak a chink in the armor of the formidable local firms. These companies do not embody a special culture that outsiders can't fit into. Instead, we're talking about an underrepresented market, and a population of buyers who, smarting from rejection, may see branch offices as a great opportunity. They're not at all xenophobic, and they will gladly talk to anyone from anywhere who can help them. It's an opening even some British law firms are hoping to seize. In late 2000, for instance, a UK firm called Osborne Clarke announced it was opening a small office in Silicon Valley.

Beck relates one story that may have significant implications for New York or other non-local law firms. It is generally assumed that one of the personality disconnects between Wall Street and Silicon Valley involves dress. The East Coast lawyers are seen as starchy and overly formal. The buyers wear blue jeans. So, the lawyers try to dress down to please the client. According to Beck, however, one big-name venture capitalist in northern California "reamed" a number of lawyers at a meeting for dressing casually. He expected more respect, and respectability, for what he was ready to pay.

"There are so many styles, you really don't know how to dress," says Beck. "I'd suggest simply asking first, when the meeting is first set up."

The Silicon Valley garment isn't seamless in any event, and the pressure on New York firms to conform to this or that standard of behavior is overstated. Professional synapses are more important. As Elizabeth Wang on the East Coast observes, the real difference between firms that can represent companies like hers, and those that can't, is the speed with which they turn over matters. She has some distrust of New York law firms because they don't instinctively understand this demand. "I can't have something 'next week,'" she says.

That, not clothes, is the real hurdle for the new firms in Silicon Valley.

BRAND NAME CUSTOMER

To what extent do smaller companies in the Old Economy have the same problems as OrderFusion or Sigma Designs in finding law firms? It's not unthinkable that such companies might also get stuck in situations where they're being unceremoniously terminated. And, complaints about lawyer unresponsiveness have long been pandemic and will predictably continue to be. However, many comparably sized Old Economy companies operate in more mature, less volatile business environments. The referral networks are sturdier and more populous. The legal needs may not be as critical. If there are no bet-the-company lawsuits looming, chances are the Old Economy companies don't have the kind of SEC needs that made Sigma's situation precipitate. Also, in many cities such as Kansas City or Miami, law firms can't as readily afford to fire the widget makers or restaurant owners. These markets are tight-knit, and too much bottom-line tough-mindedness might have deleterious effects on a firm's standing in the community.

In contrast, Silicon Valley is still a gold rush of indescribable intensity. Lawyers there work longer hours than even their counterparts on Wall Street, and sometimes they're playing for higher stakes. Any good firm in the Valley can view its market as imperiously as Cravath, Swaine & Moore views its market. No-one is surprised when Cravath is extremely selective. No-one should be surprised when Fenwick & West or Brobeck Phleger & Harrison is equally so. Companies may resent this, but they know the rules of the game and are finally willing to play by those rules.

At the same time, the Silicon Valley market can change at any moment. In August 2000, John Beck found that law firms weren't interested in talking to prospects that weren't willing to fork over 1% or 2% of their equity. In December 2000, however, law firms found that their overhead was cutting into profits. They were already compensating first-year lawyers upwards of $200,000, fully loaded with benefits and perquisites. Meanwhile, the longer-term effects of the spring 2000 stock market "correction" were being felt as one dot.com after another continued to fall by the wayside. Today, law firms are finding themselves holding lots of worthless paper. It will be interesting to see how soon they'll feel the need to show a friendlier, more receptive face to the Sigma Designs of the world.

"Law firms will wind up with a lot of paper," says Jack Martin, Vice President of Finance and Administration at Groove Networks, Inc., a company located in the midst of the technology corridor just north of Boston. Equity-sharing by law firms will turn out to have been a "fad," he believes. In general, there has been an "immature distribution of equity."

To a great extent, that immaturity reflected the culture of the venture markets over the past fifteen years. Companies "gave away too much," reflects Martin. They were preoccupied with the next financing ahead, and the next one after that. They wanted cash in their coffers, as much as possible as soon as possible. "And equity isn't cash," adds Martin.

Martin's own company has never come close to making that mistake in its relationships with law firms, but it hasn't had to. Groove brought an advantage to the table that differentiates it from both the fledgling players like OrderFusion and the global deep pockets like DoubleClick. Groove was founded by Ray Ozzie, the man who created Lotus Notes, and, for that reason, enjoys a credibility that equates with leverage. Such clout plays out in a number of ways. This start-up doesn't have to beg for a law firm. Nor does it need to be as concerned about bolstering its position at the negotiating table by dropping names like Larry Sonsini or Dick Testa.

At the close of 2000, Groove was already financed to the tune of $65 million. Founded in 1998, the company had nearly 200 employees two years later. It is developing a peer-to-peer platform for Internet communication and collaboration on which other companies will be able to build specific applications for content-sharing and other types of purposeful interaction among users.

This concept raises red flags about potential litigation in the wake of the Napster case if those third-party applications involve infringement or piracy. Martin says Groove's business model is clearly legal, although third-party suits have to be at least a consideration. Martin points out that AT&T doesn't get sued when illegal activities are carried out over the telephone, and the "economics" of a law suit against Groove in this context "wouldn't look good to plaintiff's counsel" in any event. However, the Internet is a different business culture altogether, a frontier business culture with different perceptions and expectations. As such, counsel can provide important prophylactic measures.

The real decision for companies like Groove is whether to keep such preventive work in-house or ship it to a law firm. As Martin emphasizes, it's a measure of Groove's confidence in its future that an in-house counsel, Jeff Seul, was hired early on. An alumnus of San Francisco's Farella Braun & Martel, Seul was a lecturer at Harvard Law School before he joined Groove. His very presence thus further differentiates this company from those that don't have a name like Ray Ozzie's to support its growth. Hiring lawyers in-house sends the message that Groove Networks will exist for the long haul.

Groove does share with other companies in its age group the perceived need to cast a wider net in its selection of outside counsel as it plans for future growth. According to Martin, at its inception the company never had to interview candidates in formal beauty contests. Partner Ned Martin at Piper Marbury Rudnick Wolfe has shepherded Groove since its founding. Having represented Lotus in licensing and diverse other matters related to product development, Martin was the natural choice for Ozzie's new venture.

Jack Martin, who also worked with Ozzie at Lotus where he was VP of Finance, describes Martin as a very "business-oriented" lawyer, in fact, "a great business partner." He's adeptly helped Groove navigate the capital markets. But "economics [now] dictate [the need for] competition" among outside vendors, according to Jack Martin. "Ideally," Groove would prefer to take a full-service approach with Piper, but there are geographical limitations with Piper, particularly as the company's legal needs for routine licensing and sales contract support become more widespread regionally.

It is likely this sort of thinking among its clients that propelled Piper into a fast-growth national strategy. That strategy began with the 1999 merger of Piper & Marbury on the East Coast and Rudnick & Wolfe in Chicago.[1] Not surprisingly, considering the comments of clients like Martin, the firm's managers aren't being shy in acknowledging that they want to parlay their merger into yet more growth ahead.

High-tech industry knowledge is also a consideration for Groove. As Martin points out, clients in any emerging industry require legal counsel with extremely focused understanding as diverse new licensing and trademark needs arise. In dealing with the venture capitalists, or handling most financing issues, less specificity is required. No doubt the Wilson, Sonsinis were appealing because they ostensibly offer both: Capital markets entrée plus high-tech insider knowledge.

"Ostensibly" may be the operative word. Although Wilson, Sonsini's prowess in the capital markets cannot be gainsaid, what it is really selling, as Seul points out, is its longstanding brand. "Back in the 1980s, [firms like] Wilson, Sonsini looked sexy," he says. "If we didn't have Ray Ozzie's name, we might have needed that kind of entrée too," although Seul also points out that being based on the East Coast creates a somewhat different dynamic.

---

[1] See Chapter 9 supra.

There, the specific cachet of a Silicon Valley firm isn't quite so *de rigueur*. In Massachusetts, for example, it wouldn't hurt Groove to be represented by Testa, Hurwitz, but the compulsion to bring that firm's name to the table isn't nearly as strong.

For Seul, "word of mouth" is always the best marketing. He recalls name partner Frank Farella telling him, when he was still practicing at the highly profitable Farella Braun, that the best way to develop business is to "be a damn good lawyer." Having said that, Seul attributes value to a few basic law firm marketing tactics as well. Client testimonials, for example, are impressive, especially when they don't read merely like boilerplate blurbs, but "seem to come from real living human beings."

Again, panels and substantive law firm seminars are of value to this buyer. Finally, Seul mentions public relations and targeted media strategies as potentially very effective—especially if a lawyer in a relatively insular market such as Boston is getting national coverage in an industry-related publication. As Seul puts it, "If I saw a Boston lawyer that I never heard of quoted in *Wired* or *Red Herring*, I would definitely call somebody in town I know, and ask, 'Who is this guy?'"

As Martin suggests, the ideal in-house hire presents, in one attorney, something of the same full-service capability that the great law firms feature. Seul's prior experience encompassed both cross-border negotiation expertise and represention of technology companies. He's a practiced mediator, which suggests that, if it grows, Groove may not want to be wholly reliant on outside counsel to handle disputes. At the same time, the compleat inside counsel surpasses what outside counsel offer companies like Groove in one important respect: Lawyers "must know the people" they're working with, their personal "agendas," and their professional predilections. Martin doesn't think any law firm "can have this."

As Seul describes it, the role of in-house counsel at a company like Groove is "monitoring outside and translating inside." That is not substantively different from how Old Economy corporate counsel might also describe themselves. They manage law firms, and, for the inside client, they boil down legal matters into comprehensible business alternatives.

In late 2000, Seul hired Groove's first additional in-house legal staffer. "It's hard to tell at what rate we will grow in-house," he says. "Our [future] needs are uncertain."

GLOBAL WHOLE

At almost ten times Groove's current size, DoubleClick is similarly unsure at what rate its in-house department will grow. If the Fortune 500 global companies are able to formulate some measure of their legal needs one or two years in advance, the dot.coms face much greater uncertainty about the size of their prospective markets and the volume of legal matters ahead. Right now, big guys like DoubleClick are either guestimating or just not saying.

In late 2000, DoubleClick employed fifteen lawyers worldwide, twelve of them in New York. These attorneys typically work closely on all product development, beginning with the spec phases. Their "imprint" is right there when the new service is finally posted, comments Wang.

The company's international growth has been rapid since its incorporation in January 1996, a year and a half before Wang arrived. DoubleClick has a presence in twenty-three countries, with deals occurring elsewhere where it has no offices (such as in Third World countries). The global practice is fairly decentralized, overseen by one multilingual lawyer in New York. However, there are plans to hire two new managing attorneys overseas, one in Hong Kong and one in Dublin, DoubleClick's tax hub.

Five members of the legal staff are Deputy GCs empowered to hire law firms, or at least make strong recommendations. We've seen how GCs at Old Economy companies like McDonald's also emphasize that the Associate or Deputy GCs have the direct retention power. What's notable in this New Economy context, however, is the pace of operational change. Wang herself was doing most of the interviewing and hiring as recently as early 2000. Now, although she still wants to meet partners from law firms that are under serious consideration, she'll usually do initial interviews only as a favor to somebody.

Like Groove Networks, DoubleClick is less involved in the law firm name brand game, in part because it's also an East Coast-based company. Perceptions are different on the East Coast, and names like Sonsini and Fenwick don't have quite the same mystique there. At the same time, being based on the East Coast added to DoubleClick's own mystique as a potential client. Because it's a New York company, DoubleClick was seen in the mid-1990s to presage new Internet growth markets that could rival or surpass what was coming out of Boston or Northern Virginia.

Also like Groove, DoubleClick was linked to a single legal services provider, Loeb & Loeb, when it first went public. (Loeb is L.A.-based but has a sizable New York office.) That firm had been referred by one of the venture partners involved in the initial financing. By the time DoubleClick went public in 1997, however, the company was ready to switch to one of the branded venture firms. It chose Brobeck, which has continued to handle the company's corporate and finance work as well as its executive compensation and ESOP plans.

At that point, DoubleClick was still following the dot.com tradition of letting the CEO or CFO personally hire outside counsel. Wang, upon her arrival, would seek greater diversification, and without any apparent fetish for law firms that, like Brobeck, are the identifiable New Economy brands.

When DoubleClick hired Wang, Loeb & Loeb was still negotiating customer contracts and Brobeck was handling all the corporate work. Loeb's problem, says Wang, was that it wasn't strong enough in the middle-seniority levels. "That can cost you a lot of money," she says. Legal work migrates either upward, where the rates are higher, or downward, where less experienced lawyers are naturally less efficient. Loeb worked hard to keep its share of

DoubleClick's business—it has a strong New Media group, says Wang—but lately it's only been doing real estate work for the company. The outcome might have been better for the firm had it landed a few choice laterals to fill the gaps, but apparently that wasn't in the cards. "Brobeck hires lots of laterals," comments Wang approvingly.

Like other New Economy players in their post-IPO periods, DoubleClick is obviously headed in the opposite direction from the many Fortune 500 corporations that, as we saw in previous chapters, are more often consolidating rather than expanding their lists of approved law firms. As her company's legal needs broadened, Wang deconverged dramatically, bringing on a half-dozen other law firms to share the wealth with Brobeck and Loeb.

She hired Washington, D.C.'s Hogan & Hartson for lobbying work, Kenyon & Kenyon in New York for patent litigation, and San Francisco's Kauff, McClain & McGuire as the company's employment boutique. Wilson, Sonsini does some West Coast deals whereas occasional matters also get sent to Skadden and New York's Paul, Weiss, Rifkind, Wharton & Garrison. Morrison & Foerster and Orrick, Herrington & Sutcliffe have litigated the high-profile privacy class action suits that beset DoubleClick and other large on-line companies in the advertising and marketing business. "Not a lot of law firms can handle that work," observes Wang.

DoubleClick asks outside counsel for regular monthly reviews but, as Wang describes it, the closeness with which inside and outside lawyers work on all company matters makes these periodical checks fairly routine. She does not rate-shop—we have not found one New Economy company that admits to doing so—but she does emphasize the value of DoubleClick as an ideal sample client for law firms that are still seeking wider New Economy business. Because of that leverage, Wang will always demand and get volume discounts at the beginning of a relationship. Wang is also very open to value billing suggestions.

"We want to be a good client," reflects Wang. "Easy, fun, and interesting. I want [firms'] lawyers to want to work hard for us." And, equally a matter of self-interest, she wants to see attorneys at the law firms she uses "grow" as the representation evolves.

Wang scoffs at law firm differentiation strategies. "All law firms sound the same," she avers. If she's impressed with Wilson, Sonsini's marketing, it's not because of any branding that has occurred over the past twenty years. It's the substantive aspect of that marketing that impresses her, specifically the solid informational value of the firm's web site. Wang does read firm sites, and will form distinctive impressions of a firm based on what she reads.

At the same time, she is indifferent to the online legal service exchanges that, like eLawForum, allow in-house counsel to find and vet potential retentions over the Web. Those bidding services are mainly good for "cookie-cutter" work, she says, and DoubleClick doesn't have a lot of that to bid out. She could use the exchanges to find tax lawyers, but "there are so many mediocre tax lawyers around" that she doesn't think looking online for the jewels in the rough would justify the effort. The simple lesson here is that New Economy companies aren't necessarily impressed by New Economy innovation, at least not when it comes to hiring outside counsel.

Wang is not especially attracted to the multi-disciplinary practices either. DoubleClick did use an MDP for an employment practices matter overseas, but then had to have the entire job redone from scratch. Wang does observe, though, that this failure was due more to the specific lawyer in charge, who was "altogether the wrong person for the job," and less to the fact that his organization was an MDP rather than a conventional law firm.

Finally, DoubleClick offers a good vista on the recruiting wars. As we've noted, law firms used to commonly lament the loss of talent to the dot.coms or other New Economy companies that were hiring lawyers either in a legal or business capacity. DoubleClick has certainly been a beneficiary of that trend. Some of its in-house legal staff came from other companies, but over half are law firm alumni, including four from Paul, Weiss.

However, by late 2000 the migration was slowing at least to the extent that there were more casualties among the dot.coms. Among the survivors, compensation decreased as stock values plummeted. But Wang isn't concerned about DoubleClick on this score. The company's attractions weren't ever necessarily the fool's gold pay packages prevalent elsewhere in the New Economy. "Our people were willing to take huge pay cuts to work here," she says. The lifestyle attracted them, and so did the relatively flat organizational structure.

Wang remembers one lawyer she worked with elsewhere who had such a terror of fielding questions from clients that she had contrived a strategy by which she could always avoid giving an answer. She'd simply reply to the question with another question or a request for more data before she could respond. "That is everything about this profession that I'm against," says Wang.

Like Jack Martin at Groove, Wang stresses the particular need for New Economy lawyers to understand the agendas of the people who work in this industry. It's a need that's best answered in-house. "Our lawyers don't complain about our salespeople, and our salespeople don't complain about our lawyers," Wang says. The attorneys she wants in-house must thus be great communicators as well as exceptionally skilled practitioners. Again, it's that "translation" function Jeff Seul alludes to. "Simplicity is profound," says Wang, and the lawyers who impress her usually do so by summing up their work in two or three sentences.

Retention is all in the hiring, Wang says. "I interview people, and when I describe what we want them to do here, you can see their eyes light up. [After all], this is the work they want to do," she adds. "That's why it's not been any harder to hire since April [2000]."

Woman to Woman: Does Gender-Based Marketing Work for Both Sides?

I n the last few chapters, we've essentially been alternating our discussion among purchasing sectors. The concepts of Old Economy, New Economy, and Next Economy represent only one paradigm by which the buyers of legal services have been differentiated in the last few years. The perennial lesson that marketers must learn (two or three semesters beyond Marketing 101) is how to refine and change their styles to match changes in the world around them. Marketers must understand the personality nuances of an extremely diverse client population rather than mere specific selling techniques.

For law firms, that can be a particular challenge because they're newer to professional marketing in general than most other professional services. In addition, they've had more to learn because, historically, they couldn't care less about the personalities of their buyers so long as they enjoyed a captive audience that they could mystify with legalese and pacify with opinion letters and boilerplates.

Yet it was relatively early in the evolution of legal services marketing that law firms did allow at least certain of their members to develop more personalized approaches. For example, gender-based marketing arose as women lawyers joined together to network with and target other women lawyers as clients and referral sources. This is a particularly interesting episode, and a relevant topic to address at this juncture in our discussions, for a number of reasons both narrowly professional and broadly sociopolitical. One is that gender-based marketing shows how business development must be responsive to the kind of seismic market changes discussed in the last five chapters.

As important, and equally fundamental, gender-based marketing raises the banner issue of value discussed in earlier chapters: How marketing must deliver value to the buyer to justify the time and effort for both seller and buyer. In the following discussion we'll see that a legal services marketing campaign, in which female lawyers at law firms target female lawyers at corporations, actually delivers value to male non-lawyer CEOs for reasons that are only indirectly related to the delivery of legal services.

GALVANIZING FORCES

The growth of women marketing groups among law firms was actually rather rapid during the late 1980s. Typically, strong women partners organized the other women partners at their firms into networking groups that would host regular events such as breakfasts and theater outings. They invited female associates to some or all of these events, usually on a voluntary basis.

Female in-house counsel were invited to attend and often to participate as speakers. Participants included not only the corporate decision-makers, but younger in-house women as well. Management realized that those younger women would some day be in positions of greater hiring authority or, at the very least, were worthwhile referral sources to cultivate.

Just as often, and with particularly tangible effect in terms of direct business development, non-lawyer women entrepreneurs were also targeted. Those entrepreneurs could hire outside counsel on the spot without getting clearance from a general counsel or justifying their choices to anyone besides themselves.

In a few instances, firms such as Philadelphia's Montgomery, McCracken, Walker & Rhoads and Boston's Hale and Dorr were

WOMAN TO WOMAN: DOES GENDER-BASED MARKETING
WORK FOR BOTH SIDES?

339

taking large ads in the business and legal press to spotlight their women's groups. The experiences of these two firms are particularly salutary examples. On the one hand, they're very different kinds of law firms, at least in terms of their marketplace identities. Montgomery, McCracken is very much a local and regional law firm with a strong reputation mainly in its own market. Hale and Dorr is internationally famous with a storied tradition dating back to the Army-McCarthy Hearings, and it is today one of the dominant high-tech powers in the profession. On the other hand, both firms report significantly similar approaches to gender-based marketing as well as comparably happy results over the years.

In addition, the women's groups at both firms have survived through economic upturns and downturns. Montgomery, McCracken's women's group, founded in the mid-1980s, seems, in fact, stronger now than in the past. Note, however, that a number of similar groups have not survived over the years for various reasons. Kathleen O'Brien, Montgomery, McCracken's most senior female partner who organized the women's group at her firm, points out that these groups usually depend on the ongoing commitment of strong partners. Without that commitment, the group falls by the wayside as billable hour quotas distract members or, amid the continuing profession-wide mobility, partners and associates simply move on to other law firms.

Even with the commitment of senior partners, problems arose in the 1980s and 1990s that derailed some of the women's marketing groups. Silvia Coulter, director of marketing at Hale and Dorr, points out that the rationale behind the groups was often challenged. "The implicit question was, 'Why are you just focusing on women when there's so much lost ground in terms of marketing that law firms have to pick up?'"

Yet the sheer mass of marketing initiatives by women in the legal profession was, during the 1985 to 1995 period, sufficiently voluminous and diverse to fill up a 700-page book on the subject! Deborah Graham's *Getting Down to Business:*

Marketing and Women Lawyers[1] reflected this immense national interest and activity. The author has, in the years since publication, continued to consult with law firms, including Hale and Dorr, on business development by and for women. Her career suggests that the women's groups at such firms have not merely been coffee klatches. They've included substantive training sessions as well as individualized business development planning for group members.

Kathleen O'Brien figures that, for all the economic and political pressures working against women's groups, the overall number has nonetheless increased. The briefest bird's-eye view of legal profession demographics suggests why. There are simply more women in the profession, inside and outside, than ever before. Years ago, when asked why they didn't have more women partners, law firm managers would say it was because there weren't yet enough women associates to promote. At first, that was hard to dispute. But by the early 1990s, it was a pretty lame excuse. By then the firms had had plenty of time to recruit and promote women.

Meanwhile, even the good old boys at the white-shoe firms were feeling pressure for reasons that had less to do with political correctness and more to do with bottom-line imperatives. Perhaps they could ignore the women entrepreneurs, but they couldn't ignore the women who were rising to power at some of their choicest clients or sitting on those corporate boards.

Indeed, if you simply look no further than the contents of the last few chapters of this book, you'll see women driving the inside/outside relationships at General Electric (Suzanne Hawkins), Sears, Roebuck (Bobbie McGee Gregg), Motorola (Kathleen Bryan), Ultramar Diamond Shamrock (Marylin Jenkins Milner), and DoubleClick (Elizabeth Wang). Combine the budgets for outside legal services at just these five companies and you'll see

---

[1] Graham, *Getting Down to Business: Marketing and Women Lawyers* (Little Falls, NJ: Glasser LegalWorks, 1996).

WOMAN TO WOMAN: DOES GENDER-BASED MARKETING
WORK FOR BOTH SIDES?

341

why managing partners who scoff at gender-based marketing do so at their peril.

At the same time, it's important not to oversimplify the buying-selling process, especially where such corporations are involved. As O'Brien points out, women at corporations are sometimes tougher for women at law firms to target because the buyers are under enormous pressure not to hire lawyers simply because they're women. Here, the "safety sell" cannot be ignored. If a woman at a large company hires another woman as outside counsel, and the results are disappointing, the implicit conclusion may be that it's her fault for thinking gender first and quality second.

Such women are "very sensitive to being accused of that," says O'Brien. Alternatively, if these women hire a man at a major law firm, and the work goes south, it's not necessarily their fault because they made the same choice that anyone else in the department might have made.

In the mid-1990s, O'Brien told Deborah Graham that, as Graham wrote, "female entrepreneurs have a heightened and more activist awareness . . . than female executives at large organizations."[2] Asked about that observation today, O'Brien doesn't believe the difference between the entrepreneurial and corporate sectors has changed much.

MONTGOMERY, MCCRACKEN

For many years, Katie O'Brien's focus was, in fact, more on women entrepreneurs—businesspeople who answer only to themselves— than on corporate in-house counsel. In the 1970s, O'Brien, a general business lawyer with a focus on commercial lending from the lender's side, began identifying women as client targets. More precisely, perhaps, they began identifying her. These were clients

---

[2] *Id.* at 382.

with a fairly strong feminist viewpoint, and O'Brien was one of the few women in Philadelphia at the time who enjoyed a prominent position as an outside business law counselor.

A next important step was Montgomery, McCracken's involvement in the National Association of Women Business Owners (NAWBO). One success story from the mid-1980s speaks volumes about the personal element that affects the inside/outside process, especially among independent business owners who are not enmeshed in the corporate referral networks.

O'Brien had begun representing a fairly substantial female-owned courier service. It's a telling reflection on her firm's culture that this client was developed after being brought to O'Brien's attention by the staff member in charge of Montgomery, McCracken's mailroom and messenger services. The staff member figured a businesswoman with a couple of hundred employees was right in O'Brien's strike zone. It's safe to say that support staffers don't give such business development tips to partners at most midtown Manhattan law firms.

O'Brien invited the courier owner to attend a NAWBO event that Montgomery, McCracken, along with other Philadelphia firms, was supporting with a table at the event for itself and guests. Among those guests was the female owner of an actuarial company, a friend of the courier company owner, also a fairly large company with hundreds of employees. A table or two over, another major Philadelphia firm was feting its clients and prospects. That firm had, in fact, just completed a large case for the actuarial company. The owner was a trifled miffed, wondering why she hadn't been invited to its table.

She confided to her friend, the courier services owner sitting next to her, "I just spent millions in litigation fees with them. I'd like to know why they didn't invite me."

"You're an ass," the courier services owner promptly informed her. Then she began to tell her about O'Brien. As O'Brien recalls, it was a noisy evening and she couldn't hear most of the conversation between the two women. But they were smiling and

WOMAN TO WOMAN: DOES GENDER-BASED MARKETING
WORK FOR BOTH SIDES?

343

looking her way and gesticulating. O'Brien smiled back. By the end of the evening, Montgomery, McCracken had a new client.

It was during this period that O'Brien launched the women's group at her firm. An interesting dichotomy developed. Some senior associates, and all the partners, were finding a host of gender-related issues pressing enough to warrant monthly meetings. However, at that time, the younger associates were less motivated. As Graham relates,[3] the latter were agreeable instead to quarterly meetings. Clearly, it was the older lawyers who had the battle scars. For the younger ones, the playing field was already leveler, or so they thought.

The result was that, as the older attorneys began to meet more frequently without the younger women, their concerns became much more focused on marketing and business development—not as much on lifestyle, or maternity leave policy, but on a fundamental question that older women lawyers would be more prone to ask initially. As O'Brien put it, "How do I gain power and authority?"[4]

The answer, of course, is by having a considerable business. Other factors at Montgomery, McCracken, as well as profession-wide, encouraged the further growth of these women's marketing groups during the 1990s. As O'Brien points out, the rise of the marketing director has had a direct effect, and not necessarily because these professionals at law firms often happen to be women. It's the instinct of such marketers—who have grown from $40,000 marketing coordinators in the mid-1980s to $300,000 chief marketing officers today—to ferret out new market segments to target. As the buying population changed, women naturally became an item on their agendas.

The problem, however, was that a lot of the women-owned startups weren't large enough to interest a major law firm. Today,

---

[3] Id.
[4] Id.

the issue isn't much different. With the downturn affecting startup businesses, and the drying up of venture capital, the female entrepreneurial population is still relatively limited, at least in terms of real equity.

Yet the aftershocks of the downturn have, in many instances, resulted in increased commitment to gender-based marketing at firms like Montgomery, McCracken. As the senior women lawyers at such firms perceive a smaller, more competitive market, their reaction is to redouble their efforts. Again, however, the presence of an interested senior woman partner is essential to survival. Without such a powerful female partner, it's easy to imagine law firms shifting their marketing dollars to other areas, back toward the corporate sector (where women in-house counsel are afraid to respond to gender-based marketing) and away from the leaner entrepreneurial populace.

Today, the scope of the women's group at Montgomery, McCracken has increased, and the initial resistance of the younger associates has evaporated. Forty to fifty members, drawn from all associate classes, attend each monthly meeting. O'Brien no longer leads the sessions. The hope is to nurture new leadership and achieve longevity for the group once the senior partner is no longer on the scene. And the associates determine the agendas of the meetings, which go beyond marketing and business development. Recently, for example, night security was an issue. With billable requirements steadily increasing, the firm was lobbied to hire a security officer to guard the building after dark.

The monthly meetings generally include tips on business development from the more senior women lawyers as well as formal training. Such training, comments O'Brien, is important if only because it emphasizes the importance of investing time in business development despite the rise in minimum billable hour requirements. The training includes guest appearances by clients as well as role-playing. One example might be cocktail parties. Such a training session, either through discussion or psychodrama,

WOMAN TO WOMAN: DOES GENDER-BASED MARKETING
WORK FOR BOTH SIDES?

345

would allow the younger women to understand that everyone can feel as inadequate at such events as they do.

The marketing groups thus have internal and external functions. Internally, they feature training and support groups. Externally, they offer networking forums to clients and prospects. The Montgomery, McCracken women have developed business well beyond the entrepreneurial female-owned companies with which O'Brien began. The marketing groups aggressively target the corporate community. A decade ago, the women's group was taking out full-page ads in the *Philadelphia Business Journal* to announce itself to other women in the corporate community. The firm has now abandoned that tactic. The ad space became too expensive, says O'Brien, and the benefits were hard to assess.

The shrewder, more focused approach is still all about networking. One successful idea involved regular breakfast teas. These events focused on the in-house community to such an extent that the guest speakers would always be a female general counsel or other female client representative. No Montgomery, McCracken lawyers served as featured presenters. Instead, the firm was hosting events where it was, for all intents and purposes, merely a facilitator that allowed in-house women lawyers to network with each other.

To some extent, this approach can at least begin to overcome the resistance of in-house women to hiring law firm women. Outside counsel can get on the in-house radar screen without being conspicuously self-promotional. In fact, O'Brien says she's able to trace specific new business to virtually every breakfast tea the firm sponsored over a period of a few years, notwithstanding the ostensible risks that women who report to men may run by hiring women at law firms.

O'Brien admits she initially resisted the idea of these breakfast events as "too fluffy," but they were so successful that the firm no longer needed to sponsor the events. The in-house women began their own networking groups under the aegis of the Philadelphia Bar. Now O'Brien wants to revisit the idea, and start up a new series of breakfast meetings because there are new in-house women, and new female GCs, in town.

"Whatever they [the in-house guests] might hear from the speakers would be of value to them," says O'Brien, because the content will be disinterested wisdom from one of their own. The value of these breakfasts was enhanced because the speakers only spoke for five or ten minutes. The rest of the time was devoted to questions and answers from the audiences, providing additional opportunity to focus in on what the attendees really wanted to hear and talk about. The attendees, drawn from a broad spectrum of local businesses, would have the opportunity to sell themselves as well—to another company, for example.

We are indeed beginning to answer the fundamental question with which we began: *Of what value to the buyer is this kind of marketing?* The value equation, which we explored in Chapter 4, once again plays out on two levels. First, there's the value provided to the business entity that will pay the legal fees. Second, as the sales trainers also emphasize, there's the value that sellers discreetly provide to individual buyers. By providing a veritable job forum for in-house women, law firms such as Montgomery, McCracken create allies. The participants are performing services on behalf of women who may some day be clients or referral sources. At the very least, they're already friends.

At some large companies, like banks, women employees and executives don't even get a chance to exchange ideas with each other. They usually don't have the time, or the space, to discuss their professional/personal issues. Again, on the value-added side of the marketing ledger, Montgomery, McCracken takes different women from the same company to dinner and a show. These women are non-lawyer decision-makers who, under the auspices of the firm, are being given a chance to communicate comfortably with each other.

Here we seem to be a long way from Jeffrey Kindler's warning (in Chapter 9). The McDonald's GC cautioned that, if you take him to a basketball game, he might be glad to go, but your

WOMAN TO WOMAN: DOES GENDER-BASED MARKETING
WORK FOR BOTH SIDES?

347

gesture will likely backfire. In fact, he'll hesitate to send you any work at all afterward. He won't want his professional judgment to be affected or to appear affected. Kindler, like other powerful buyers, recommends value-based marketing instead: the seminar or newsletter that shows off your knowledge and skill while at the same time leaving him and his department with something of lasting professional usefulness.

Yet it can be argued that the networking of women's groups like Montgomery, McCracken's isn't necessarily different from what Kindler has commended. Networking may not serve the same function as an advisory bulletin about some new statutory development affecting client companies. However, exposing clients to other clients—or, in the case of the large company, to their own corporate colleagues—also delivers value by simply providing a forum that they can put to good use. As the sales trainers advise, the best sellers take themselves out of the picture entirely.

HALE AND DORR

At Hale and Dorr, we find a fairly even balance of women corporate counsel and women entrepreneurs as target clients. The entrepreneurial targets aren't surprising: Hale and Dorr is well-known for developing high technology business both before and after the 2000 downturn. It's inevitable that women buyers will be turning up in those markets, locally and nationally. By the same token, Hale and Dorr partner Joan Lukey, one of the lawyers spearheading the firm's women's initiative, is an employment litigator with a strong "Older Economy" client base.

One difference between Hale and Dorr and Montgomery, McCracken is that Lukey, the president of the Boston Bar Association, leads a separate women's group that draws on female lawyers from all the major Boston law firms as well as from large local and regional companies. The group is called "ISOS," i.e., "inside/outside." As Lukey notes, it just so happens that "isos" is also the Greek word for "equality."

Twenty women sit on the ISOS steering committee, including women from CVS Corporation, the City of Cambridge (across the Charles River from Boston), Boston Gas Company, Sappi Fine Paper, and Houghton Mifflin Company. Hale and Dorr thus has a two-fold gender-based campaign that includes its own internal women's marketing group as well as ISOS.

The five-year-old ISOS, which was founded by Lukey, convenes four times a year. The members include women lawyers from the ten or so largest Boston firms as well as a diverse in-house contingent. The group has been criticized for excluding smaller firms. "That was never the intention," says Lukey. Instead, "we were looking to involve law firms that have very similar problems and goals in common."

Guest speakers from a variety of backgrounds appear at the ISOS meetings. Steering committee members hold separate meetings as well. ISOS has gotten some attention outside Boston, in the ABA publication on women lawyers called *Perspectives*, for example, but the specific focus is mainly local. (Law firm members are not on the extensive ISOS mailing list, since each firm handles group-related communications internally.)

The approach is similar to what we saw at Montgomery, McCracken in that the value equation is based on networking. Lukey emphasizes the opportunity ISOS provides for younger women to meet senior attorneys. Because Lukey is Boston Bar President, her motives go beyond Hale and Dorr. "It's always good for lawyers to have new [professional] communities to be a part of," she says, so ISOS helps fulfill the Bar leader's obligation to build them.

Moreover, because all the major Boston firms are involved, the marketing focus is even subtler than at Montgomery, McCracken. "We're careful not to steal each other's clients," says Lukey. Some of the companies who attend the meetings are already using more than one of the member firms anyway. As such, a lot of the marketing that goes on is to existing clients and referral sources at other law firms.

WOMAN TO WOMAN: DOES GENDER-BASED MARKETING
WORK FOR BOTH SIDES?

349

But there are more direct new business benefits as well. For example, one firm may have a conflict in representing its client in a particular matter, and another firm is on hand to pick up the slack. Just being at a meeting thus increases the chances of getting hired to handle a pending matter, especially for litigators like Lukey. Litigation work is episodic, after all, and new business development is often a function of being in the right place with the right people at the right time.

As we noted, Hale and Dorr has its own internal women's marketing group (as does at least one other ISOS member, Foley, Hoag & Eliot). Here, too, there are both internal and external agendas. Internally, Hale and Dorr associates are included in monthly lunches where senior attorneys like Lukey give first-hand accounts of their own business development successes. Cross-selling is also a frequent topic. At the very least, says Lukey, associates should be taught to look for the "cues" when dealing with clients—that here is a good opportunity to tell the client about another Hale and Dorr practice group or area of expertise, and to offer to put the client in touch with the appropriate partner.

But associates were not included when Deborah Graham led a women's marketing training course in 2000. The firm did not want to put too much business development pressure on lawyers too early, which is fairly interesting considering how aggressive Hale and Dorr has been in its business development regimen over the past few years. (Lukey has also steered her female partners to ClientFocus, a marketing consulting firm headed up by Sara Holtz, a former in-house counsel at Sara Lee Corporation.)

Externally, we find Hale and Dorr women sponsoring public events where they can interact with women clients, both in-house counsel and business owners. As an example of the latter, Hale and Dorr supports the Commonwealth Institute, an organization serving local entrepreneurs. In return for its support, Hale and Dorr ran a series of breakfast meetings in 2000 attended by women members who run companies worth between $250,000 and $50 million.

Lukey and Coulter both strongly defend the notion of gender-based marketing on a value basis. The interplay with their colleagues at law firms helps give the in-house lawyers "a sense of their careers," says Lukey, in that they might move from one company to another, or perhaps join a law firm. Similarly, it's expected that some of the women from the firms may want to know more about working in-house and the alleged "lifestyle" benefits of doing so.

"Women relate better to women than men do to men," avers Lukey, at least in terms of how they share professional problems and provide personal help. "They make truer friends. And women simply need more help because of their gender."

If the professional trends continue, and demographic patterns progress apace, the gender burden may begin to slowly shift. Male lawyers could very well be at a disadvantage because many of them lack the mutually supportive instincts that Lukey describes, and because they cannot acknowledge their need for professional guidance as openly as their female colleagues.

Certainly some men will be at a marketing disadvantage. Silvia Coulter, who was a prominent marketing consultant before joining Hale and Dorr, recalls one law firm that called on her because its male partners were fretting about their inability to sell to women. It was in the mid-1990s, at a firm about the same size and of comparable stature to Hale and Dorr. Coulter led a seminar and discussed some tried-and-true relationship building techniques.

One supposes this to be the great ancient promise held out by feminist thinking back to Aristophanes: That, at some levels, the reins of power will be held more humanely because of the influence of women and that, at the same time, it will simply be bad for the bottom line to buck such humanizing trends.

But the value to the client implicit in gender-based marketing goes beyond job counseling and personal career advice. It directly affects clients' keenest economic self-interest as well. Those women from the Commonwealth Institute are learning from the Hale and Dorr women they meet how to increase their access

WOMAN TO WOMAN: DOES GENDER-BASED MARKETING
WORK FOR BOTH SIDES?

351

to venture capital. (Hale and Dorr, along with Testa, Hurwitz & Thibeault, has the same bead on VC in New England that Brobeck Phleger or Wilson, Sonsini has in Silicon Valley.)

For the larger corporate clients, those who sit on the ISOS steering committee, the benefits are different but equally tangible. A male CEO can take great comfort knowing that women at law firms are marketing themselves to the women in his law department, just because it's good for business. Take CVS, a member of the ISOS steering committee, as an example. As Lukey points out, a majority of CVS consumers are women. Some day an attorney might have occasion to be speaking publicly on behalf of the company. The attorney's gender won't be lost on the client's paying customers.

In a gender discrimination case, the gender of the defendant's lawyer has an obvious impact on public sentiment. In court, female defense attorneys have tremendous impact on juror perceptions, regardless of the kind of lawsuit. Lukey says that jurors have told her as much after a trial. But in a gender discrimination case, the jury will certainly connect the dots, according to Lukey: If the company is prejudiced against women, why would they allow a woman to defend it in a case where the exposure could be tens of millions? They wouldn't just do it for cosmetic purposes, not when the risks are so high. They must have genuine respect for qualified women.

The more input from women in the professional services sector, the better clients will deduce how their customers are thinking, regardless of whether their female counselors actually have public visibility or are trying cases in court. Companies want females on their boards of directors in any event, and female board directors want to see more females handling important company matters.

Women at law firms who sell legal services by being helpful to in-house women are delivering signal value to the corporation by just showing up at the tea party. We are indeed a long way from Jeff Kindler's gratuitous basketball tickets. In fact, we're at the heart of the client service concept before we've even been hired.

THE CORPORATE MANDATE

In talking about the value that gender-based marketing produces for the buyer, we're clearly talking about many things. Gender-based marketing provides personal support, on a person-to-person basis, from one woman to another woman who happens to be working in-house, and who then (hopefully) becomes a lifelong ally of the seller.

Gender-based marketing also provides value to the client company as a whole. If nothing else, that value should extend to the actual quality of the professional services delivered. In the legal field, this value-added affects both litigation and business practice. Lukey has pointed out the potential impact of a female litigator on a jury. O'Brien articulates the diversity potential for deals as well.

"Every transaction involves personalities," she says. As a result, every transaction is potentially enhanced when it involves a pool of different personalities. The give-and-take between human beings can make transactions go well or go badly. Optimal staffing means you can pick and choose your players and, the more options you have, the better for you and the better for your client.

The same gender diversity that may prove threatening to an in-house female lawyer, who doesn't want to be blamed for a bad retention decision based solely on gender, can thus turn out to be a lifeline as well. It's a "delicate balance," adds O'Brien. If a major law firm trots out nothing but white males at a beauty contest, it's offensive, and may not serve the client's legal objectives either. Conversely, if the firm takes a preponderance of women to a dog-and-pony show because the client is female, that's an equally injudicious cheapening of the inside/outside dynamic.

Ideally, perhaps, the safety sell may also be diversified if, for instance, the brand-name law firm that the company will want to hire as its best bet in any event also has the foresight to seal the deal by including women and minorities on its team. To be sure, minority issues, racial or otherwise, justify a separate chapter. We have focused in this chapter on gender because these women's

WOMAN TO WOMAN: DOES GENDER-BASED MARKETING
WORK FOR BOTH SIDES?

353

marketing groups have existed as discrete law firm marketing entities with their own ongoing business development strategies. There do exist networks of minority-owned firms that have thrived in recent years, offering corporations a real choice in a variety of practice areas. But there are practically no ethnically or racially based marketing groups at the larger establishment law firms and—for all the eager efforts to spotlight top minority lawyers— one suspects we won't soon be seeing African-American or Hispanic marketing contingents within the major U.S. firms.

Finally, gender-based marketing serves the corporate client for very practical reasons as well. O'Brien is candid enough to allow that some companies can "more easily achieve diversity among their vendors than among themselves." Generally speaking, though, Fortune 250 companies are fortuitously headed in the same direction as their law firms, accounting firms, and other providers.

In Detroit, for example, the Big Three have added top African-American professionals to their in-house legal (and other) staffs, including black GCs. At the same time, they have pressured all their law firms to hire more African-American associates and make the best ones partners. In survey after survey, we find that firms in Detroit are inevitably leading the nation in their minority lawyer numbers, including partners. This may be partly a function of the high percentage of blacks in Detroit proper and the Detroit-area MSA.

The aforementioned number of female decision-makers just at the law departments we've covered in this book suggests that a similar phenomenon has occurred with respect to women. As Lukey points out, given a choice between equally talented female or black attorneys, on the one hand, and white male attorneys, on the other, CEOs will generally hire the former. This is a business decision that they've learned to make almost instinctively. The world speaks to businesses and businesses relay the message to their lawyers.

Consultants: How They Help Law Departments Run Themselves, Hire Law Firms, and Manage Relationships

Law firms, more than law departments, have begun increasingly relying on outside consultants in the last decade. In large measure this reliance is due to the intensification of the competitive environment during these years, as well as to a persistent insecurity that lawyers tend to have about their own business skills. Professional encouragement from disinterested outsiders, as well as the market knowledge they offer, has thus become a most saleable commodity.

At the same time, in order to enjoy credibility in the guild-like culture of legal practitioners, these outsiders often should be lawyers themselves. They do not need merely an "Esq." after their names; some experience practicing law, running a law firm business, and marketing to clients is often—although not always—*de rigueur*.

Yet there's been an interesting bifurcation among the consultants who serve the profession. Very few of them work both sides of the fence. Marketing consultants help law firms target in-house buyers, define the needs and instincts of those buyers, and close the deal. But these consultants do not, in reality, work much with in-house counsel themselves. In some cases they may claim they do because it enhances their sales pitch to be able to say, "We talk on a regular basis with the buyers of legal services throughout the world. We advise them on best practices. We advise them, in fact, on how to buy legal services."

In reality, that claim is somewhat specious. The leading consulting firms that service law firms usually only have one person on staff who concentrates on law departments. Everybody else handles mainly law firms. It's hard to imagine that that one person maintains a sufficient informational flow with his or her colleagues on the law firm side to dramatically affect the substance of what they're advising those firms about the marketplace. If I were a managing partner, I would not be especially impressed by or attracted to a consulting firm just because it has one or two people working full time with my potential clients.

The consultants who advise law firms will make their dutiful appearances at ACCA conferences, or they may arrange speaking engagements for themselves or panel spots in the in-house-oriented programs sponsored by *Corporate Legal Times.* It's just marketing. The fact is, many law firm consultants have never worked closely with corporate buyers at all.

There are a number of subtle wrinkles here. For example, many law firms expect outside consultants not just to advise them about the marketplace, or to train them on how best to sell their services, but to actually provide referrals and even recommendations that lead directly to new business. Indeed, some law firms have been rather cynical in their use of consultants, as if the consulting fee is nothing more than a finder's fee. All the other advice that is delivered is written up in a report and left to rot on the marketing director's shelf.

The better consultants immediately disabuse law firms of this hope of direct referrals. Others, less forthright, let firms think it's a possibility, or will even try to go out and generate the referrals. In-house counsel are well-advised to avoid such consultants for the obvious reason that they are not disinterested. It's an odd dynamic, to be sure: Consultants target in-house departments not so much in the hope of getting their work, but because they want to be perceived by their real clients, the law firms, as players in the in-house ballpark. In recent years, headhunters have been taking the same tack. Many of them will tell you that corporations are now representing a bigger and bigger percentage of their business. In most cases, it's simply not true.

The consultants are hoping to create that appearance because 1. in-house slots are sometimes easier to fill, and the cash turnover is faster, and 2. they want to impress their law firm clients with their in-house savvy.

In at least one case, that strategy backfired. One recruiter, naturally speaking on condition of anonymity, confessed that her law firm clients believed her in-house work was very substantial, but they grew distrustful as a result. This occurred when many lawyers were leaving firms and seeking refuge in corporate law departments. The recruiter's law firms were therefore worried the recruiter might change course and recruit their associates on behalf of the alleged corporate clientele. Had she been a little more honest, and not marketed dubious in-house connections, she'd have been spared the headache of having to retrench and convince law firms that it was still safe to deal with her.

Conflicts are an incessant problem for consultants who advise law firms, less so for those who advise law departments. The conundrum for law firms is that they want and need the market knowledge of the outsiders they hire, but that kind of market knowledge can only be gained by the outsiders having worked with competitors, and on issues that are strategic, sensitive, and confidential. For law firms, the ideal consultant, apparently, is someone who *used* to work with competitors, but doesn't anymore, and never will again.

With law departments, the conflicts are less direct and often nonexistent. Even advising departments in the same industry does not necessarily raise a red flag. Citicorp and Chase Manhattan, for example, have historically been so different in how they're structured, with the former highly decentralized and the latter more concentrated in the corporate home office, that their management issues and objectives do not conflict. Further, it's not a direct conflict for the same consultant to help both run their legal services more efficiently because the departments don't directly compete in that arena. Such assistance is nothing like helping two banks both develop more profitable consumer loan programs.

For in-house departments, a few best practices for hiring outside consultants are as follows:

- *Make sure the consultant has enough experience as a legal practitioner so that he or she can bring first-hand experience to the inside/outside dynamic.* The consultant relationship isn't just another vendor relationship, after all, and advisers who treat it as they might treat the company's relationships with a realtor or a software company won't provide much more than surface assistance.

- *Don't hesitate because the consultant has helped someone else in your industry.* To the contrary, that's a plus because it implies familiarity with the specific industry problems faced by your in-house lawyers. The potential conflicts are usually just technical at worst.

- *Select someone who focuses exclusively, or nearly exclusively, on law departments to guarantee his or her disinterestedness.*

- *Be wary of consultants who are especially eager to help name the law firms you hire.* After all, many of these consulting groups have numerous law firm clients. The consultant ought to be eager to prove that he or she does *not* want to promote any particular choice for outside counsel.

- *Keeping in mind the foregoing, be careful not to discourage consultants from recommending a law firm based on what they've heard on the street, or because the consultant is impressed with a firm's answer to an RFP or a performance during a beauty contest interview.* Full disclosure is the key. Consultants who acknowledge a personal interest in helping a law firm are showing you that they're pretty ethical, and can generally be trusted.

- *Specify or focus the consultant's charge if possible.* Hire one consultant to help you interview firms in a convergence process. Hire one to help you decide whether or not to log hourly time. Hire one to help you decide how big the department ought to be. Hire one to help you restructure reporting relationships.

There are two interrelated signs of a superior consulting group. First, do the consultants ask you plenty of questions? Consultants who don't have probably arrived with packaged solutions that are not tailored to the client's needs. Getting you to talk at length not only helps them do a better job, it also helps you understand your own situation with greater clarity. Sometimes, it's worth the price of admission to simply invigorate your own thinking by being responsive to an outsider's intelligent questions.

Second, how much work are they leaving for you to do on your own? It ought to be a lot. A superior consultant only begins the process; he or she does not mix a magic elixir that, with one gulp, soothes the corporate aches and pains. A simple example from the author's experience in a media/marketing firm might be instructive. At our firm we bring some knowledge of the buyers to the table (as, hopefully, this book should confirm). But we also ask our law firm clients to identify not only the decision-makers who work for their clients and prospective clients, but also what print media those decision-makers read. Then we can take steps to get our lawyers quoted in the places where the people they want to impress are most likely to read about them.

Consultants don't know who those decision-makers are, or what they read. Why should we know? It's our clients' job to find out for us. That's a big chore for them, but if a consultant doesn't leave you with a lot of work to do on your own behalf, he or she hasn't left you with much.

At the same time, the in-house law consultant is, or ought to be, a conspicuously different kind of a person than a law firm consultant—just as a general counsel is, or ought to be, a more confident businessperson than even the managing partners of great law firms. Corporations run top-down, not flat, and the consultant must be comfortable in such an environment. The consensus-building skills that consultants utilize at law firms might not be quite so important at a corporation. Conversely, too much time spent helping law firms re-engineer partner/associate relationships might hinder consultants from dealing astutely with the hierarchical arrangements in force at in-house departments.

A CASE IN POINT

Rees W. Morrison typifies the in-house legal specialist who is currently serving corporate America, and a look at how he does business will provide a telling case study on who such specialists are and what they do. Morrison has worked as a consultant with what was then called PriceWaterhouse and, later, Arthur Andersen. Currently, he is a partner at the Newtown Square, Pennsylvania-based Altman Weil, which specializes in the legal profession. Previously, he was a bankruptcy lawyer practicing for six years at three New York firms including Weil, Gotshal & Manges. He acknowledges that his associate career was not stellar. "[But] I have immensely more credibility as a consultant for having practiced so long—indeed, simply for having a Columbia law degree plus an LL.M from New York University."

We are profiling Morrison not because he is necessarily the best, but because he certainly typifies this particular cottage industry. In addition, by profiling a consultant like Morrison, we'll see certain common themes emerge regarding how in-house legal managers hire outside advisors in general. There are telling similarities and differences in how law departments go outside for help with their legal problems, on the one hand, and their management concerns, on the other.

Altman Weil is an example of the sort of consulting firm discussed above. It focuses on law firms at the most strategic levels, including mergers. There are a number of ancillary services such firms provide. For example, as we mentioned in Chapter 1, Altman Weil has even dabbled in online bidding forums. But its real meat and potatoes is in helping law firms survive and expand.

When you call Altman Weil and ask about corporate law departments, Morrison is the man you'll get. Morrison does mention other Altman Weil consultants such as Daniel DiLucchio and James Wilber, who are active in this area. Together, the three men have thirty years of service to law departments, although DiLucchio himself will refer callers such as this writer to Morrison.

As Morrison expresses it, law departments typically call him, or other consultants, if they need expertise, manpower, or objectivity. Expertise means that law departments are looking for someone who can tell them what other law departments do to manage outside counsel, invest in technology, restructure, or install knowledge management systems. Morrison indicates that usually law departments are pleased when the consultant has worked in their industry before, although the management issues involved are more universal than clients usually realize.

As for manpower, sometimes law departments simply are not staffed to handle a competitive bidding process, or management skills training. They realize they need to supplement their resources with an external advisor.

"Objectivity" drives law departments to hire a consultant who can step back and look at encrusted processes with neutrality. In response, Morrison will provide overall diagnostics of a department. Note that in this context, like a good doctor, consultants may unearth problems the department has not been thinking about, and did not actually call the consultant to address. The in-house manager's challenge is to recognize when outside advisors are churning work by looking in areas that will increase their hours and their fees, versus when the prophylaxis is genuine.

Consultants such as Morrison base their reputations on honest instinct; they'll only snoop in corners where they believe important problems might actually be lurking. We've seen how ambivalent in-house managers feel about proactive legal services— rereading employee manuals that don't need to be reread, or auditing patent portfolios that don't need to be audited. A key point with both the consultants and outside counsel is billing.

Prophylaxis is always more trustworthy on a flat fee rather than an hourly basis, whereas some "diagnostics" might simply be an excuse for flagrant overutilization and resulting excessive billing.

Morrison, it should therefore be noted, bills on a flat fee. Whatever other points are relevant to the hourly/non-hourly billing debate, it would seem that—at least for work such as "audits" or "health checks" that often invite hourly abuses—flat fees are an in-house manager's best friend. And this would seem true whether those managers are shopping for outside legal help or for a consultant's analysis of the department's organization and management.

"Objectivity" also means that consultants are both impartial and strictly confidential. These are two especially important considerations when the consultants do client satisfaction surveys or benchmarking studies. The goal is to simultaneously protect the integrity of the data and still complete the process. The fact that in-house departments conduct client satisfaction surveys has additional resonance for outside counsel. As we've discussed, such surveys are a proven and yet underused marketing tool for law firms. If law department managers are often hiring professionals like Morrison to ascertain internal satisfaction with how their departments are doing their jobs, it means they value that process. This is a familiar strategy for in-house managers and, as such, one that many of them expect from their own vendors, including law firms, even if they don't say so.

Although consultants can directly influence how law departments purchase outside services, Morrison points out that this is an "exceptional circumstance." As we've suggested, it ought to be exceptional, since an overemphasis on helping departments hire law firms might compromise the consultants' crucial objectivity.

Some need for input on outside hiring might arise if there is a competitive bidding project or a convergence process. Then the consultant could suggest names of law firms or give pointed feedback on how competing law firms are handling themselves in the beauty contest. But "decisions about outside counsel are the domain of the law department and rarely tread upon by consultants," insists Morrison. Much more commonly, consultants recommend procedures—such as budgeting, electronic billing, evaluations, and referrals from regional counsel—that indirectly affect whom the law department chooses to retain.

Not surprisingly, Morrison agrees that, with law department consulting, conflicts rarely arise. To the contrary, broad experience with other companies is the "selling point. It's what they value the most." Nor has Morrison experienced conflicts because of Altman Weil's law firm clientele. As far as he's concerned, for example, online bidding or the MDPs are viable options for his law department clients, as they are for the mainstream law firms that represent the lion's share of Altman Weil's business.

It may indeed be a common experience among diverse consultants (including the firm in which this writer is a partner) that the conflicts issue does often get raised, but only during the business development phase. Afterwards, it is common that the issue hardly ever arises. If a consultant is any good at all, most clients just stop worrying about it.

Historically, there have been dubious instances of consulting firms that recommend vendors in which they had a direct vested interest. Altman Weil, says Morrison, avoids such conflicts by not investing in, say, case management systems, and by not having strategic partnerships with the companies that develop or sell them. However, such "conflicts" are often manageable if the consultant fully discloses the extent of the relationship when he recommends the product or service.

NUMBERS GAMES

"Metrics" thread their way through Morrison's work repeatedly, more so than with other consultants in his field. Benchmarking projects are all about metrics. The numbers tell all when Morrison examines profession-wide staffing ratios such as paralegals per lawyer. Morrison then compares those ratios to the ratios of other similarly sized departments, or departments of whatever size in the same industry. (Surveys are thus a crucial preliminary data-gathering tool for consultants such as Morrison.)

If there is a significant variance, the natural next step is to ask why. In some cases, there's a good reason for the variance. In other cases, money is being wasted or lawyers are being undersupported. Metrics can demonstrate the efficiency of a law department, or they can expose vulnerabilities. And they are crucial to compensation decisions, for obvious reasons.

Metrics also play an important role in re-examinations of the inside/outside relationship. For example, Morrison looks at concentration ratios, or what percentage of the total spending is going to what percentage of the law firms on the corporate approved list. Those numbers will have a decisive impact on the decision to initiate a convergence strategy.

From May 2000 to May 2001, Morrison worked with approximately two dozen law departments, a workload he describes as pretty typical. Fees for these projects are fairly predictable, although they seem to be somewhat lower than fees charged by consultants to law firms. Projects of $20,000 to $40,000 constitute the bulk of Morrison's business. Some small ones, such as departmental retreats, might be billed at only $2,000 to $5,000. The occasional very large project exceeds $100,000.

We've noted that, for the sort of "diagnostic" work often undertaken by consultants, a flat fee arrangement deters time-keeping abuses and attempts to solve nonexistent problems. In general, Morrison finds that law departments prefer the "certainty of a fee proposal on those terms." It also works from the consultant's point of view as well because it makes the consultant feel more efficient. Only once has Morrison ever felt "abused" by a company trying to extract more work from him than the fee agreement warranted.

These clear-cut arrangements with consultants are a striking contrast to the turmoil and controversy surrounding value billing with law firms. Departmental managers apparently have a much easier time creating value-based billing arrangements with a consultant such as Morrison than with outside legal counsel. One reason is that law firms are often taking on work that requires many, many attorneys, and fair flat fees are hard to determine in those situations. Morrison himself acknowledges that he finds it difficult to help law departments devise alternatives to hourly rates when they retain outside counsel.

But there may be another factor working here as well. Clients may like the "certainty" of a flat fee when it comes to consultants, but hourly rate-shopping for outside legal services is, as we've noted in this book, easier to justify to the corporate bean counters. Hourly rates are a different type of certainty: The certainty of knowing that, however much we may get bilked by a law firm in the long run, it won't be because we struck a disadvantageous fee arrangement at the get-go. We had the "certainty" of competitive hourly rates. (How were we to know that the lawsuit would take an extra year or two to resolve?)

DISINTERESTED PARTICIPANT

Convergence projects are infrequent in Morrison's experience. He has completed seven of them since 1998. However, they also tend to be the most lucrative projects. In each of those competitive bidding projects, Morrison was retained at the start to guide the law departments as they thought through and wrote the RFPs, sent them out, analyzed the responses, and chose a law firm.

One example was Morrison's work with the Ingersoll-Rand Company. The goal was to choose a single law firm to handle all that company's intellectual property work except for litigation. Morrison was one of a troika that included the GC and the Chief Patent Counsel. The selection process was a six-month job during the spring and summer of 2000 that began with the solicitation of proposals from about twenty law firms. The finalists were interviewed intensively by Ingersoll-Rand. Morrison attended three meetings for which the three finalists each sent in two or more partners. He "may have asked some questions also." Morrison put together pros and cons for the three finalists, but the final decision was naturally the GC's.

Here, though, is the cusp of the conflict issue, at least theoretically: What relationship does Altman Weil have, or may want to have, with the finalists? If there is already any relationship, is there a sufficient firewall between Morrison and his colleagues back at Altman Weil who are busy marketing themselves to law firms?

Actually, says Morrison, the same dynamic applies here in terms of conflicts and potential conflicts as when in-house managers look to their consultants for broad experience in dealing with other law departments. Again, such experience is a "selling point." The GCs and Associate GCs who hire outside counsel want outside advisors who can help them identify the likeliest law firm candidates. Full disclosure is still the crux: So long as the consultants tell their clients that they have worked, or want to work, for particular law firms, "the clients can decide for themselves if there is a disabling conflict." So far that has not happened, in Morrison's experience.

One issue related to outside counsel that Morrison does see as becoming a greater concern is law firm profit levels. This is a touchy subject, one to which Morrison figures law department consultants may be able to make a contribution via metrical analysis. Clearly, there are different levels of law firms, and the margins that Wachtell Lipton expects won't have much to do with the profits that insurance defense firms typically earn. However, within the category of, say, IP boutiques, there are enough numbers to crunch to have some influence on how departments can negotiate fees either on an hourly or non-hourly basis.

It's difficult for consultants like Morrison to handle more than five simultaneous projects, simply for scheduling reasons.

Nevertheless, at Morrison's seniority level, there is always more than one project under way at any one time. Yet Morrison's business is not highly leveraged. For most projects, Morrison himself does the bulk of the actual work. In part, this hands-on approach reflects Altman Weil's relatively small size. Also, clients are specifically looking for Morrison's expertise, without a lot of back-up busy work. In addition, Morrison simply prefers consulting to managing other consultants.

Here, of course, is the main difference between the Altman Weils or Hildebrandts or the solo-shop consultants, on the one hand, and the Big Five, on the other. The Big Five all do in-house legal consulting, which, as they expand into providing legal services, no doubt raises yet another knotty conflicts question.

Just as when they hire law firms, in-house managers need to think about what kind of leverage they really need from the outside provider. Some types of legal practice are naturally "de-leveraged" and partner-intensive: Employment counseling or trusts and estates are examples. Others, such as multi-jurisdictional litigation, obviously require breadth and depth of resources.

It reflects some bias on this writer's part, but one wonders how much more value a leveraged management consultancy could bring to a law department client, compared to what somebody like Morrison can accomplish alone. True, client interviews can be time-consuming and extensive, but how far down any food chain should we go in interviewing key corporate personnel about the efficiency of their house counsel? Such investigation is still sensitive work, however voluminous, and, it seems, best left to senior advisers.

COMPANY BY COMPANY

Another natural difference between law firm consultants and law department consultants is in the tactics they use to market themselves, and how they present themselves to the market.

Naturally, there are generic similarities as well. Both stress speaking and writing. In particular, Morrison stresses the value of authoring books.[1] "There is a powerful effect in the phrase, 'He wrote the book on it,' especially when it's literally true," says Morrison.

Speeches are potent for a different reason. Audiences get a palpable sense of the speaker, especially during the question-and-answer period, when they can gauge how well he or she can respond extemporaneously. Even at a subconscious level, prospective clients are deeply affected by this sense of how a consultant behaves in an impromptu setting. "I give every talk I can," quips Morrison.

The powerful difference between how the two consultant types market themselves lies in the substance of what they write and speak about. Morrison is a particularly good example on the law department consulting side because his writings are about metrics. He's preoccupied with refining the best methods to ferret about specific information. He will discuss such questions as, "What is an industry norm for paralegal/lawyer leverage?" But it's the question that's ultimately important as a methodological tool. The actual answer is significant mainly to the corporate client at the time the metrical research is being conducted. In his writings, and in his speeches, Morrison is less interested in presenting the answers to such questions as salient trends. The trends may change in a flash anyway.

In contrast, law firm consultants, in order to demonstrate market wisdom, talk extensively in public about trends. Their law firm clients must sell to survive, so presumably they need to be acutely sensitive to those trends. Similarly, law firms are constantly restructuring themselves, often via merger. What other law firms are doing around the world is therefore of continual interest to them.

Law departments also must know what other law departments are doing, but not necessarily in order to copy them or follow suit in any way. They are much more constrained by the

---

[1] See his own book, which is chock full of sample metrics: Morrison, *Law Department Benchmarking: Myths, Metrics, and Management*, 2d ed. (Little Falls, NJ: Glasser LegalWorks, 2001).

umbrella corporate organization. Even if Law Department X may envy and wish to emulate Law Department Y, that may never be possible because of the business models ordained by the corporate client.

Despite his focus on benchmarking, and the metrics that support it, Morrison does not therefore perceive overarching trends affecting how law departments ought to proceed. What does happen, he adds, is that "idiosyncratic implementations by certain law departments get disproportionate publicity." In the late 1980s, for instance, Continental Bank got a great deal of attention because it shut down its law department altogether and outsourced most of its legal work to Mayer, Brown & Platt. Some Continental lawyers wound up working at Mayer, Brown. But not a single major company followed suit.

Journalists, who need something to write about, "fuel the preoccupation with the new," says Morrison. But management is an art, not a science. "My feeling is that many techniques are available and are underutilized," adds Morrison. "So law departments do not need to quest for novelty. They need to implement effectively what is already available."

Again, the art of management itself is paramount. "Systems approaches to management, which are at the base of seemingly new ideas, fall short of changing people's behavior and incentives," says Morrison. The last two decades are littered with ideas, both good and bad, that went nowhere because they were nothing but ideas. TQM was a benchmarking adaptation that corporations went wild over, but imposing an efficient regimen on de-motivated people proved of limited value. Among the more precise ideas, task-based billing was attractive not only because it mandated cost control, but because it could seemingly operate without human interference. As Morrison points out, however (and, as we saw in Chapter 7, companies such as Prudential discovered), there's always a need for motivated implementation by actual people.

"Eventually, a human being has to interpret whether a law firm is performing appropriately for the money spent," says

Morrison, regardless of whether or not a consultant applies predetermined task codes. "It may sound squishy, but I am realizing more and more that much of law department management revolves around changing the way human beings think, more than around the technologies and techniques that they apply."

Cost control is one overarching theme for everybody, adds Morrison, and so is head count constraints. But those are such well-established facts of corporate life that they do not bear separate mention as hot trends. However, one trend that Morrison points to could have a decisive impact: In-house practice rules could change. There is considerable pressure to admit inside lawyers in jurisdictions other than those where they passed the bar. If this happens, corporations will have something closer to the flexibility that law firms enjoy due to the reciprocity that applies to firms in most states. Such flexibility could certainly affect how law departments retain law firms. There won't be the immediate reflex of scrambling to find outside counsel in some other venue. Companies will tend to ask, "Can we do this ourselves without calling somebody for a referral in Portland, Maine, or Portland, Oregon?" Especially if the matter is a relatively simple one, flying in-house counsel to another jurisdiction will certainly be a simpler, less expensive option.

Morrison figures the future will include one ineluctable trend likely to affect in-house practice: More high technology, and at increasingly rapid rates of implementation. He mentions greater use of portals, a gradual acceptance of knowledge management efforts, perhaps technology literacy standards, and a continuing struggle to provide seamless services to overseas offices. Indeed, among the consultants that specialize in in-house work, technology is a constant focus to the extent that it's really the main area where some consultants work on behalf of law departments.

It may be that too much market knowledge tends to encourage pat answers: Other 300-lawyer law firms are merging, so you'd better too. Or, other law departments have converged, so what are you waiting for? "Just as I have learned to mistrust broad generalizations about law departments and the trends that affect them, I try to avoid preconceived notions about what works best," says Morrison.

Generally, though, Morrison tends to favor certain best practices as most often applicable in a variety of in-house settings. One is internal time-tracking, which a majority of corporate law departments still avoid. Of the departments with over forty lawyers, Morrison estimates that one-third of them track time, but, of those, many do not charge back that time as departmental overhead.

Morrison also tends to recommend budgeting outside costs and reducing the number of law firms that undertake the bulk of the company's work. Yet there are no absolutes, only the "needs and circumstances of the client."

Even with the near-absolutes (and one might expect the budgeting of outside legal costs to fall into that category), it's not the consultant's job to stand in judgment of the client. There are certain practices that firms are likely to accept, as well as some commendable ones that they will never adopt. "So much depends on what they believe in, and on their history," says Morrison. "If you cannot adapt yourself to that, you will not be successful."

"Oftentimes, I find myself describing what other law departments do and then helping clients fashion a solution that mixes their own ideas and the new ideas that I bring. In many ways, my work is to facilitate thinking on the part of clients—thinking that has been stimulated by external ideas and objectivity. I strongly disagree that any consultant can thrive with a preconceived set of answers for most situations. To the contrary, we need as many ideas in our quiver to bring to bear as appropriate."

It's altogether laudable, for example, that both departmental managers and the consultants they rely on have never advanced unyielding standards about the balance of legal services that ought to be performed inside versus outside. However, the nature of the work done by consultants like Morrison tends to favor the flow of work inside. This is not because of any general principle that that's where the work ought to be done.

Clearly, the work ought to be done where it can be done most efficiently, and the mission of the consultant is just that—to increase efficiency.

"The thighbone of inside management is connected to the hipbone of outside counsel usage," says Morrison. "A company can either produce its legal services from inside, purchase them from outside, or forego them altogether. Thus, one can assume a hydraulic function: The more you press down with resources inside, the less you need outside resources. Accordingly, everything done to change the productivity and effectiveness of inside counsel reduces to that degree the need for outside counsel."

In other words, an efficiency expert working inside will, by definition, increase the flow of legal matters that goes inside simply because that's where he happens to be.

Although the buying and selling of legal services comprises a unique dynamic, there are certain fundamental issues that mark professional services in general. It therefore seems appropriate to conclude these discussions with a look at how the consulting profession interfaces with in-house legal practice and, by inference, with law firms.

For corporate counsel, the debate on hourly rates versus flat fees seems interminable. The leverage riddle seems similarly imponderable. Finally, as they re-examine their own internal management systems, as well as their approach to hiring and managing outside counsel, the in-house buyers must navigate a welter of what Rees Morrison has somewhat deprecatingly called "novelty" ideas.

If the legal profession can learn something from how the MDPs have handled these challenges, their own consultants can provide similar lessons in organizational survival. The future may belong to those law firms and law departments that are amenable to learning from other professional services. The consultants teach, not just by advising, but by their example of efficient practice and fair billing.

The Final
Victory?

L et's go back to that conference we mentioned in Chapter 5. It was a 1999 get-together of the College of Law Practice Management in Denver. For one of the sessions, the attendees were broken out into a half-dozen groups. Included in these groups were lawyers and consultants from all over the world who had been working in or for law firms for much of their professional lives.

The moderator put some sheets of paper on each table, and participants were asked to draw the law firm of the future. Working independently, none of us drew a picture of a coherent single organization. Instead, we all drew some version of the same concept. We drew big circles labeled "clients," with lots of little circles labeled "law," "accounting," "engineering," etc., surrounding the clients.

In every drawing, there were naturally lines connecting the big circle to each small circle. Some of the drawings also had lines connecting each smaller circle to other smaller circles.

By that time, the multi-disciplinary firms (MDPs) were already center stage, and it seemed clear that the breadth of those global behemoths had decisively affected all our collective visions of the future. Yet, MDPs aside, what we were drawing also betokened the final triumph of the buyer in the inside/outside dynamic. After all, not only was the client center stage, the discrete entity called "law firm" was hardly there at all.

In fact, it wasn't there at all. Only the service itself —"law" as just one orbiting tributary—was visible.

What an immense journey from the first conference, in 1986, of the American Corporate Counsel Association (ACCA) that we've mentioned in these pages. At that conference, all the talk was about how to dignify life in-house. How to hold your own with big-shot law firms. How not to be ashamed to be a client!

The predominant theme of this book is that the buying and selling of legal services ought to be predicated on value. If you sell, make the selling itself worth the buyer's time. That's how you infuse the free market system with conscience and quality. In fact, the sales trainers even talk about how sellers should take themselves out of the picture altogether when they sell. The Denver drawings suggest that, at least in the legal profession, the sellers, as discrete entities, may soon be as extinct as the dodo.

Is such an extreme outcome salutary? From the corporate point of view, it probably is. What matters is the service rendered, not the form or consistency of the service provider. If maximum value requires the disappearance of the thing we call law firms, then goodbye and good luck!

From the corporate buyer's perspective, that is one possibly logical and welcome outcome of all the trends that we have discussed in this book.

But I would be remiss not to qualify this conclusion somewhat.

Law firms are bizarre places. They are seldom pleasant places. It takes a special kind of person to thrive in an environment dominated by 100 or 200 "self-entitled" owner-operators. Yet from society's viewpoint, rather than a corporate point of view, these organizations have been hothouses that the world may need. These organizations were founded by people like Louis Brandeis and Wendell Wilkie. In the past half-century, they've produced people like William O. Douglas and Archibald Cox.

Maybe law firms are no longer capable of nurturing such genius. So maybe it no longer matters if they survive or not. But I'm quite certain that the pure client service sensibility that we find at the MDPs will never produce *anything but* client service.

Amid all the studied contempt for the old-fashioned "guild mentality," and all the fashionable glib impatience with lawyers' reluctance to self-promote, there's a real danger that something of transcendent value is at risk.

LARRY SMITH, a principal of Levick Strategic Communications, is one of the nation's leading law firm consultants in the areas of public relations and strategic media communications. He is a frequent speaker to law firms and professional groups and has written for and edited numerous legal publications, including *Of Counsel*, a management report for law firms and their clients on strategic planning and business development. Before focusing on law, Smith was a journalist and ghostwriter whose credits included political biographies and military history.